day trips® from
portland, oregon

help us keep this guide up to date

We would love to hear from you concerning your experiences with this guide and how you feel it could be improved and kept up to date. Please send your comments and suggestions to:

editorial@GlobePequot.com

Thanks for your input, and happy travels!

day trips® series

day trips® from portland, oregon

first edition

getaway ideas for the local traveler

*to desiree —
happy day tripping!*

kim cooper findling

gpp®
travel

Guilford, Connecticut

Editor: Kevin Sirois
Project Editor: Heather Santiago
Layout: Joanna Beyer
Text Design: Linda R. Loiewski
Maps: Design Maps Inc. © Morris Book Publishing, LLC.

Library of Congress Cataloging-in-Publication Data is available on file.
ISBN 978-0-7627-6961-2

Printed in the United States of America
10 9 8 7 6 5 4 3 2 1

contents

about the author

Nationally-published writer Kim Cooper Findling grew up on the Oregon Coast, spent several years in the Willamette Valley, and has lived in Central Oregon for 16 years. Her work has appeared in many publications including *Travel Oregon, Horizon Air, Oregon Quarterly, Alaska Air, Sky West, Central Oregon Magazine, The Best Places to Kiss NW,* and *High Desert Journal*. See www.kimcooperfindling.com.

acknowledgments

This book would not have come to fruition without the support and assistance of many others. First to thank in a cosmic shout-out is the Pacific Northwest, for existing as such a diverse, fascinating, and richly beautiful place. I am unbelievably fortunate to reside and write here. I extend appreciation to Kevin Sirois, of Globe Pequot Press, for signing me to this task and guiding me through it. I owe thank yous to dozens of Oregon and Washington tourism and travel professionals who contributed to these pages—far too many to name here. Personal thanks to Beverly, Bob, Joanne, Katherine, Romy, Tim and Trish for suggesting your favorite destinations to add to these pages. Endless gratitude goes to my husband Karl, for reacting to this project with such enthusiasm and support, not to mention grocery shopping and heaps of extra parenting hours. Finally, hugs and thanks to Libby and Maris, for not resenting the fact that I was totally absorbed elsewhere but instead bragging on the playground that mom was writing a book. I am so very lucky.

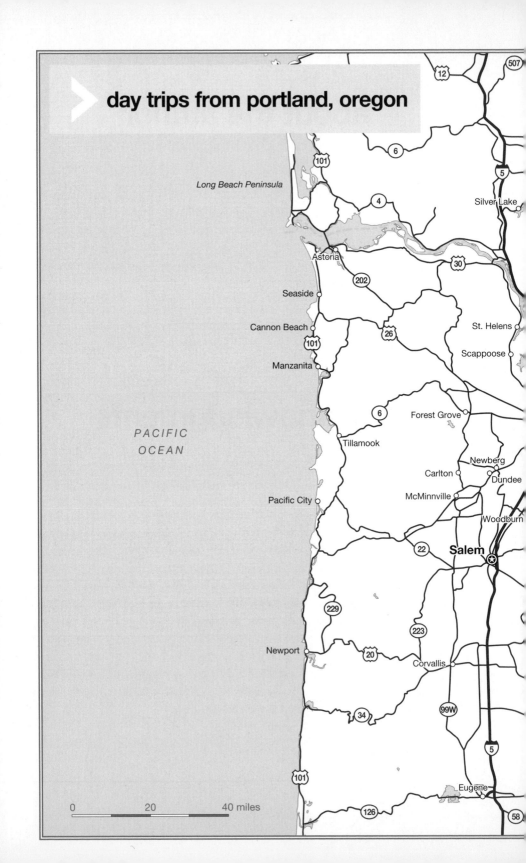

day trips from portland, oregon

introduction

Not so long ago I was at a Portland concert venue in the pouring rain. We're talking buckets of rain—the kind of relentless rain that only falls in the Pacific Northwest. Sheets of water fell from the sky, water cascaded from our hair in waterfalls, we stood in puddles. But to look at the crowd, you'd never have guessed at any discomfort. Everyone was grinning and leaping about to the music, entirely undaunted by the weather. I mentioned this to my sister, laughing. "It's Portland," she shrugged. "Everyone's happy."

Portlanders are generally a happy bunch, and that's because we live in a great place. This is a city with the very best to offer in terms of culture, dining, entertainment, and the outdoors—and yet, Portland doesn't take itself too seriously. It's a city that wears fleece, sips coffee from funky ceramic mugs, and carries a raincoat to a rock concert. You never need to leave Portland because it's so comfortable and fun.

But leave we do. After all, we are descendents of the pioneers. Even the expansive acres of Forest Park and antiques shops in Multnomah Village can't substitute for the veritable wilderness and historical small towns that lie just beyond Portland's borders. When wanderlust strikes, Portland reveals its other primary advantage. We're so close to so many awesome places! The beach—an hour away. The mountains—an hour away. The fertile farms of the Willamette Valley—an hour away. The end of the Oregon Trail—an hour away. North America's most famous volcano—an hour away. Wine country—yes, an hour away.

In fact, there's so much beyond the city limits, you may not know where to start. The greater Portland area is rich with beauty, culture, and possible exploration. That's where this book comes in. Here you'll find more than 20 day trip ideas, each under a three-hour drive from Portland. Some visit one action-packed town and help you narrow down what to see there. Other trips cover two to four smaller towns, some more action-packed than others. Each trip is just a little bit different; each destination offers its own unique flavor. We suggest attractions, restaurants, shops, and outdoor destinations that might tickle your fancy. You'll find more options than you could possibly cover in one day, so pick and choose as you please. Should you find you want more of a certain city, check out the lodgings section—each trip has one, if appropriate.

Our intention is that in these pages you'll find nearly everything you need to blast out of town for a day-long adventure. A few words of wisdom to the savvy traveler, however. First—take a map. Even if your car is equipped with a GPS system or your smart phone is loaded with MapQuest, these systems aren't foolproof and don't always include smaller or newer roads. In these cases, a paper map is an invaluable tool. If you have time, it's also a good idea to highlight the places you really want to see in your chosen day trip ahead of time and call ahead to check on hours of operation, necessary reservations, and the like. Especially in Oregon and Washington's smaller towns, hours vary seasonally, and small shops and restaurants change and even close permanently without warning.

With that in mind—get out of town! Take a hike, drink some wine, gaze upon the bucolic countryside, pick a pumpkin, buy an antique chiffarobe, eat some ice cream, walk the beach, eat some huckleberries, go windsurfing, hug a tree, hit the surf. Whatever you do, have a great time day trippin'! Then return to the most comfortable city in the US, kick back, and plan your next adventure.

using this guide

Day Trips from Portland, Oregon is organized by general direction from Portland: north, northeast, east, southeast, south, southwest, west, and northwest. Listings in the Where to Go, Where to Shop, Where to Eat, and Where to Stay sections are arranged in alphabetical order, unless otherwise specified. If several places in a given town offer similar opportunities, listing titles highlight broad categories (e.g., "wineries") rather than the names of specific businesses or locations. Each stop on every day trip includes a Where to Go listing, but Where to Shop, Where to Eat, and Where to Stay are only included when there are appropriate listings worth visiting.

scheduling your day trip

Half the fun of day tripping is planning. Many a workday can be endured by imagining what fun you'll have come the weekend and an unencumbered day—just you and the open road, maybe a pal or two along for the ride, nowhere to go and all day to get there. As you fantasize about your next day trip, keep these things in mind. Saturday is often a better choice than Sunday to day trip in the Pacific Northwest, as, especially in smaller towns, many shops, destinations, and restaurants close up shop on Sunday or are open for limited hours. If your heart is set on a certain destination, call in advance to check on hours and plan your trip accordingly. If you have the luxury of day tripping mid-week, doing so can be a fabulous option. The crowds are thinner during the week, yet most services are open. That said, be aware that many tourist-dependent businesses in smaller towns choose to close shop mid-week, often on Monday or Tuesday, in order to accommodate the majority of travelers and yet still have a break themselves. A little foresight can help you to choose the best day to hit most of your selected destinations.

hours of operation

Many businesses change their hours frequently or seasonally. Hours of operation are frequently included in these pages, but be aware that this information may change without notice. Phone numbers and, when possible, websites for each listing are included here so that you can access current information on your own. Also, small businesses can be known to change location or phone number at whim. If a phone number turns out to be out of service, call information or try a web search. Keep in mind, too, that many businesses close on major holidays, even though that information may not be indicated in these pages.

pricing key

The price codes for accommodations and restaurants are represented as a scale of one to three dollar signs ($).

Most businesses take credit cards these days, but you can't always be guaranteed of this convenience. Should a business require cash only, in most cases they can direct you to a nearby ATM to access cash, which will sometimes assess a small banking fee. You will only pay sales tax in Washington (the percentage varies by area), not Oregon, and some Washington attractions may have already factored sales tax into their pricing schema.

restaurants

The price code used here is based on the average price of dinner entrees for two, excluding drinks, appetizers, dessert, tax, and tip. (Oregon has no sales tax; Washington does and it varies by county and city). You can typically expect to pay a little less for lunch and/or breakfast, where applicable. If the business only serves lunch and/or breakfast, the code has been applied to those meals.

$ Less than $20
$$ $20 to $35
$$$ More than $35

accommodations

This book is intended primarily for those who wish to venture out of the city for just a day or half-day. However, overnight accommodations are included in many sections for those who wish to explore an area further. You wouldn't be the first to find yourself at the beach or in the mountains and not ready to leave yet. Accommodations included here are almost all local hotels and bed and breakfasts. Large national chains are typically not included, though many of the larger cities in this book do have chain hotels. Other cities in this book are too small for a chain—some are too small for any other lodging. In that case the Where to Stay section has been omitted. Each day trip does not include accommodation listings for every stop, though typically at least one stop per day trip includes a suggested overnight lodging. With few exceptions, most towns in each trip aren't more than 40 minutes apart, and many are much closer.

The following price code is used for accommodations throughout this book. It is based on the average price of a one-night stay in a standard, double-occupancy room, before taxes. This price does not include state and city hotel taxes, which vary but are typically around 8 percent. City taxes vary, and are typically lower in smaller towns. Keep in mind that lodging prices often change seasonally or between the weekend and mid-week. Summer pricing is almost always higher, and weekends are very frequently more expensive, as well.

$ Less than $100

$$ $100 to $200

$$$ More than $200

driving tips

In general, Oregon and Washington have good signage, and navigation between towns should be fairly straightforward. That said, especially in more rural areas, signage is more intermittent, roads narrower, more winding, and not as well lit. Drive cautiously and keep your eyes open for road changes and directional signage.

In the winter, many of the destinations included in this book can be subject to stormy weather. The beach can be windy and incredibly rainy; the mountains snowed in. Occasionally some of the roads in this book are closed due to weather conditions. Always travel with caution in the winter, and plan ahead. For road closures and weather information, call the **Oregon Department of Transportation Trip Check** at (800) 977-ODOT or check it online at www.tripcheck.com. Always stay on marked, plowed roads. If you aren't sure where you are or which way to go, ask for directions. It doesn't hurt to carry water, blankets, and food when traveling in the Pacific Northwest in the winter. A cellular phone is always handy—charge it up before you leave!

There are many differences of which day trippers should be aware between travel in Oregon and travel in Washington. Oregon is one of the last states in the nation in which travelers are not allowed to pump their own gas. Wait for an attendant and ask him or her for the gas type and quantity you desire. In Washington, gas is pump-your-own. Oregonians might find this an uncomfortable practice—ask for help if you aren't sure how to operate a gas pump.

Maximum highway speeds vary by state, too. Oregon's I-5 tops out at 65 mph, while Washington's I-5 allows speeds up to 70 mph. State highway top speeds vary, too. In Oregon you won't see any allowed speeds over 55 mph on rural highways; Washington may allow higher speeds. The best practice is to stay alert, pay attention, and obey the posted signs.

Keep in mind that speed limits can change abruptly from one town or stretch of highway to the next. While it's important to heed speed limits at all times when driving, be particularly cautious when passing through construction zones, where speeding ticket fines can be double the normal (already high) fine. Many smaller highways in these trips pass directly through small towns, necessitating a speed limit change on either end. Respect the residents of these towns, and avoid getting pulled over by a police officer, by slowing down appropriately.

Mileage is calculated, in most chapters, from the **Portland City Center.** Depending on from which specific part of Portland you begin your day trip, mileage and directions will vary. Use a good city or state map, or electronic navigation system, to determine how to best merge onto major arterials out of town from your exact starting point.

Another thing to keep in mind is that car travel isn't your only option for many of these day trips. Portland's Tri-Met bus system services many of the communities included in this book. See www.trimet.org. Another option is your bicycle. Many of the smaller more rural roads and destinations in this book are simply perfect for road biking. Be safe and wear a helmet, please.

highway designations

For consistency's sake, this book typically refers to state highways with "OR," "WA," or "SR" followed by the highway number (e.g., OR 20). In many cases, that number will be followed by a cardinal designation (e.g., OR 20 E). In some situations, multiple highways run along the same path. In other cases, the same highway may have more than one name. OR 26 W, for example, is also known as the Sunset Highway. The road in Washington State that leads to Mt. St. Helens is known as WA 504/Mt. St. Helens Way NE/Spirit Lake Highway. A good map, GPS, or mapping service like Google Maps or Mapquest can help you sort things out.

area codes

The northwest corner of Oregon uses the area code 503. This area extends south to Salem, southwest to Pacific City, east to Mt. Hood, and southeast to Detroit. Beyond those parameters, in Oregon, the 541 area code is the most prevalent, though you will also see the area code 458. In Washington, the areas covered in this book almost all use 564, though some north of Longview may use 509 or 360. Cell phone prefixes, obviously, vary widely.

where to get more information

Day Trips from Portland, Oregon attempts to cover a variety of interests and destinations, but those looking for additional travel information can contact the following agencies by phone, mail, or the web. Keep in mind that online reviews can be contradictory, as everyone experiences places differently. Call directly or stick with advice from respected travel organizations.

for general travel information:

Oregon Department of Transportation
Intelligent Transportation Systems
800 Airport Rd. SE, Room 81, Salem, OR 97301
(800) 977-ODOT
www.tripcheck.com (for hotels, food, attractions, and road condition information)

Oregon State Tourism
Travel Oregon and MEDIAmerica
715 SW Morrison, Suite 800, Portland, OR 97201
(800) 547-7842
www.traveloregon.com
Request a copy of *Travel Oregon*'s magazine and travel guides.

Washington State Tourism
tourism@cted.wa.gov
(800) 544-1800
www.experiencewa.com

AAA Oregon
600 SW Market St., Portland, OR 97201
(503) 222-6767 or (800) 452-1643
www.aaaorid.com

AAA Washington
4301 E Fourth Plain Blvd., Vancouver, WA 98661
(360) 696-4081
www.aaawa.com

Oregon.com
Oregon Interactive Corp.
P.O. Box 727
611 NE 3rd St., McMinnville, OR 97128
(503) 296-5644
www.oregon.com
Oregon-related vacation and tourism information.

for camping & recreation information:

Oregon Parks and Recreation Department, State Parks

725 Summer St. NE, Suite C, Salem, OR 97301

Main: (503) 986-0707

Reservations: (800) 452-5687

Information: (800) 551-6949

www.oregon.gov/OPRD

http://park.info@state.or.us

Washington State Parks and Recreation Commission

1111 Israel Rd. SW, Olympia, WA 98504-2650

(360) 902-8844

(888) CAMP-OUT

www.parks.wa.go

for information on farms & wineries:

Pick Your Own

www.pickyourown.org

This website features a listing of pick-your-own farms near you.

Oregon Farmer's Market Association

P.O. Box 13272, Portland, OR 97213

(503) 525-1035

www.oregonfarmersmarkets.org

Washington State Farmers Market Association

P.O. Box 445, Suquamish, WA 98392

(206) 706-5198

www.wafarmersmarkets.com

Oregon Wine Center

1200 NW Naito Pkwy., Suite 400, Portland, OR 97209

(503) 228-8336

www.oregonwine.org

Wines Northwest

P.O. Box 87575, Vancouver, WA 98687

(360) 604-1205

www.winesnw.com

The Pacific Northwest's guide to wines and wine country.

north

day trip 01

north

the city to the north:
vancouver, wa

vancouver

When it comes to West Coast cities, Vancouver is often overlooked. With a population of 165,000, Vancouver is smaller and less glamorous than Portland and Seattle. And on an international scale, Vancouver, British Columbia, is the better known of the two Pacific Coast Vancouvers.

But when it comes to history, Vancouver, Washington, has all three other cities beat. Vancouver was established in 1857, a few years after Portland but long before Vancouver, B.C., or Seattle. And at that point, Vancouver had already been long inhabited by white settlers at the historic Fort Vancouver trading post.

In modern times, Vancouver is recognized for its culinary scene, including one of the Northwest's oldest farmers' markets, highly acclaimed restaurants, and an emerging wine region. Vancouver is also a budding hub for fashion design and boutique shopping. The downtown area continues to undergo a revitalization effort that has transformed it into a very popular and attractive destination.

Still, Vancouver's primary draws are its history and natural surroundings. Ft. Vancouver National Historic Site is one of the most visited historical destinations in the West. Much of the city fronts the massive, impressive Columbia River, and to the north is rich farmland, forests, old railroads, and wildlife. Vancouver was Washington's first city and remains its fourth largest today. As a day tripper, you'll find much to like about this city to the north.

getting there

Vancouver is directly north of Portland, just over the state line into Washington. Vancouver city center is 10 miles north of Portland City Center on I-5.

where to go

Chelatchie Prairie Railroad. NE Railroad Avenue, Yacolt; (360) 686-3559; www.bycx .com. In logging boom days, this railroad line transported logs to Columbia River ports. Pulled by a 1929 ALCO 2-8-2T steam locomotive, the train today transports sightseeing passengers through scenic northern Clark County from Yacolt to Mouton Falls and Chelatchie Prairie and back. Special events include casino nights, murder mysteries, staged hold-ups, Christmas tree trips, leaf peeper trips, and barbeque trips.

Clark County Historical Museum. 1511 Main St.; (360) 993-5679; www.cchmuseum .org. The history of Clark County is on display at this Vancouver museum housed in a former Carnegie Library, built in 1909 and listed on the National Register of Historic Sites. Exhibits include a Native American gallery, railroad display, American military memorabilia, an old country store, country kitchen, and doctor's office. This museum is also the place to pick up a walking map for Tour through Time, a walking tour of Vancouver's historic properties. Open Tues through Sat 11 a.m. to 4 p.m. Admission to the museum is free on the evening of the first Thurs of each month from 5 p.m. to 9 p.m. during the museum's after hours program.

Esther Short Park Glockenspiel. 6th and Columbia Streets; www.ci.vancouver.wa.us. In a corner of this huge downtown park you'll find a hidden treasure—the Salmon Run Bell Tower and Glockenspiel. The bells for this magnificent public artwork were cast in the Netherlands and shipped in. There are four 5-foot-long bronze jumping salmon on the tower and several jets that spray water down the column. A Chinook Indian story is inscribed in the basalt column around the base of the tower and a fully animated three-scene glockenspiel depicts the Chinook Indian legend daily just after the bells ring at noon, then every 2 hours until 8 p.m.

Fort Vancouver National Historic Site and Visitor Center. 615 E Reserve St.; (360) 816-6200; www.fortvan.org. When the Lewis and Clark Expedition came through this region in 1805, Meriwether Lewis wrote that the Vancouver area was "the only desired situation for settlement west of the Rocky Mountains." But the first permanent European settlement did not occur until 1824, when Fort Vancouver was established as a fur trading post of the Hudson's Bay Company. This bustling fort became the center of political, cultural, and commercial activities in the Pacific Northwest. Today, interpreters in period clothing reenact mid-19th century daily life at the reconstructed fort. Open daily. The Visitor Center is free to enter; Fort Vancouver admission is $5 for a family, $3 for adults, and free for youth under the age of 15.

Officers Row. 750 Anderson St.; (360) 992-1800; www.fortvan.org. Where else in the Northwest can you stroll past 22 preserved Victorian homes on the National Historic Register? Built in the mid- to late 1800s, these beautifully restored homes were constructed to house US Army officers stationed with their families at Vancouver Barracks. The O. O. Howard House is home to the Visitor Information Center and is open to the public. The Grant House features a restaurant by the same name. The Marshall House offers tours and an exhibit on General George C. Marshall, its most famous resident. Group tours available. No admission fee.

Pearson Air Museum. 1115 E 5th St.; (360) 694-7026; www.fortvan.org. Aviation history is on display at Pearson Air Museum, located at the oldest continually operating airfield in the US. Exhibition areas offer a collection of vintage airplanes, interpretive displays, an interactive children's center, theater presentations, and a gift shop. Open 10 a.m. to 5 p.m. Wed through Sat. Free admission for children under the age of 6.

Pendleton Woolen Mills. 2 17th St., Washougal; (360) 835-1118; www.pendleton-usa .com. The Pendleton tradition of making quality woolen blankets in Native American motifs extends back to 1909. Visitors to this mill today can tour the facilities and see firsthand 100 percent virgin wool go through the state-of-the-art dye house, spinning and weaving, and finishing process. After the tour, shop the Mill Outlet Store and select from Pendleton's array of quality menswear, womenswear, distinctive Indian blankets, and fabrics. Group tours available.

Pomeroy Living History Farm. 20902 NE Lucia Falls Rd., Yacolt; (360) 686-3537; www .pomeroyfarm.org. Period-dressed interpreters help visitors experience 1920s farm life with activities like washing clothes, feeding livestock, grinding grain, and making rope at this farmstead registered on the National Register of Historic Places. Take a tour through the 6-bedroom log home. Open the first full weekend of the month, June through Sept, and special event weekends. Hours are 10 a.m. to 5 p.m. Sat, 1 p.m. to 5 pm. Sun.

Ridgefield National Wildlife Refuge and Cathlapotle Plankhouse. 1071 S Hillhurst Rd., Ridgefield; (360) 887-4106; www.ridgefieldfriends.org. The Ridgefield National Wildlife Refuge consists of more than 5,000 acres of vital migration and wintering habitat for spring and fall migrating birds. The mild winter climate and wetlands along the Columbia River create ideal resting and feeding areas for 180 species of birds such as Canada geese, sandhill cranes, great blue herons, swans, shore and song birds, and a variety of waterfowl. Visitors can see these and other wildlife while driving the 4-mile auto tour or hiking along the 2-mile Oaks to Wetlands Wildlife Trail. On site at the location of Cathlapotle, one of the largest Chinookan villages in the area, you will also find a full-scale replica of a Chinookan-style cedar plankhouse. This Lewis and Clark historical site is where the Corps of Discovery camped in November 1805 and again in March 1806. Visitors to the plankhouse learn about

> ## walk it off
>
> *With more than 40 miles of urban walking trails, it's no wonder Vancouver's Clark County received the Walkable Community Award from* Walking *magazine. These two trails are the most popular, and actually can be walked as one if you are feeling ambitious.*
>
> - ***Discovery Loop Trail.*** *The 2.3-mile loop begins on East Evergreen Street and winds through Ft. Vancouver National Historic Site, Officers Row, and downtown Vancouver, joining the Waterfront Renaissance Trail at Vancouver Landing. Sights along the way include Ft. Vancouver, Pearson Air Museum, Providence Academy, and Esther Short Park.*
>
> - ***Waterfront Renaissance Trail.*** *From downtown, head south on Columbia Avenue to pick up the trail at the waterfront. This 4-mile, 14-foot-wide shared-use trail connects downtown to the retail shops and restaurants along the Columbia River waterfront. The trail passes the plaza and a 7-foot tall statue dedicated to Ilchee, a Chinook Indian chief's daughter. There are many parks and picnic areas along the way.*

the culture and habitat of this area's original inhabitants. Refuge and trails open year-round. Plankhouse only open seasonally—call ahead to check for hours of operation.

Wineries. Lucky you—there are so many wineries in the Pacific Northwest, a good number of them in the Vancouver region. We've chosen just a few to name here, but there are many more. See www.visitvancouverusa.com/wineries for a complete listing.

Bethany Vineyards. 4115 NE 259th St.; (360) 887-3525; www.bethanyvineyardand winery.com. Bethany Vineyard and Winery, voted Best Winery in Clark County in 2009, combines the best traditions of winemaking with the nearly perfect growing climate of southwest Washington to produce a wine with distinct flavor and character. Visit the winery and tasting room, bring a picnic lunch or have the folks at Bethany Vineyards prepare one for you, then take a stroll through the beautiful lakeside vineyard. Open Sat from 11 a.m. to 6 p.m., Sun noon to 5 p.m., and by appointment.

East Fork Cellars. 24415 NE 10th Ave., Ridgefield; (360) 607-8430; www.eastfork cellars.com. The rich, alluvial soils and temperatures moderated by the East Fork of the Lewis River provide the outstanding characteristics of these estate wines. East Fork Cellars specializes in creating wonderful blends of red varietals and offers a "Blend Your Own" program where you can make and private-label your own special wine. The vineyard grows pinot noir, pinot gris, and chardonnay. Open Tues through Sat 11 a.m. to 7 p.m., and Sun noon to 7 p.m.

English Estate Winery. 17908 SE 1st St.; (360) 772-5141; www.englishestatewinery .com. English Estate Winery makes a wide variety of award-winning wines from its own pinot noir and cabernet sauvignon vineyards. Winemaker Carl English takes great pride in the arts of wine grape growing and wine-making. The quaint European-style buildings, towering trees, and seasonal flowers at this winery make a perfect setting for tasting wine. Open tasting hours are Apr through Dec, Fri, Sat, and Sun, noon to 6 p.m.

where to shop

Agave Premium Denim and Apparel. 6210 S 11th St., Ridgefield; (360) 887-5400; www .agavedenimoutlet.com. A favorite among stars such as Mark Wahlberg, Zooey Deschanel, and Courtney Cox, Agave Denim opened an outlet store, design studio, and warehouse in Ridgefield in 2010. This stylish shop is definitely a stand-out in the local shopping scene.

Downtown Camas. www.downtowncamas.com. The downtown area of Camas, just east of Vancouver, is truly a treasure to be found. The quaint, tree-lined street running through the heart of the city boasts a variety of shops, eateries, and the fully restored Liberty Theater (circa 1927), all within walking distance of one another. The eclectic boutique shops here offer antiques, ladies' fashions, accessories, jewelry, and home decor and have attracted the attention of professional shoppers Joe Apodaca and Jermonne Swendell. Some highlights include:

Chateau Lauren. 339 NE 4th Ave. Fabulously beautiful interior design store.

Camas Antiques. 305 NE 4th Ave. More than 50 booths with antiques and collectibles.

Painless Ric's Tattoo Studio. 315 NE Birch St. What's a day trip without a commemorative tattoo?

Lily Atelier. 237 NE 4th Ave. Gorgeous high-end apparel.

Uptown Village. 1701 Broadway; www.uptownvillage.com. The upper Main Street area of Vancouver offers a mixture of antique stores, gift shops, restaurants, and boutiques. Seasonal activities and festivals are scheduled throughout the year here. From downtown Vancouver, head north on Main Street.

Vancouver Farmers' Market. Esther Short Park, 6th and Columbia Streets; (360) 737-8298; www.vancouverfarmersmarket.com. From Apr through Oct each year, the street adjacent to Esther Short Park comes alive with more than 150 vendors offering local produce, plants, arts, and crafts. Food booths offering local and international specialties keep the crowd well fed while entertainers provide live music. This is the place to pick up local produce, arts, and culture.

where to eat

Beaches. 1919 SE Columbia River Dr.; (360) 699-1592; www.beaches.simplehelix.com. Beaches is a casual and fun dining establishment located on the banks of the Columbia River offering great views, especially in the summer. Chicken, steak, seafood, rice bowls, pizza, sandwiches, and a full and happening bar in a tropical-themed space transform a night out into a mini-vacation. $–$$$.

The Grant House. 1101 Officers Row; (360) 906-1101; www.thegranthouse.us. This place has been called "Vancouver's Best Kept Secret," but that might not last for long if the Grant House keeps getting the press it deserves. Set on the scenic Officers Row, this restaurant offers lunch and dinner as well as an extensive collection of single malt scotches, whiskies, bourbons, and more than 200 wines. Large windows overlook lovely grounds; in the summer, enjoy the outdoor patio or veranda. $$–$$$.

La Bottega. 1905 Main St.; (360) 571-5010; www.labottegafoods.com. La Bottega, located in the Uptown Village section of downtown Vancouver, is a local's favorite. Wine lovers and foodies gather here to enjoy monthly special wine dinners with menus that change seasonally. La Bottega is also a deli. Stop in for a large variety of quality meats, imported cheeses, oils, vinegars, sauces, pasta, soups, entrees, and more, as well as retail beer and wine. Open Mon through Sat for lunch and dinner. Closed Sunday. $$–$$$.

Lapellah. 2520 Columbia House Blvd.; (360) 828-7911; www.lapellah.com. The name Lapellah comes from the trade language used in the area in the 1800s and means "to cook or roast over an open fire." Similar to a language made up of words from many cultures, Lapellah's menu is a melting pot of foods. The restaurant features a full bar, an open kitchen, and a wood-fired grill. Dishes range from grilled Carlton Farms rib eye steak to New Orleans BBQ shrimp, but each is great. From the creation of dishes to the handmade interior, Lapellah takes a sustainable approach to dining. Open Mon through Thurs 11 a.m. to 10 p.m., Fri and Sat 11 a.m. to 11 p.m., and Sun 10 a.m. to 10 p.m. (brunch 10 a.m. to 2:30 p.m.). $$$.

Roots. 19215 SE 34th St.; (360) 260-3001; www.rootsrestaurantandbar.com. Brad Root's flagship restaurant Roots was voted by *Bon Appétit* magazine as "one of the best spots around the country for a romantic winter dinner." Dishes like seared duck breast with pumpkin risotto, cattail creek lamb shank with goat cheese polenta, and fish and chips with mac n' jacks beer batter keep guests coming back. Open for lunch and dinner 7 days a week. $$–$$$.

Tommy O's Pacific Rim Grill. Downtown Bistro: 801 Washington St.; (360) 694-5107; Eastside Grill: 4101 SE 192nd Ave.; (360) 892-2484; www.tommyosaloha.com. At Tommy

O's, the vibrant, rich flavors of the cultures that compose the Pacific Rim serve as the inspiration for fresh and flavorful food. With influences from Honolulu to Hong Kong, Chef Tommy Owens designs specials featuring innovative and locally sourced organic ingredients. The downtown location is open for breakfast, lunch, and dinner 7 days a week. The eastside location is open for lunch and dinner every day. Call for details. $$–$$$.

where to stay

The Heathman Lodge. 7801 NE Greenwood Dr.; (360) 254-3100; www.heathmanlodge .com. This relaxing, rustic getaway in a mountain-like setting delivers a tranquil retreat brimming with Northwest ambiance. The Heathman Lodge is a very big hotel, popular with conferences and weddings. There is a pool, spa, and health and fitness center on site. Hudson's Bar and Grill serves delicious foods of the Pacific Northwest and bakes all of its pastries and breads in their own kitchen. $$.

Hilton Vancouver. 301 W 6th St.; (360) 993-4500; www.hilton.com. It's true that this is a chain hotel, but the Hilton Vancouver is a relatively new facility, part of downtown Vancouver's renaissance efforts, across the street from Esther Short Park and truly one of the best places to stay in town. The boutique-style Hilton Vancouver offers 226 guest rooms and 10 suites that are exceptionally furnished. $–$$.

day trip 02

north

the mighty columbia:
scappoose, st. helens

scappoose

The name Scappoose comes from the Chinook Indian language and means "gravelly plains." This region of Oregon, which fronts the southern shore of the Columbia River as it approaches the Pacific Ocean, once served as prime Indian hunting grounds. The rich riverfront soil, plains of wild grass, wetlands, and waters of the Columbia nurtured herds of elk and deer, spawning salmon, and flocks of upland birds. The bounty of wildlife astounded Lewis and Clark during their 1804 to 1806 travels, and later captured the attention of migratory fur traders, who came here to trap the beaver that lived in the rivers.

The fur trade died out long ago, but dairies, farming, and logging thrived as commercial endeavors in this region through the middle of the 20th century. Today, Scappoose is largely a bedroom community for Portland, as well as a popular weekend getaway.

Visitors still come to see the rich biodiversity and wildlife. Perhaps the biggest attraction to the Scappoose area is Sauvie Island—the largest island in the Columbia River. Because of its size and rich ecosystem, the island is the perfect destination for so many activities—biking, hiking, bird watching, hunting, boating, and kayaking. Sauvie Island's Columbia River beaches are the best riverfront sandy beaches in the greater Portland area, and fill up with families seeking a dip in the Columbia when the weather turns hot. Sauvie Island is also home to small farms, pumpkin patches, roadside produce vendors, and farmers' markets. In the summer and fall especially, thousands of Portlanders drive

north day trip 02

N

0   5   10 miles

Kalama

WASHINGTON

30

503

Woodland

Columbia
City
St. Helens

5

Vernonia

Warren

Ridgefield

OREGON

Columbia River

Sauvie
Island

47

Scappoose

Sturgeon
Lake

502

30

Vancouver

6

47

5

26

47

26

8

Hillsboro

Portland

99E

8

Forest
Grove

Cornelius

Beaverton

5

Tigard

47

219

99W

the short distance to this bucolic, beach-fronted, Pacific Northwest version of an island paradise.

getting there

Take I-405 north to the exit for US 30 W/St. Helens. Follow US 30 north out of Portland, through the industrial area and railroad switchyards that line the Columbia River. Soon, US 30 will become more rural. Scappoose is 20 miles north of Portland on US 30.

where to go

Crown Zellerbach Trail. The trailhead is located approximately 2 miles off US 30 on Scappoose-Vernonia Road. Part of the Rails to Trails program, this scenic trail connects Scappoose with Vernonia, where it connects to another popular and well-developed trail, the Banks-Vernonia Trail. Great for walking, jogging, bicycling, and horseback riding, the CZ Trail, as it is known, is a point of community pride and a great way to see the countryside and get some exercise at the same time. It's also mostly flat terrain, making it a great place to take kids.

Joy Creek Nursery. 20300 NW Watson Rd.; (503) 543-7474; www.joycreek.com. This 7-acre nursery has hundreds of plants for sale, offers classes, and can even dispatch a landscape gardening design team to your home to create the garden of your dreams. Open 7 days a week, 9 a.m. to 5 p.m., Mar through Oct, or by appointment. Please call 24 hours in advance to arrange to visit the nursery during the winter.

Sauvie Island. Sauvie Island lies approximately 10 miles northwest of downtown Portland and is accessed by a sole bridge from US 30. The island's unique character as a wildlife area, agricultural community, and recreational destination so close to the Portland metro area makes it a highly prized destination for visitors. The island is situated between the Columbia River to the east, the Multnomah Channel to the west, and the Willamette River to the south. At 26,000 acres, it is the largest island along the Columbia River—an island so large it has its own rivers, lakes, islands, and sloughs, and even a small school and a volunteer fire department.

Sauvie Island is also simply very beautiful. As visitors cross the bridge, a serene vista of fields, trees, and the Cascade Range spreads out before them. If the day is clear, folks spot Mt. Rainier, Mt. St. Helens, Mt. Adams, Mt. Hood, and Mt. Jefferson. Fruit (mostly berries), vegetables, flowers, and pumpkins are all available on the island for you-pick. If you are in a hurry or don't wish to pick your own produce, roadside farm stands sell just about everything grown on the island.

In the fall and winter, the island hosts over 150,000 migratory ducks and geese. The wildlife area is open to the public mid-Apr through Sept and closed to hunting permit only over the wintering months. Sun-and-sand seekers migrate to Walton Beach, accessed via Reeder Road and about 9 miles from the Sauvie Island Bridge. The beach is a mile long—be aware that beyond that is the area called Collins Beach, which in grand Pacific Northwest tradition has been considered clothing-optional since the 1970s. Also be advised that all beach parking is subject to Sauvie Island Wildlife Area parking permits, which are available at all the stores on the island and cost just a few dollars. Vehicles without a permit are subject to a ticket costing around $75.

Destinations on Sauvie Island actually use Portland addresses. The northernmost tip of the island reaches nearly to Scappoose, but there is no connecting road to the mainland on that end of the island. Services are limited on the island, as you might expect, but there are a few stores and small businesses, mostly at the southern tip of the island near the bridge. Here is a sampling:

Bella Organic Farm. 16205 NW Gillihan Rd.; (503) 621-9545; www.bellaorganic .com. Bella Organic is a certified organic farm on 100 acres of organic ground. This young and growing farm's goal is to promote responsible farming practices. A large variety of organic fruits and vegetables including strawberries, heirloom tomatoes, beefsteak tomatoes, blueberries, blackberries, zucchini, green beans, carrots, garlic, sweet corn, cucumbers, and asparagus is available you-pick and already picked. Open June through Nov.

Columbia Farms. 21024 NW Gillihan Rd.; (503) 621-3909; www.columbiafarms u-pick.com. This large farm has been on the island for ages and offers 8 different types of berries on over 80 acres, all available for you-pick. Visitors also find flowers, tomatoes, pumpkins, and all types of fall decor items. Open June, July, Sept, and Oct.

Island Cove Cafe and Market. 31421 NW Reeder Rd.; (503) 621-9300. One of the few places to get food on the island, this little market offers a menu of local sustainable dishes that guests can eat inside or outside on the patio, or take to go. Located on the east side of the island near the beaches, Island Cove Café and Market also offers market supplies, Oregon Department of Fish and Wildlife (ODFW) parking permits, and fishing tackle. Summer hours: 9 a.m. to 7 p.m. every day from May to Oct. Winter hours are 9 a.m. to 5 p.m. Wed through Sun.

Sauvie Island Lavender Farms. 20230 NW Sauvie Island Rd.; (503) 577-6565; www.sauvieislandlavenderfarm.com. This beautiful farm pays homage to a Victorian garden with lovely paths leading to a flower-filled arbor where visitors can view four snow-capped mountain peaks and hundreds of acres of nursery and farmland. Purchase lavender bouquets, sachets, essential oils, and more. The farm is only open seasonally, but you can shop online all year.

Scappoose Bay Kayaking. 57420 Old Portland Rd., Warren; (503) 397-2161; www .scappoosebaykayaking.com. Itching to get out on the water? This shop is your source for water access to the beautiful Scappoose Bay, offering kayak sales, tours, and rentals. Guided journeys include a wetland tour, slough tour, and lighthouse tour. Rentals include recreational kayaks in single, tandem, or pedal-powered styles, each popular with first-timers for their safe, flat bottom designs. Touring kayaks are also available in both single and tandems for more advanced paddlers. Try a canoe; ask about Sailyaks.

where to stay

Scappoose Creek Inn. 53758 W Lane Rd.; (503) 543-2740; www.scappoosecreekinn .com. Two beautifully restored farmhouses sit on this early 1900s-era dairy farm, where they've been transformed into a lovely bed and breakfast. The adjacent barn, once the site of one of the largest Prohibition-era busts in the region for housing a massive still and producing bootleg liquor, is now an event hall that can host up to 150 people. A tree-lined drive leads to this peaceful retreat for a romantic or personal getaway, where rooms are decorated with country charm and farm-inspired knick-knacks. $–$$.

st. helens

Most travelers don't find many reasons to drive US 30 unless they are en route to Astoria, putting the small town of St. Helens solidly off the beaten path. But this little city makes for a great close-at-hand escape from the big city, and is the perfect day trip for those seeking the quirkiness and comforts of a visit to an old-fashioned small town.

Don't be fooled, though—St. Helens is more than antiquated. This is one cool hamlet. In fact, it might be your kids who drag you here. Why? Because St. Helens has appeared in many films, including most notably the pop culture vampire saga sensation *Twilight*. That little factoid has put this place on the map, and tours and tourist attractions have sprung up to accommodate the masses who come here seeking a glimpse of scenery from the movies.

Those who aren't *Twilight* maniacs will still find plenty to enjoy in St. Helens. The Olde Towne area located along a 3-block stretch of First Street on the waterfront is eclectic and includes shops, restaurants, an old courthouse, and a theater. On a clear day the tops of Mt. St. Helens, Mt. Adams, and Mt. Hood frame the scenery.

getting there

From Scappoose, continue north along the Columbia River on the Lower Columbia River Highway/US 30. St. Helens is 8.5 miles from Scappoose. Turn right on Columbia Boulevard and follow it for 1.5 miles into Olde Towne St. Helens, on the riverfront.

where to go

Captured by Porches Brewery. 40 Cowlitz St., #B; (971) 207-3742; www.capturedby porches.com. These beer makers might be a bit tricky to track down, but it's worth it if you can pull it off. All beers from this relatively new brewery are made with regionally grown,

> ## movin' and groovin'
>
> *In the summer, this little port town comes alive. The outdoor amphitheater at Columbia View Park, right on the Columbia River near Olde Towne St. Helens, hosts outdoor concerts Thursday nights beginning in June. This "13 Nights on the River" series also includes an open air market with dinner options from local restaurants as well as variety of merchandise vendors. Summer evenings are balmy and gorgeous here, and this is a great opportunity to take a little sunset escape from the bustle of the city. See www.travelcolumbiacounty.com for more information.*

locally malted organic grain. The Invasive Species IPA is available all year, and there's always at least one other beer available seasonally. Captured by Porches brewery proper doesn't have a tasting room, but the brewery serves beer from their MoPub Bus, parked in the summertime until Halloween at Kruger's Farm Market (17100 NW Sauvie Island Rd.) on Sauvie Island. Call for details during the rest of the year. About that name—Captured by Porches is what happens when good friends get together with good beer. They end up captured on a porch whiling the night away. Wherever you find these folks, be aware that they probably won't be serving any food—unless you, like so many of us, consider beer a food.

Fishing the Columbia with Dan's Guide Service. Warren; (503) 816-6803; www.fishwithdan.com. River mouths make excellent fishing grounds because waters of different temperatures collide. There's plenty of that going on here around St. Helens, where several tributaries enter the Columbia River and the Columbia's mouth itself is so close by. Experienced guide Dan Warren loves to take folks fishing in these marvelous waters. Try your luck catching salmon, steelhead, or sturgeon, depending on the season. Guided trips run approximately $175 per person.

Halloweentown. Olde Towne St. Helens in October; www.halloweentownblog.com. Even before *Twilight,* St. Helens had earned itself a frightful reputation. The films *Halloweentown* and *Behind the Mask* were also filmed here. Each October, the small town turns itself over to all things scary and becomes Halloweentown. Every weekend for the entire month, larger than life scarecrows line the streets, shopkeepers turn into witches, ghosts and ghouls prowl about, and even the historic courthouse square becomes just a little . . . creepier. Costumed visitors earn discounts at local shops. Now that's electrifying.

Sand Island. Not many public parks are in the middle of a river. This 40-acre manmade island is a lovely, developed park totally surrounded by water. But Sand Island has a major catch—you can only access it by boat. If you are ambitious enough to row out, you'll find camping, volleyball, birding, and all manner of artistic inspiration on Sand Island. The ecosystem is a mix of cottonwood forest and grassy areas, and here you'll find campsites, pit toilets, fire pits, picnic tables, nature trails and one large picnic shelter. Though there are trash barrels scattered around the island, the official policy is "Pack it in, pack it out." Bring your own boat or rent one from Scappoose Bay Kayaking (www.scappoosebaykayaking .com).

The Twilight Tour. Here's what you've all been waiting for—the *Twilight* Tour! (What's that you say? You have no idea what *Twilight* is? Oh. It's one of the biggest pop culture phenomena of the past decade—a teen vampire romance taking place in the Pacific Northwest.) Several St. Helens locations were used for the filming of *Twilight*. You can find a full list plus a map at www.goseeoregon.com/guide/55-twilight-film-locations or www.travelcolumbia county.com. Here are the top three filming locations plus a couple of *Twilight*-related retail shops to tempt your bloodthirsty little palate.

Filming Locations:

Edward Saves Bella Honorary Parking Lot. 225 S 1st St. This parking lot has views of local murals and was the location of Edward's brave saving of Bella from a gang of threatening thugs. It's also a great place to park your car while you tour St. Helens.

Bella's House. 184 S 6th St. The quaint home where Bella lived with her father is actually a private residence on a dead end. Please park at the bottom of the hill and walk up to take pictures from the street.

Thunderbird and Whale Bookstore. 260 S 2nd St. This building served as the bookstore that Bella visited to research vampire life, but in real life it's a private business. Observe from a distance.

Shops:

Experience Twilight. 294 S 1st St.; (503) 396-5488; http://experiencetwilight.com. Here's the place to find an insider's scoop on St. Helens' *Twilight* movie locations, hand crafted *Twilight*-inspired collectibles, jewelry, T-shirts, and more. Get your Bella and Edward on here. Open Tues through Sat 10 a.m. to 5 p.m.

Jilly's Beverly Hills Shopping. 294 S 1st St.; (503) 396-5488; www.jillyssthelens .com. Women's outfits and accessories ranging from modern to the '50s, hippie to bellydancer, Old Hollywood to New Wave. Jilly's prom dresses and fairy wings were used in the *Twilight* dress shop scene, when Bella and her friends were shopping for prom dresses. Jilly is usually in the shop, and she loves Twilighters and telling stories about how she met Robert Pattinson.

where to eat

Dockside Steak and Pasta. 343 S 1st St.; (503) 366-0877; www.docksideontheriver .com. Right near Columbia View Park is this restaurant, with a menu that extends to fine seafood dishes, classic Italian entrées, steaks, great burgers, and interesting nightly specials. The patio has views of the Columbia River and the Cascade Range. Open Mon through Sat 11 a.m. to 9 p.m. and Sun 4 to 8 p.m. $$.

Houlton Bakery. 2155 Columbia Blvd.; (503) 366-2648; www.houltonbakery.com. This sweet little bakery serves fabulous pastries, lovely lunches like roast pork loin with cara-melized apples and corned beef and braised red cabbage, fresh baked bread, and Pacific Northwest coffee. This is a good place to take a breather from downtown strolling, and also to take the kids. Open Tues through Sat 9 a.m. to 4 p.m. $.

Klondike Restaurant and Bar. 71 Cowlitz St.; (503) 366-2634; www.klondikerestaurant .com. Serving the finest American food including sandwiches, seafood, steaks, mashed potatoes, and baked potatoes with the works in cozy, warm surroundings with charm and history. Fabulous house-made desserts are here to tempt you, too. $$–$$$.

where to stay

Nob Hill B&B. 285 South 2nd St.; (503) 396-5555; www.nobhillbb.com. Listed on the National Register of Historic Places, this home was built in 1900, giving it historic charm, yet it has been updated with modern conveniences and transformed into an inviting bed and breakfast. Guests have the choice of three romantic guest suites, each of which is luxurious and beautiful. The home also offers large gathering rooms with cozy couches. A full gourmet organic breakfast is served each morning in the formal dining room. $$.

worth more time

Vernonia. The charming little community of Vernonia is about 20 miles west of St. Helens as the crow flies. This quaint little town that sits at the lower elevation of the Coast Range mountains is a very popular day trip destination, particularly for road cyclists, who find the barely traveled roads that lead here to be friendly for their sport. Additionally, two trails designed for biking (as well as walking) terminate here—the Banks-Vernonia Trail, which begins in Banks, and the Crown-Zellerbach Trail, which begins in Scappoose.

Whether you arrive by car or by bike, you've earned the right to lunch at the **Blue House Café** (919 Bridge St.; 503-429-4350), which serves Greek and Mediterranean foods in a light, open space. Vegetarian and meat dishes with organic and local ingredients make everyone happy here.

If you decide you want to sleep over, try **Rock Creek Bed and Breakfast** (1162 State Ave.; 503-429-2503; www.rockcreekbb.com). This 2-story vintage mill house is an attrac-tive, appealing spot to spend the night, and its surrounding perennial gardens are simply gorgeous. Another option is **The Old Mill House** (487 Arkansas Ave.; 503-429-0952) which has 3 charming rooms with their own baths with shower, and access to drinks, treats, and books on the same level. A phenomenal breakfast is whipped up for guests and served to them in the formal dining room.

To get to Vernonia from St. Helens, return to Scappoose on US 30 and take a right on the Scappoose-Vernonia Highway. After 20 miles, take a left on OR 47/Nehalem Highway N, and continue 5 miles into Vernonia.

northeast

day trip 01

northeast

living volcanoes:
silver lake, wa; toutle, wa

silver lake

Once upon a time Mt. St. Helens was known for its perfect shape. Now it's known for its massive crater. On May 18, 1980, the beautiful mountain in the North Cascade Range blew its top. Everyone who was living in the Pacific Northwest remembers that event—ash fell in a radius of hundreds of miles. The eruption caused the largest landslide in recorded history. Winds reached over 300 miles per hour, and the valley below the mountain was instantly scoured by heat, wind, ash, and rock. Many folks lost their lives, as did countless wild animals.

Today, Mt. St. Helens is still treated with the reverence and awe that it earned that cataclysmic day. But in the 30-plus years that have passed, the area has also become a testament to the power and beauty of nature and the ability of the land to make a rapid recovery. Earth that was once practically annihilated has transformed into a green landscape once more, and bright flowers and green seedlings have taken their place where once there was only ash and mud.

Silver Lake is the first town off of I-5 en route to Mt. St. Helens. Though it's just a few miles off the very busy north-south interstate between Portland and Seattle, this small town feels alpine and rustic. You can feel the weight of the vast wilderness ahead, pulling you out of the city and into a terrain that is both lush and austere.

Though in a different way than years ago, Silver Lake remains a recreational playground. Visitors come here every year for skiing, spelunking, hiking, camping, horseback

N

0 5 10 miles

Kid Valley

504

Toutle

Silver Lake

Silver Lake

Castle Rock

Johnston Ridge Observatory

Mt. St. Helens National Volcanic Monument

506

505

5

411

4

Longview

Kelso

WASHINGTON

Cougar

Swift Reservoir

Yale Lake

Kalama

30

Ariel

503

Woodland

Columbia City

St. Helens

Warren

Ridgefield

Yacolt

5

Battle Ground

502

Columbia River Gorge Nat'l Scenic Area

503

Sauvie Island

Scappoose

Sturgeon Lake

205

500

OREGON

5

Vancouver

30

Camas

Washougal

14

26

84

Bridal Veil

Hillsboro

Portland

Fairview

Gresham

8

Beaverton

5

99E

205

219

Columbia River

riding, and more. Fishing is very popular—Silver Lake is one of the best largemouth bass lakes in Western Washington, and also boasts crappie, bluegill, trout, catfish, and edible carp. Tourism thrives here—thousands of people a year find that they just have to get a glimpse of that amazing Mt. St. Helens.

getting there

From Portland, take I-5 north towards Seattle. Continue for 55 miles. Look for WA 411 S/ WA 504 E exit, exit 49, towards Castle Rock/Toutle. Turn right onto WA 504/Mt. St. Helens Way NE/Spirit Lake Highway. Continue for 6 miles into Silver Lake.

where to go

Silver Lake/Mt. St. Helens Visitors Center. Milepost 5 on WA 504. This is the first of four Mt. St. Helens Visitor Centers, and one of the most convenient for its proximity to I-5. The center features walk-through interpretive exhibits and award-winning theater programs that educate the visitor on events before, during, and after the 1980 eruption. Kids love the walk-through volcano model, and grown-ups love the bookstore, which offers books on flora and fauna local to the area and the Washington Cascades as well as, of course, the natural history of Mt. St. Helens. Nearby, a 1-mile nature trail and the Silver Lake wetlands provide opportunities to observe waterfowl, wildlife, and native vegetation against the backdrop of Mt. St. Helens. Open daily 9 a.m. to 5 p.m. from May 16 through Sept 30. Open daily 9 a.m. to 4 p.m. from Oct 1 through May 15 (except for Jan through Mar, when the center is closed Tues and Wed). Closed major holidays.

Seaquest State Park. 3030 Spirit Lake Hwy.; (888) 226-7688. Seaquest State Park is a 475-acre, year-round camping park on Silver Lake. The beautifully forested park hugs over a mile of Silver Lake shoreline. Visitors enjoy 1 mile of trail on this shallow wetland 3,000-acre lake and 6 miles of woodland trails for hiking and bicycling. There are spectacular views of wildlife, Silver Lake, and the surrounding area from the campground and surrounds, as well as children's play areas and playing fields. Great seasonal fishing, boating, and swimming are available nearby.

where to stay

Blue Heron Inn. 2846 Spirit Lake Hwy.; (360) 274-9595; www.blueheroninn.com. Choose from 7 intimate, beautiful guest rooms, each featuring simple floral decor, a queen-size bed, a full bath, and a private balcony overlooking Mt. St. Helens. A spacious parlor offers a fireplace to relax next to and comfy chairs to sit in. With the room comes a full country breakfast, served each morning in the expansive dining room. $$.

Lakeview Lodgings. 240 Lakeview Dr.; (360) 274-7482; www.mtshelenslodging.com. This cozy lodging offers 3 cabins at very affordable rates. Done up in western mountain

> ## cloudy with a chance of a ruined day trip

I visited Mt. St. Helens for the first time over 15 years ago. In 1980, when I was a child living with my family on the Oregon Coast, the explosion had been positively major news. Not only was it the primary story in the papers and on television for weeks, but, although we were 300 miles from the mythic mountain, volcanic ash fell in my own backyard.

By the time I finally ventured to Mt. St. Helens as an adult, a visit to the West Coast's most famous volcano was long overdue. A friend and I drove north from Portland on I-5 on a fair day in June, wound our way through the mountainous terrain of WA 504, and emerged at the rim to gaze upon . . . a thick bank of low-hanging clouds completely enveloping the crater. We couldn't see a thing. This is, after all, the Pacific Northwest. Clouds happen.

*One of the advantages to today's world is that there are high-tech tools to use to check the weather in advance of a much anticipated day trip. Check **www .noaa.com** for general weather conditions in the Mt. St. Helens region or try the Mt. St. Helens Volcano Cam, **www.fs.fed.us/gpnf/volcanocams/msh,** for an image of the crater itself in live time. Things might change during your drive, but at least you'll have a better shot at getting a crystal clear view of that awesome crater.*

decor with wood paneling and deer and elk patterned fabrics, these rustic cabins have log beds and fireplaces. Views of Mt. St. Helens are lovely from this Silver Lake–front location. $–$$.

Silver Cove RV Resort. 351 Hall Rd.; (877) 380-7278; www.silvercoveresort.com. Open to the public year-round, this is one of the nicer RV parks you'll visit. Large lots with hookups for RVers are here, of course, but there are also cabins for rent and a recreational facility with laundry, kitchen, and restrooms. Silver Cove itself has several canals, big enough for small watercrafts, that lead to Silver Lake. $.

Silver Lake Resort. 3201 Spirit Lake Hwy.; (360) 274-6141; www.silverlake-resort.com. This motel is basic in decor and amenities but has many charms. Views of Silver Lake, Mt. St. Helens, and the surrounding forest are pleasant. Some rooms have spa tubs and fire-places. But the pièce de résistance is that because the resort is quite literally on the lake, you can fish directly from your balcony. Now that's living. $$.

toutle

Once a thriving timber town, these days Toutle survives primarily on tourism. Like Silver Lake, Toutle is one of the last outposts before the secluded grandeur of Mt. St. Helens and its surrounds. With a population of less than 1,000, Toutle is a quiet place most of the time, but summer brings throngs of visitors. Especially during the 30-year anniversary of the Mt. St. Helens eruption in 2010, visitation to this little town thrived.

For your purposes, day tripper, Toutle is essentially the last place to pick up food and gas to keep you going on your journey to the famous mountaintop. It's also the site of overnight lodging, a couple of restaurants, a quirky roadside attraction or two, and plenty of scenic beauty.

getting there

From Silver Lake, travel east on Spirit Lake Highway/WA 504, 5 miles to Toutle.

Keep in mind that should you choose to drive to the rim of Mt. St. Helens, you will continue another 41 miles past Toutle. Aside from the last small town, Kid Valley, just a few miles past Toutle, you won't find any more towns. Therefore, the destinations in this Toutle section are not all in Toutle proper, but extend along WA 504 past Toutle. Not all destinations use street addresses per se; we've used milepost designations when appropriate to help you keep your bearings. There is only the one road, however, so you are highly unlikely to get lost.

Note: Kid Valley, just past Toutle, is the last place to gas up on the way to Mt. St. Helens.

the road(s) less traveled

*This day trip focuses on the northern rim of Mt. St. Helens and attractions en route, along WA 504. This is the most popular route to the mythic mountain, but be aware that there are two other roads that access Mt. St. Helens. **WA 503** comes in from the southwest and offers the opportunity to see the historic Cedar Creek Grist Mill, hike to the summit of Mt. St. Helens, and explore Ape Cave, a natural wonder consisting of two tubes through which lava traveled below the Earth's surface. **WA 99** provides access to the mountain from the northeast, and allows visitors access to spectacular Spirit Lake and other hiking and exploration options. See www.visitmtsthelens.com or a good Washington State map for more details.*

where to go

Bigfoot and the Buried A-Frame. Milepost 20 on WA 504, Kid Valley. This is definitely the spot to fill up your own personal quirk quota. First off is the Mt. St. Helens Bigfoot statue—a 28-foot-tall, concrete statue of the famous Sasquatch (who some say lives here, and others say was killed in the volcanic eruption), with detailed fur and a goofy grin. After you've had your photo taken with the big guy, check out the buried A-frame house nearby. The mud from the Mt. St. Helens eruption reached speeds of up to 70 miles per hour on its way down the mountain. By the time it reached Kid Valley, it had slowed to a leisurely 20 miles per hour—still plenty fast enough to destroy homes in this forest. This A-frame house—newly built at the time—wasn't destroyed, but was filled with 200 tons of silt, mud, water, and ash. Today you can see it stuck in place half underground as it was over 30 years ago, and even venture inside.

Coldwater Lake Picnic Area. Milepost 45 on WA 504. Before the eruption of Mt. St. Helens, Coldwater Lake didn't exist. A massive landslide created a natural dam that henceforth collected water: voilà, a lake. Coldwater Lake Recreation Area offers opportunity to explore the lake's origins and current flora and fauna. Restrooms and picnic tables are available. Several hikes originate here, as well. The Birth of a Lake Trail is a leisurely quarter-mile stroll on an interpretive boardwalk. The Hummocks Trail is a 2.4-mile loop through house-sized boulders. The Lakes Trail is a 9-mile round trip to the end of Coldwater Lake and back.

The Forest Learning Center. Milepost 33 on WA 504; (360) 274-7750; www.mountst helens.com/Forest-Learning-Center. Within months of the 1980 eruption of Mt. St. Helens, Weyerhaeuser Corporation began hand-planting 18 million seedlings. Today, the Forest Learning Center allows visitors to walk through a lifelike forest, experience an eruption chamber, and learn about forest recovery, reforestation, and conservation of forest resources. Interactive exhibits and a virtual helicopter tour video are indoor attractions; outdoors is a volcano playground for the kids. Open Fri through Sun from May 14 through Sept 6 from 10 a.m. to 4 p.m. Admission is free.

Hoffstadt Bluffs Visitors Center. Milepost 27 on WA 504; 15000 Spirit Lake Hwy.; (360) 274-5200; www.hoffstadtbluffs.com. This grand lodge-like facility is one of the largest post and beam structures on the West Coast and offers a family-friendly restaurant, expansive gift shop, meeting rooms, and event space all overlooking the gorgeous Toutle River Valley and Mt. St. Helens. Inside the center is the Memories of a Lost Landscape exhibit, which interprets what life was like at Mt. St. Helens before the blast. Outside, a paved walking path will take you through a memorial grove planted in 2000 in memory of the 57 people who perished in the May 18, 1980 eruption. The gift shop offers apparel, 30th anniversary items, Mt. St. Helens jewelry, ashware, glassware, and books. This is also the spot to catch a helicopter tour—the Visitors Center partners with Hillsboro Aviation to offer tours from the sky with views of Spirit Lake and the crater of Mt. St. Helens. Helicopter tours are only offered seasonally. Visitors Center open every day 9 a.m. to 4 p.m.

Johnston Ridge Observatory. Milepost 52 on WA 504; 21500 Spirit Lake Hwy.; (360) 274-2140. Sitting high atop a bluff just 5.5 miles from the Mt. St. Helens crater at an elevation of 4,314 feet is this magnificent visitor center and observatory. This facility is the closest you can get to the mountain by car when driving in from the west, and these are the best views of Mt. St. Helens and much of the 1980 blast zone available, aside from those you'd get in a helicopter. Here you can enjoy spectacular scenery including the lava dome, crater, pumice plain, and landslide deposit. A wide-screen theater presentation and interpretive displays depict the sequence of geologic events that changed the landscape. Discover the art and science of monitoring an active volcano and predicting eruptions through various displays and also read eye-witness accounts from eruption survivors. This is also the place to access the eruption trail—a 1-mile hike that offers a picture perfect view of the 1-mile-wide and 2,000-foot-deep crater. The visitor center is open daily from 10 a.m. to 6 p.m. May through Oct. Closed in winter. A Monument Pass is required and can be obtained at the center.

where to shop

Drew's Grocery and Service Station. 5304 Spirit Lake Hwy.; (360) 274-8920. This full grocery store and service station in Toutle has been turned into a hot spot by location alone. It's basically the last place to get hot deli food, hunting and fishing licenses, beer and wine, an ATM machine, fresh coffee, and ice before the meandering drive to Mt. St. Helens. Stop in for some road food and fill up the gas tank.

where to eat

Fire Mountain Grill. Milepost 27 on WA 504; 15000 Spirit Lake Hwy.; (360) 274-5217; www.hoffstadtbluffs.com. High-backed booths and wooden floors adorn the inside of this spacious restaurant at Hoffstadt Bluffs Visitors Center. In the summertime, sit outside on the spacious patio with umbrella-shaded tables. The menu offers burgers, salads, coconut prawns, and sandwiches like BLTs and grilled turkey and cheddar. Open 7 days a week, 11 a.m. to 4 p.m. in the winter, 11 a.m. to 7 p.m. in the summer. $.

19 Mile House. 9440 Spirit Lake Hwy., Kid Valley; (360) 274-8779. As the name implies, this restaurant is located at the 19-mile mark of WA 504. It's a rustic riverside joint with lots of atmosphere. The kitchen turns out good food, including the specialty/monstrosity the St. Helens Burger, which consists of a quarter-pound beef patty, a fried egg, a slab of ham, both cheddar and pepper jack cheeses, a pile of fresh local greens, onions, tomato, and a special house sauce. But make sure you save room for dessert—the 19 Mile House is famous for their fresh cobblers, including blackberry and strawberry-rhubarb. Yum. In good weather, eat outside on the veranda and gaze upon the Toutle River. $.

where to stay

Eco Park Resort. 1400 Spirit Lake Hwy.; (360) 274-7007; www.ecoparkresort.com. Cabins, RV spots, tent sites, and yurts are all options at this lodging, the closest to the blast zone. Everything is clean and very inviting, and horseback tours and the like can be arranged right from here. The restaurant goes by the amusing name Eco Park Backwoods Café and serves hearty, delicious food to prove it. Great burgers, logger stew, and rib eye steaks will keep you going, whatever Mt. St. Helens adventure you pursue. Don't miss a bite of the homemade pie. Group box lunches are available to go. $–$$.

Kid Valley Campground. 9360 Spirit Lake Hwy.; (360) 274 9060; www.kidvalley.com. Full RV hookups, partial hookups, tent sites, picnic area, bath house with showers, forested hiking trail on site, and a convenience store and gas station nearby make this lovely campground a popular destination. The Toutle River, adjacent, and Green River, nearby, have both recovered from the volcanic mudflows and offer great steelhead and salmon fishing. $.

east

day trip 01

east

wonderful waterfalls:
bridal veil, cascade locks,
stevenson, wa

bridal veil

Bridal Veil is a blink-and-you'll-miss it sort of place, with a good excuse. The natural spectacle that is the Historic Columbia River Highway sizzles with enough powerful beauty to distract even the most astute visitor from the services and amenities of a township. Boasting a dozen waterfalls, views of the magnificent Columbia Gorge, and a lush green Pacific Northwest forest, the drive along the historic highway is not to be missed.

It's also a drive with history. In the early 1900s, Samuel Hill, the "Father of the Columbia River Highway," invited Samuel C. Lancaster, a renowned engineer from Tennessee, to assist him in the construction of a road that would allow travelers to pass as close to the river and the gorge as possible. Both men agreed on one thing—the natural splendor of nature should not be marred by the road, but instead enhanced. As many lovely spots should be accessed as possible. They stayed true to this vision, and therefore the road is a narrow and meandering one that was ultimately abandoned by most travelers for the smooth sailing of the faster, newer I-84.

However, the romance of the Columbia River Highway remains undeniable, and many travelers enjoy this passageway each year. It is absolutely one of the most scenic drives in the Pacific Northwest.

This day trip begins at the start of the Historic Columbia River Highway in Troutdale, passes through the small town of Bridal Veil, and continues for the duration of the west

east day trip 01

N

WASHINGTON

Cougar

Swift
Reservoir

Yale
Lake

83

90

Ariel

503

Yacolt

Battle
Ground

Columbia River
Gorge Nat'l
Scenic Area

Cascade Range

502

503

Stevenson

14

14

Beacon Rock
State Park

North Bonneville

Skamania

Cascade
Locks

500

205

5

Vancouver

Camas

Washougal

Columbia River

14

Dodson

Multnomah Falls

84

84

Bridal
Veil

84

Portland

Fairview

Troutdale

Crown Point

205

Gresham

99E

5

Milwaukie

Damascus

212

Sandy

OREGON

224

26

205

Gladstone

Estacada

99E

Canby

213

Aurora

211

0   5   10 miles

Mt. Hood
National
Forest

section of the Highway before crossing the Bridge of the Gods and looping back west on the other side of the Columbia Gorge in Washington State. You can make the trip a loop.

getting there

The Columbia Gorge Highway begins in Troutdale. To follow it in its entirety, take I-84 E out of Portland, and then take the 257th Drive exit (exit number 17/Kane Road). Turn right on NE 257th and watch for signs for the Columbia Gorge Highway, which will be a left turn just after the Outlet Mall. From that location, in Troutdale, Bridal Veil is 15 miles past Crown Point (or a total of 29 miles from Portland).

Alternately, to proceed directly to Bridal Veil without seeing Crown Point or the first section of the Columbia Gorge Highway, take exit 28 off of I-84 and turn right into Bridal Veil. But this is not recommended. This trip is meant to be Sunday-drive-style—take it slow and easy and don't skip scenery for speed.

Note: This road is one of those that might be closed in inclement weather. If you are traveling in the winter, check www.tripcheck.com ahead of time for road condition information.

where to go

Crown Point Vista House. Eleven miles east of Troutdale on US 30; (503) 695-2240. Crown Point is a promontory that stands 733 feet above the Columbia River and offers stunning panoramic views. The Vista House, built in 1916, is a lovely masterpiece with a marble interior and brass fixtures. Here you will find a public restroom—in fact, that's about all you'll find, save for expansive beauty. It's enough. Hours vary by season and according to weather.

Hiking. The Columbia River Gorge is Portland's hiking Mecca. In addition to trails associated with the waterfalls (below), the **Eagle Creek Trail** (12 miles round trip), **Herman Creek Trail,** and **Pacific Crest National Scenic Trail** are all accessible from this part of the Historic Columbia Gorge Highway. Pick up a map at the Multnomah Falls Lodge or grab one in town before you leave to plan a hike of the duration and difficulty for which you are in the mood. In addition to food, water, and good shoes, bring a jacket—it is often rainy and windy in the gorge, in all seasons.

Multnomah Falls Lodge. 50,000 Historic Columbia River Hwy.; (503) 695-2376; www.multnomahfallslodge.com. At this lovely old lodge at the base of Multnomah Falls you'll find a visitors center, where you can learn natural and cultural history of the Columbia Gorge and pick up tips about hiking and other recreation in the area. If it's meal time, visit the restaurant, where authentic Northwest cuisine is served in a rustic, romantic environment. Open 7 days a week, but hours vary seasonally. Call for details. Note: this is not an overnight lodge, only a day lodge.

Waterfalls. One of the most famous aspects of the Columbia Gorge Highway is its string of beautiful waterfalls, most of which are accessible by car. Some require a short hike, and in fact, each of these is a great excuse for a short hike. Many of these trails are well traveled and family friendly. Pick up a map from Multnomah Falls Lodge for hiking trail details. Rather than list these waterfalls alphabetically as is the style standard for this book, here they are listed in the order you will encounter them, assuming you are driving east on the highway from Portland. This isn't a comprehensive list, either—see www.waterfallswest .com for more falls and hikes.

Latourell Falls. This falls is unique among the best-known Columbia Gorge waterfalls, as it plunges over a rocky cliff, falling straight down from an overhanging basalt cliff instead of tumbling over rocks. From the parking area, walk a short distance up the trail to a viewpoint or walk about 0.1 mile to the base of the falls.

Bridal Veil Falls. As pretty as its name, and probably the second most popular waterfall in the gorge. A short hike from the parking lot will take you to a viewpoint.

Multnomah Falls. As the granddaddy of the Columbia Gorge waterfalls, Multnomah Falls is one of the most visited destinations in the state of Oregon. This means that, while you shouldn't miss stopping here, don't expect to be alone. Walk to the viewing area located in a carved-out opening in the rock face, or for an even closer view, walk another several hundred feet up the paved trail to reach Benson Bridge, which spans the falls at the first tier. For a little more solitude, hike up to the top of the waterfall (2 miles round-trip), where you can catch a glimpse of other waterfalls and the spectacular Columbia River.

Oneonta Gorge. A trail climbs up this gorge and leads to Lower Oneonta Falls, Middle Oneonta Falls, Upper Oneonta Falls, and Triple Falls. Worth the hike if you have time.

Horsetail Falls. Easily accessed and including a swimming-sized pond, Horsetail Falls is a great place for a picnic. From here, hike a quarter-mile up the trail to reach the lovely Ponytail Falls.

where to shop

Columbia Gorge Premium Outlets. 450 NW 257th, Troutdale; (503) 669-8060; www .premiumoutlets.com. On your way to witness scenic beauty and a glimpse of the history of the Northwest, why not do a little shopping? You are going to have to drive right past this outlet mall and its 45 outlet stores, including Harry & David, Izod, and Jones New York, anyway. Just try to resist. Open Mon through Sat from 10 a.m. to 8 p.m. and Sun from 10 a.m. to 6 p.m. Extended hours during the holidays.

where to eat

Tippy Canoe Bar and Grill. 28242 E Historic Columbia River Hwy.; (503) 618-9661. This place has been around forever, as evidenced by the rough-hewn wood paneling and old-school Native American motif. But this roadside tavern-turned-family-friendly place has been renovated and is under new ownership. You'll find friendly service and excellent seafood, though it can be expensive. In the summer, Tippy Canoe offers outdoor seating. $$–$$$.

where to stay

Bridal Veil Lodge. 46650 E Historic Columbia River Hwy.; (503) 695-2333; www.bridalveil lodge.com. Bridal Veil Lodge was a popular stopping point in the heyday of early motor touring. Back in the day, which was right around 1926, it was called Bridal Veil Lodge and Auto Camp and 50 cents would get a good hot meal of roast pork, mashed potatoes, and vegetables fresh out of the garden. For another buck-fifty, you could pull the Ford around back and pitch a tent, or tuck your family into one of the snug cabins or rooms in the lodge. Today the lodge welcomes guests with the same warmth and hospitality, and a bit more modern style. $$.

McMenamins Edgefield. 2126 SW Halsey, Troutdale; (503) 669-8610; www.mcmenamins .com. The McMenamin brothers have been busy these past 20 years sweeping the Pacific Northwest for abandoned buildings with lots of heart and potential, which they harness, renovate, and transform into masterpieces of hospitality. Edgefield is one such place, and plenty of reason to make your day trip an overnighter. This sprawling facility was built in 1911 as the county poor farm. Poor no longer, today Edgefield is a National Historic Landmark and destination for thousands of visitors every year. The hotel oozes charm and houses more than 100 European guest rooms, fine dining in the Black Rabbit restaurant, 2 golf courses, pampering at Ruby's Spa, an on-site glass blower, and a full-sized music venue. There's always a party happening somewhere here. $–$$.

cascade locks

Cascade Locks is one of the oldest towns on the Columbia River, first taking root in 1853 when three white families settled here alongside the Indian families who already lived here. For as long as there had been people in the Pacific Northwest, Cascade Locks had already been a destination.

Before the installation of the Bonneville Dam, a massive stretch of rapids ran by Cascade Locks on the Columbia River, described by Lewis and Clark as the "great rapids of the Columbia." Native Americans used the site to fish in the frothy water created by the falls. The river also served as the region's main highway, clear up until the 1930s when the first roads were built. Travelers heading west by water would be forced to stop here to portage—the churning waters were 2.5 miles long and so vicious that even seasoned Indian canoers and

French-Canadian trappers often had to pull out of this part of the river. Some early Oregon settlers tried to run the rapids on makeshift rafts, atop which they'd perched their wagons. Many lost the supplies they had brought all the way across the continent—others lost their lives.

Today, Cascade Locks is still primarily a stopover for the weary traveler, as well as a quiet and scenic mountain village home to about 1,000 people. For the day tripper, it's the site of the lovely Bridge of the Gods and the impressive Bonneville Dam.

getting there

From Bridal Veil, continue east on the Historic Columbia River Highway to its terminus, just before Dodson. Merge onto I-84 E and continue east to Cascade Locks/US 30 exit, number 44, and continue into Cascade Locks. Total mileage from Bridal Veil to Cascade Locks is 17 miles.

where to go

The Bridge of the Gods. The original bridge of the gods was formed about 29,000 years ago when a mountain on the Oregon side of the river near Cascade Locks caved in, letting loose a massive slide that filled the river with 270 feet of debris. This event blocked the Columbia River and created a natural dam. Over the years, erosion slowly dug at the base of this dam, eventually tunneling through and leaving a natural bridge above. These events gave rise to a local Native American legend about "the bridge of the Gods." The modern-day Bridge of the Gods is a manmade structure, completed in 1926 as the third oldest bridge on the Columbia River. Its high perch above the river and delicate appearance, not to mention the fact that it's one of few toll bridges in the Pacific Northwest, make it as legendary as the legend that gave it a name. The bridge is open to motor and foot traffic and crosses from Cascade Locks, Oregon, to Stevenson, Washington. There is a $1 toll for passenger cars, $2 for dual-axle trucks.

Bonneville Fish Hatchery. 70543 NE Herman Loop; (541) 374-8393; www.dfw.state.or .us. Located right near Bonneville Lock and Dam, the Bonneville Fish Hatchery receives an average of 1 million visitors a year from all over the world. Built in 1909, the hatchery raises 8 million fall Chinook, 1.2 million coho, 200,000 summer steelhead, and 60,000 winter steelhead annually. Tour the grounds and visit "Herman the Sturgeon" swimming in Kelly's Pond. He's big. Also on site is the Bonneville Gift Store, open in the summer only, which sells refreshments, gift items, and educational materials about fish, wildlife, and the gorge area. All proceeds benefit Oregon's fish and wildlife. The hatchery is open year-round and is free of charge.

Bonneville Lock and Dam. Accessed from either side of the river: OR 84, exit 40; WA 14, MP 40; (541) 374-8820; www.nwp.usace.army.mil/locations/bonneville. I once knew someone who made Bonneville Dam the primary destination of their honeymoon—a concept I found mystifying until I actually saw the place myself. Whatever your opinion of dams as hydroelectric power generators, this place is a sight to behold. Watch fish migrate through underwater fish-ways and roam a 5-level facility that includes an observation deck, exhibits, a large theater, and all-glass exterior walls that allow a panoramic view of the Columbia River Gorge. A short walk leads to a viewing area inside the first powerhouse. Open 9 a.m. to 5 p.m. daily.

Cascade Locks Marine Park. 355 WaNaPa St.; (541) 374-8427. This 23-acre marine park and adjacent 3-acre island is on the National Register of Historic Places and is owned and operated by the Port of Cascade Locks. The park includes 3 historic houses that were formerly lock tenders' homes, the *Oregon Pony* (the first steam engine operated in the west), access to fishing on the Columbia River, picnic and pavilion area, a marina, and a visitor's center. The marine park is also home to the Columbia Gorge Sternwheeler. Within the park is the Cascade Locks Historical Museum, which features information, photos, and artifacts on the history of the Columbia River Gorge. The Museum is at Marine Park Port House #1. There is also a cafe and campground in this expansive park. Call (541) 374-8619 for more information.

***Columbia Gorge* Sternwheeler "Landmarks of the Gorge" Cruise.** (503) 224-3900; www.portlandspirit.com. *Portland Spirit* offers many dinner trip cruises all over the Columbia River. The *Columbia Gorge* Sternwheeler departs from Cascade Locks and provides voyageurs with outrageous views of the gorge from the perspective of the river. Glide past such natural and historic landmarks as Multnomah Falls, Beacon Rock, and Bonneville Lock and Dam. A 5-hour tour runs Wed June through Sept, includes lunch and gratuity, and costs $84 for adults, $64 for seniors and children.

where to eat

Pacific Crest Pub. 500 Wanapa St.; (541) 374-9310; www.pacificcrestpub.com. This is a good old-fashioned pub and grub joint in a boardinghouse built for Bonneville Dam workers a century ago. Pizza, burgers, and nachos are served alongside regional craft brews from Walking Man Brewery, Mt. Hood Brewery, Deschutes Brewery, and Widmer Bros. While you're here, pick up a jar of the extra-hot horseradish that Pacific Crest Pub has been known for since 1965. Open for lunch and dinner; open hours and days vary seasonally. $–$$.

stevenson

Stevenson is Cascade Locks counterpart to the north—another Columbia River city born on servicing travelers. Over 90 percent of Skamania County is protected public land, making this area a beautiful forested retreat. Hiking is great here; the views of the Columbia River and the Oregon side are outstanding. In the summertime, look for huckleberries on the trail you choose to explore.

On Stevenson's waterfront, athletes perform water sports like kiteboarding and wind-surfing. In town, you'll see a glimpse of history. Lampposts designed to look like old gas lamps sit out front of old restored buildings that date back to the early 20th century. Stevenson also boasts one of the region's best attractions, the Columbia Gorge Interpretive Center Museum, which provides further insight into this river city's history.

When you've had your fill of the outdoors and education, kick back in one of Stevenson's great restaurants or two luxury resorts and rest up for your next adventure.

getting there

Stevenson is 4 miles north of Cascade Locks across the Columbia River via the Bridge of the Gods. There is a $1 toll for passenger cars.

(To complete this day trip as a loop, after your time in Stevenson, follow SR 14 east to Vancouver and take I-5 south back into Portland, a distance of about 50 total miles from Stevenson.)

where to go

Beacon Rock. Ten miles west of Stevenson on SR 14. This giant monolith, named by Lewis and Clark in 1805, is traversed by a 0.75-mile trail to the top. Despite the steepness, an average hiker can reach the summit in less than 30 minutes, earning the right to spectacular views of the river and gorge. It's a don't-miss.

Columbia Gorge Interpretive Center and Museum. 990 SW Rock Creek Dr.; (800) 991-2338; www.columbiagorge.org. A glimpse of the history of the people of the Columbia Gorge. Exhibits here cover first people, transportation, military, and harvesting resources. There is an enormous fish wheel that sits in a spectacular open, windowed room in this multi-level facility. Open daily 10 a.m. to 5 p.m.

Dog Mountain. Twelve miles east of Stevenson on SR 14. Both intermediate and experienced hikers will enjoy Dog Mountain. This very steep 6.5-mile round trip hike offers great views of the Columbia River and, come springtime, a gorgeous display of wildflowers.

Hamilton Mountain. Eight miles west of Stevenson on SR 14. This trail offers a 7.5-mile loop for only the most experienced hikers, but families and beginners can walk just 1.25 miles up the trail to view Rodney Falls and the Pool of the Winds.

where to eat

Big River Grill. 192 SW 2nd St.; (509) 427-4888; www.bigrivergrill.us. The food here has been described as "high-end roadhouse" and "approved by the sturgeon general." Garlic shrimp, spaghetti with homemade meatballs, and Thai peanut chicken are delicious and not fussy, with big, bold flavors and large portions. The chef buys local produce and products when possible. The building, built in 1910 and reportedly once home of a brothel, has oodles of character. $–$$.

Granny's Gedunk Ice Cream Parlor. 296 SW Second St.; (509) 427-5584. An old-fashioned ice cream parlor featuring Umpqua Ice Cream, homemade waffle cones, milk shakes, espresso drinks, and mini doughnuts. This little gem is only open Apr through Sept—call for hours and details. $.

130 Bar and Grill. 130 SW Cascade Ave.; (509) 427-0161. Fine dining and casual fare on the waterfront, with a spacious deck to enjoy seasonally and beautiful views of the river and mountains. Open for lunch and dinner 7 days a week, plus brunch on Sun. $–$$.

Walking Man Brewery. 240 SW First St.; (509) 427-5520; www.walkingmanbrewing.com. This little brewpub has yummy beers with original names. Barefoot Brown, Biped Red, Flip-flop Pilsner, and Crosswalk Wheat are made fresh and are available on tap, alongside other examples of Walking Man's best. Ravioli, spring rolls, Greek salad, clam strips, and all kinds of pizzas round out the menu. Open for dinner Wed through Sun. $$.

where to stay

Bonneville Hot Springs Resort and Spa. 1252 E Cascade Dr., North Bonneville; (509) 427-7767; www.bonnevilleresort.com. This lovely resort offers extravagance and wilderness wrapped up in one. A European spa traps local hot-spring waters, while a central outdoor courtyard with waterfall adds ambiance. Each room offers a private balcony; suites have a bubbling mineral water hot tub. There is also an on-site restaurant and lounge and gorgeous gardens. Historic photos line the walls. This resort has been a favorite for many for a long time. $$–$$$.

chauffeured day trippin'

Here's your day-trip-with-personal-driver option. **Martin's Gorge Tours** *offers wine, wildflower, and waterfall tours of the Columbia River Gorge, and will even pick you up at a handful of Portland downtown hotels or the gorge hotel, Ska-mania and Bonneville Hot Springs Resort. Afternoon wine tours of the Gorge and Hood River Valley are offered daily, year-round; Morning Wildflower Tours are offered weekends from Mar through June; and morning waterfall tours are offered mid-week year-round and weekends July through Feb. Tours run from $59 to $99 per person. For more information contact Martin's Gorge Tours at (503) 349-1323 or see www.martinsgorgetours.com.*

Skamania Lodge. 1131 SW Skamania Lodge Way, Skamania; (509) 427-7700; www
.skamania.com. Seemingly in the middle of the lovely Pacific Northwest woods is this gorgeous lodge and resort. A majestic building holds 254 guest rooms boasting either a com-
manding view of the Columbia River Gorge or the lush forests of the Cascade Mountains.
The whole place is draped in extravagant native landscaping, and several courtyards offer
natural respite. Three restaurants are on site, including the award-winning Cascade Room
with expansive views of the gorge and Columbia River. For lighter fare or a drink, visit the
River Rock, which has great views, too. Greenside Grille is located outdoors by the 18-hole
golf course. Skamania's great room has towering ceilings, an enormous fireplace, and—you
guessed it—great views. This lodge is a very popular site for weddings. If you are lucky,
you'll spot a bridal party out the windows while you dine or drink. $$–$$$.

day trip 02

east

fertile valley:
hood river

hood river

Hood River is one of those mythical places—a day trip so excellent that you might just never want to leave. Located on the Columbia River at the intersection of the Cascade Range, Hood River sits smack in the middle of gorgeous scenery and is an outdoor recreation paradise to boot.

The winds here in the Columbia River Gorge reach gale forces, and Hood River has been a world-renowned destination for windsurfing and kiteboarding since the advent of these sports. Mt. Hood looms behind the city, offering opportunities to ski, trek, hike, mountain bike, and more. Mt. Adams is in view to the north. The Hood River itself tumbles fetchingly from the south to the Columbia, providing opportunities to fish as well as kayak and whitewater raft. Across the Columbia is the White Salmon River in Washington state, and even more recreational opportunities.

But Hood River isn't just for the outdoor junkie. The fertile slopes of Mt. Hood as they approach the river give birth to much of Oregon's fruit crop. There are 15,000 acres of orchards in the Hood River Valley, producing mostly apples, pears, and cherries. These are harvested each fall, but those orchards explode with vibrant blooms each spring. Other farm-fresh foods are available in the spring, summer, and early fall.

The town has dozens of lovely historical homes dotting its steep sloped streets. Great little shops and restaurants fill up the charming downtown area, which is great for walking

and offers views of the river from its higher vantage points. Wineries surround the city. The weather is even good—sunnier and warmer more often than this city's west-of-here counterparts.

The many charms of Hood River haven't escaped notice, and the city has been named to many "Best City" and "Top Town" lists, including in *Outside* and *National Geographic Explorer* magazines. Still, the population has grown only modestly in the past 10 years, and Hood River remains a lovely small town in an unbeatable setting.

getting there

Hood River is 60 miles east of Portland on I-84. Take exit 63 toward Hood River/City Center.

where to go

Windsports. Since the dawn of windsurfing, Hood River has been recognized as one of the world's best spots to catch the wind. Wind sports have flourished and evolved here, into sailboarding, kiteboarding, wakekiting, and more. If you want to try one of these sports, this is the place, and there are several vendors to help. Beginners are welcome—in fact, the Hood River Port Commission built a protected harbor for learning windsurfers called The Hook. If the thought of windsurfing terrifies you, or you'd rather just keep your feet on dry terra firma, the waterfront is still a worthy destination. The action on display here is awesome to watch.

For rentals and lessons, check out one of these shops.

Big Winds. 207 Front St.; (541) 386-6086; www.bigwinds.com. Big Winds is the largest lesson and rental center in the Columbia River Gorge. This is your source for windsurf, kiteboard, and stand up paddling rentals and lessons.

Brian's. 100 E Port Marina Dr.; (541) 386-1423; www.brianswindsurfing.com. Windsurfing and kitesurfing lessons from an instructor with 20 years' experience, located right near the water.

Hood River Water Play. 100 E Port Marina Dr.; (541) 386-9463; www .hoodriverwaterplay.com. Windsurfing, kiteboarding, wakekiting, stand up paddle boarding, and catamaran paddling—these folks offer rentals and lessons for the gamut.

Mt. Hood Railroad. 110 Cascade Ave.; (541) 386-3556; www.mthoodrr.com. The Mt. Hood Railroad was built in the early 1900s and served as an economic lifeline for the valley, carrying fruit and forest products to market and later functioning as a passenger train. Today the railroad is simply a really fun way to pass an afternoon or an evening. The rail route south out of Hood River offers great views of the Columbia River, forests, meadows, and fruit orchards. Trips are offered day and night, and many include a live narration that covers local history and key points of interest. In addition to standard sightseeing tours, the railroad offers several themed trips, including a murder mystery dinner train and Western train robbery trip for adults and *The Polar Express* and *Thomas the Tank Engine* experiences for kids. Prices vary by trip and age—expect to pay between $25 and $80 for adults. All aboard!

The Hood River Fruit Loop. (541) 386-7697; www.hoodriverfruitloop.com. The Fruit Loop isn't a breakfast cereal—it's a 35-mile scenic drive that begins and ends in Hood River, passing through the valley's orchards, forests, and farmlands. This is a great way to see the Hood River Valley's best bets. Sample delicious fruits and take your favorites home, visit a winery, bury your nose in fields of fragrant lavender, meet a pack of alpacas, and savor delicious baked goods. There are more than 30 destinations listed in this do-it-yourself driving tour, including Lavender Valley Lavender Farm, Nelson's Blueberry Farm, Packer Orchards, the Gorge White House (you-pick flowers, strawberries, blueberries, and table grapes), Cody Orchards Farm Stand, Smiley's Red Barn (produce), and Cascade Alpacas Yarn and Fiber. Download a map before your day trip at www.hoodriverfruitloop.com or call (541) 386-7697 to have one sent to you in advance.

Western Antique Aeroplane and Automobile Museum. 1600 Air Museum Rd.; (541) 308-1600; www.waaamuseum.org. One of the largest collections of still-flying antique airplanes and still-driving antique automobiles in the country is located right here in Hood River. That makes this place a great destination for the aircraft, automobile, motorcycle, tractor, military jeep, and engine aficionado. Open daily 9 a.m. to 5 p.m. Free admission for active military and children 4 years of age and under.

Wineries. There are at least a dozen wineries in the Hood River area and many more in the entire Columbia Gorge—more than we could list here. See www.columbiagorgewine.com for a complete listing, but here are a few to get you started.

> **Cathedral Ridge Winery.** 4200 Post Canyon Dr.; (800) 516-8710; www.cathedral ridgewinery.com. Cathedral Ridge was named Oregon Winery of the Year in 2007 and winemaker Michael Sebastiani has been named one of the top winemakers of the year. The winery as a destination has been identified as one of the best for picnics, weddings, and wine tasting. This winery produces chardonnay, rosé, pinot noir, zinfandel, and more. Open daily.

> **Naked Winery.** 102 2nd St.; (541) 386-3700; www.nakedwinery.com. With labels like Dominatrix Pinot Noir, Shag Chardonnay, and Vixen Syrah, the folks at Naked have proven that they aren't shy. Neither are their wines. Open 7 days a week with live music on the weekends.

> **Pheasant Valley Vineyard and Winery.** 3890 Acree Dr.; (541) 387-3040; www .pheasantvalleywinery.com. Pheasant Valley is the Hood River Valley's first organic winery and bottles pinot gris, chardonnay and pear wine, pinot noir, zinfandel, and

more. There is a small cottage available for lodging on the premises, but it books out quickly. Call for details. Open 7 days a week except for the month of January, when Pheasant Valley is closed.

Springhouse Cellar. 13 Railroad Ave.; (541) 308-0700; www.springhousecellar.com. These folks started making wine in the springhouse at their old homestead above the Columbia River. Just a few years later they have a winery and tasting room located in a converted 1920s cannery in downtown Hood River. Every wine they make is available in refillable bottles. Open daily.

where to shop

Anana's Boutique. 206 Oak Ave.; (541) 386-1116; www.ananas-boutique.com. Custom gowns and dresses for very special occasions are available here, in designs that reflect clean lines, color, and high quality fabric. Most of Anana's clothes are machine washable and colorfast, and she also stocks other clothes as well as jewelry, shoes, and accessories. Clients can expect direct and honest consultation for which style and colors flatter them.

Made in the Gorge Artist Co-op. 403 Oak St.; (541) 386-2830; www.angelfire.com/art /madeinthegorge. As is true of so many stunning places to live, Hood River is home to many fine and talented artists. This gallery brings many of them together. It's a great spot to find handmade pieces of art from jewelry to pottery, sculpture to handbags. Open 7 days a week and staffed by a member artist.

Melika. 316 Oak St.; (541) 387-4400; www.melika.com. Where does the girl kiteboarder buy her clothes? At Melika, where performance activewear, waterwear, and accessories come with plenty of practical style. The Melika mission is to share the inspiration of the Pacific Northwest lifestyle with women everywhere. This Oregon-based company has grown beyond Hood River; shopping at this store is a special treat. Open 7 days a week.

Parts + Labour. 209 Oak St.; (541) 387-2787; www.parts-labour.com. This little boutique is a modern lifestyle boutique specializing in progressive urban clothing for women by designers from Hood River, Seattle, and Portland. Shoppers who prioritize personal style and artistic expression over conventional fashion will love Parts + Labour. Open daily.

The Ruddy Duck. 504 Oak St.; (541) 386-5050; www.ruddyduckstore.com. This 2-story family-owned and operated retail store offers the latest in men's, women's, and children's clothing, shoes, toys, gifts, accessories, and housewares. The wooden walkway leading in the front door of this cheerful shop is like a magic carpet—it will take you into a world of wonderful surprises. Open daily.

Silverado. 310 Oak St.; (541) 386-7642; www.silveradogallery.com. One of my favorite shops anywhere. Silverado has jewelry for everyone, in a wide range of styles and prices. Many local and regional artists are represented and pieces vary from contemporary to traditional. It's hard to leave this shop without buying something. Come with a Christmas list, and don't forget yourself.

Twiggs. 305 Oak Ave.; (541) 386-6188. This art and jewelry store is cool just to walk into, what with all of those vintage displays and an open, modern vibe. A series of glass cases surely holds more treasure than you can carry home. I bought some truly spectacular earrings here a couple of years ago and can't wait to shop here again next time I am in Hood River.

where to eat

Bette's. 416 Oak St.; (541) 386-1880; www.bettesplace.com. Bette's makes Hood River's breakfast and serves it all day. The huge menu offers eggs Florentine to omelets to cinnamon French toast, as well as sandwiches, soups, and salads. Bette's loves kids and has the extensive children's menu to prove it. Open 5:30 a.m. to 3 p.m. daily. Reservations accepted for large groups. $–$$.

Brian's Pourhouse. 606 Oak St.; (541) 387-4344; www.brianspourhouse.com. This 1-story Colonial-style white clapboard restaurant exudes small town charm and high-style class. The atmosphere is dignified and friendly, with oil paintings and fresh flowers in abundance. The eclectic menu boasts porterhouse steak, sushi, and fish tacos. Open for dinner 7 nights a week. Brian's stays open late, until midnight, with a special menu after 10 or 11 p.m. $–$$$.

Celilo. 16 Oak St.; (541) 386-5710; www.celilorestaurant.com. Seafood, pasta, and steaks are served creatively with an emphasis on local foods at this downtown restaurant. The menu changes with the season but the quality is always top notch. Celilo makes every attempt to buy naturally raised products and organic products when available, and even converts their used vegetable oils into biodiesel to burn in the company car. Open for lunch 11:30 a.m. to 3 p.m. and for dinner starting at 5 p.m. $$–$$$.

Full Sail Brewery. 506 Columbia St.; (541) 386-2247; www.fullsailbrewing.com. Back in 1987, when the Hood River windsurfing craze was really in full swing and microbreweries were just starting to pop up all over the Pacific Northwest, some folks with a dream bought the old Diamond Fruit cannery in downtown Hood River and turned it into a brewery. Full Sail today brews and bottles lots and lots of beer every year, including an amber ale, IPA, pale ale, and a handful of seasonal brews. The menu at the Tasting Room and Pub offers yummy upscale pub food, including artichoke dip, Thai chicken wings, clam chowder, pulled pork, and bratwurst. If the Imperial Stout brownie served with Tillamook vanilla ice cream and caramel sauce doesn't put you over the edge, the Session Black float with three scoops of Tillamook vanilla ice cream served in a pint glass and topped with award-winning Session Black Lager will. The Tasting Room and Pub is open daily from 11:30 a.m. to 9 p.m. for lunch and dinner. Brewery tours are available daily, free of charge at 1, 2, 3, and 4 p.m. $$.

North Oak Brasserie. 113 3rd St.; (541) 387-2310; www.hoodriverrestaurants.com. In the cellar of a downtown building is this cozy Italian restaurant, just waiting for you and your hungry tummy. Nosh on roasted garlic and brie soup, garlic mashed potato tacos, grilled lobster ravioli, and veal scaloppini in a warm atmosphere with great service. $$.

Stonehedge Gardens. 3405 Cascade Ave.; (541) 386-3940; www.stonehedgegardens .com. This romantic restaurant is located on 6 acres not far from downtown. Housed in a restored home, built in 1898, with several intimate dining rooms and a patio featuring more than 6,000 square feet of Italian stone on 5 different levels with seating for up to 200 people. Crab cakes, gorgonzola sirloin, and seared ahi tuna are some menu options. $$–$$$.

3 Rivers Grill. 601 Oak St.; (541) 386-8883; www.3riversgrill.com. Northwest cuisine with French flair and award-winning wines can be found at this downtown restaurant. Try the beet salad, seared scallops, gnocchi, or trout piccata. The 3 Rivers Grill strives to use local and organic produce and products whenever available. $$–$$$.

where to stay

Columbia Gorge Hotel. 4000 Westcliff Dr.; (800) 345-1921; www.columbiagorgehotel .com. This hotel falls into the "to die for" category. Built in 1921, it's a magnificent villa perched on a scenic cliff over the Columbia River, once a favored retreat for the rich and famous like Clara Bow, Rudolph Valentino, Shirley Temple, and Theodore Roosevelt. Rooms overlook the river or the gardens surrounding Phelps Creek. Each is decorated with Victorian period style artwork and furnishings; some offer brass or canopy beds and fireplaces. The outdoor gardens are themselves a feast for the senses, displaying gorgeous flowers in the spring and adorned with over 500,000 dazzling white lights in the winter. The fine dining restaurant offers breakfast, brunch, lunch, dinner, and happy hour, but open hours and days vary seasonally. A seafood martini, chopped salad, seafood cioppino, and a lovely steak called the New York Madagascar are all delicious dining options. If you can't afford a room or dinner or don't have time, stop by for a drink. It's worth it just to see the place and soak up the Gorge's history. $$$.

Hood River Hotel. 102 Oak Ave.; (541) 386-1900; www.hoodriverhotel.com. This old hotel is on the National Register of Historic Places and many of its original features have been restored, including the lofty ceilings, expansive windows, brass elevator gate, and marble-faced lobby fireplace. Rooms are cozy and done up in Victorian floral decor. The restaurant, Cornerstone Cuisine, specializes in a "freestyle" interpretation of national culinary trends by way of a full-service breakfast, lunch, and dinner menu. Hotel: $–$$. Restaurant: $$–$$$.

Inn at the Gorge. 1113 Eugene St.; (541) 386-4429; www.innatthegorge.com. The Inn at the Gorge is a lovely 1908 Queen Anne house in uptown Hood River with classic furnishings.

The back patio is inviting; the wraparound porch is too, and has 23 columns surrounding it. Overnight guests enjoy a full breakfast that might include fresh fruit, tarts, muffins, omelets, or eggs Benedict. Perk: lift tickets to Mt. Hood Meadows ski area are discounted for guests, and the inn even offers storage space for your sports gear. $$.

Oak Street Hotel. 610 Oak St.; (541) 386-3845; www.oakstreethotel.com. This renovated 1909 beauty is now a classic 9-room hotel and one of the few hotels in Hood River within walking distance to restaurants, cafes, movie theaters, and the marina. Rooms are lovely with hand-forged queen bed frames and oak leaf–adorned bedside tables. Fresh pastries are baked right in the hotel and offered in a buffet style breakfast, along with Oak Street Hotel roast coffee, an assortment of teas, juice, and fresh fruit. $$.

Villa Columbia. 902 Oak St.; (541) 386-6670, (800) 708-6217; www.villacolumbia.com. A villa is a large, luxurious house—this 1911 masterpiece fits the bill. Elegant, European-style guest rooms, many of which offer views of the Columbia, are comfortable and lovely. Breakfast is included and can be requested to-go for those itching to get outside and explore the Columbia River Gorge. $$.

worth more time

Husum, Washington, is on the White Salmon River 11 miles north of Hood River and makes for a pretty drive and fun extra jaunt from Hood River. Federally protected as a wild and scenic river, the White Salmon River is one of the most beautiful rivers in the state. Several companies offer whitewater rafting and kayaking journeys here. Try **Wet Planet Rafting** at (509-493-8989 or www.wetplanetwhitewater.com) or **All Adventures** (509-493-3926 or www.alladventuresrafting.com) to take a ride on these tumultuous waters. After the ride, have lunch or dinner at **Husum Riverside B&B, Patio Cafe and Icehouse Bar,** which serves heart-healthy and delicious Mediterranean dishes with plenty of meat and vegetarian choices in an old ice house and on a large brick patio. You can stay overnight there, too—it's the former site of the Husum Hotel, founded at the turn of the century (866 WA 141; 509-493-8900; www.gorgerooms.com). Nearby you'll also find the **Husum Highlands B&B** (70 Postgren Rd.; 509-493-4503; www.husumhighlands.com). Country charm abounds here, with antique furnishings, wood floors, and high ceilings distinguishing this Victorian home. The grounds are lovely and popular for weddings, with a gazebo and views of the White Salmon Valley. Breakfast is included in a night's stay and dinner is offered for an additional price.

day trip 03

east

the end of the oregon trail:
the dalles

the dalles

Until the Barlow Toll Road opened over Mt. Hood in 1945, The Dalles was considered the end of the land route of the Oregon Trail. When emigrants reached the mighty Columbia River at this location, they had no choice but to load their wagons onto wooden rafts and float to Oregon City—a dangerous undertaking to say the least. Not surprisingly, some of these travelers chose to simply stay put, and a city was born.

First incorporated by the Oregon Territorial Government in 1857 as Dalles City, The Dalles is Oregon's fourth oldest city. The Dalles ultimately became an economic hub of the Pacific Northwest, linking the Columbia River, the Cascade Mountains, and major transportation routes between Eastern and Southern Oregon and Washington State.

But long before all of that, the place earned its name. French-Canadian fur trappers noted the tall basalt columns at the site, created by ancient lava flows and the passage of the Columbia River through Celilo Falls, and called them "Dalle"—French for flagstone. These columns are no longer as visible as they once were, and the falls itself is gone—submerged by the creation of the Dalles Dam in 1957. Still, The Dalles remains a destination for history buffs and outdoor recreationalists.

east day trip 03

getting there

From Portland, The Dalles is an 81-mile drive due east along the Columbia River on I-84. Take exit 85 towards City Center/The Dalles.

where to go

Columbia River Discovery Center. 5000 Discovery Dr.; (541) 296-8600; www.gorge discovery.org. The structure and surroundings here are as much of a destination as the exhibits and collection. Sitting in one of the oldest continuously occupied areas in North America with immediate proximity to one of the largest rivers on the continent as well as the Lewis and Clark and Oregon Trails is this stunning facility and interpretive center. The building is situated on a 54-acre point of land adjacent to the Columbia River and the Historic Columbia River Highway, and won an American Institute of Architects Honor Award for its appealing design. An incredible stone entryway is cut through by a stylized rock "river" across the floor, which leads to exhibits interpreting 40 million years of natural history, 10,0000 years of cultural history, and 150 years of modern history of the Columbia Gorge. Explore the history of the Columbia, its native peoples, the Lewis and Clark expedition, and travelers on the Oregon Trail. Hundreds of American Indian baskets from throughout the Pacific Northwest are on display, and live raptor shows occur daily. Outdoors, the grounds have been restored with native vegetation and include paved hiking and biking trails, a pond, and scenic overlooks. The Basalt Rock Café serves lunch and snacks; hours vary seasonally. The museum is open 9 a.m. to 5 p.m. 7 days a week year-round.

The Dalles Dash. The Dalles Chamber of Commerce, 404 W 2nd St.; (541) 296-2231; http://thedalleschamber.com. Geocaching is a high-tech treasure hunting game played throughout the world by adventure seekers equipped with GPS devices. The Dalles Dash is a 12-cache password geocache hunt. Pick up a password at the Chamber of Commerce, follow the hunt, find the password on the cache lid, write it in the passport, and return to

pick a bushel

The major agricultural product of The Dalles is sweet cherries, produced here in quantities of thousands of pounds annually for both domestic and overseas markets. More than 6,000 acres of sweet cherry trees grow around the city, and in the spring, boy aren't they beautiful. Two local orchards you might visit are **Orchard View Farms Inc.** *(4055 Skyline Rd.; 541-298-1481) and* **DJ Orchards** *(3750 Pleasant Ridge Rd.; 541-296-9302). Call for details about visiting seasonally to pick up a bushel of Rainiers or Royal Annes.*

the chamber to receive a commemorative The Dalles Geo-Coin. GPS devices can be rented at the chamber for free.

Fort Dalles Museum and the Anderson Homestead. 500 W 15th St.; (541) 296-4547; www.fortdallesmuseum.org. When Fort Dalles was established in 1850 as Camp Drum, the site was the only US Army fort on the Oregon Trail between Fort Laramie and Fort Vancouver. Today, a single remaining building endures as Oregon's oldest history museum. Take a tour of the grounds as well as pioneer and military artifacts, antique wagons, and vehicles. On site, visitors can also tour an old fashioned Swedish log homestead built in 1895. In the summer, Fort Dalles is open daily from 11 a.m. to 4 p.m. In the winter, the site is only open Fri, Sat, and Sun, 11 a.m. to 4 p.m. Call for details.

Klindt's Booksellers. 315 East 2nd St.; (541) 296-3355; www.klindtsbooks.com. Given that you are holding this actual paper book in your hand instead of travel researching online, I am going to assume that you are at least a little bit of a book junkie. If that's the case, then Klindt's might just be your number one destination in The Dalles. Klindt's first opened its doors in 1870 and is the oldest bookstore in Oregon. The space has all of the charm to prove it. Browse through original bookshelves, cabinets, and squeaky wooden floors to discover all sorts of titles, both brand new and old and out of print. Whether you are searching for mystery or memoir, cooking or cartography, Klindt's automatically provides the history and romance.

Old St. Peter's Landmark. 405 Lincoln St.; (541) 296-5686; www.oldstpeterslandmark .org. Built in 1897, dedicated in 1898, and saved from demolition in 1971, this magnificent structure is open free to the public for tours. Gaze on brilliant stained glass windows, listen for the clear melodic tones of the old church bell, feel serenity in the lovely interior of this Gothic brick church. Open Tues through Sat, free admission.

Pulpit Rock. In the intersection of E 12th and Court Streets. This 12-foot-tall rock historically stood next to the Methodist Wascopam Mission, where it was transformed into a natural pulpit by missionary preachers hoping to get their word across to Native Americans. One of the missionaries who preached from Pulpit Rock was mission founder Reverend Jason Lee, whose repeated trips back east in the 1830s and 1840s to spread word of the value of the Oregon Territory are said to have triggered the mass emigration that would follow. Today this rock stands in the middle of the street in the center of The Dalles. Every year at Easter, the surrounding streets are closed and Easter services are offered at the site.

The River Front Trail. Access from downtown at Union Street, at the I-84 underpass, and at the Columbia Gorge Discovery Center. This relatively new trail is a highlight of downtown. Extending for 10 miles along the south bank of the Columbia River on The Dalles waterfront, this trail gets you as close to the river as you are going to get and takes bicyclists and pedestrians past Taylor Lakes, Klindt's, The Dalles Marina, and Riverfront Park. Interpretive

ghosts of celilo

*Eleven miles east of The Dalles on I-84 is **Celilo Village,** a community of Native Americans on the Columbia River. It sits at the former site of Celilo Falls, a gorgeous force of nature that had for centuries been a spiritual destination and salmon fishing hub for Native Americans. Celilo Village was a major cultural and trading center until it disappeared along with Celilo Falls due to the creation of The Dalles Dam in 1957. The US Army Corps of Engineers promised to rebuild the village, but it wasn't until 2006 that the Corps provided funding for a new tribal longhouse. Today a couple of hundred people live here, most members of the Yakama Nation or Confederated Tribes of Warm Springs. As they did generations ago, residents engage in ceremonial, subsistence, and commercial fishing for salmon, steelhead, and sturgeon in the Columbia River. The village and longhouses are open to the public for the Celilo Salmon Bake, to celebrate the arrival of the first spring Chinook salmon in April, and for other events annually. For information contact The Dalles Chamber of Commerce at (541) 296-2231 or see www.thedalleschamber.com.*

signs pop up now and then, providing information on the Lewis and Clark Trail, Rock Fort, and The Dalles.

where to eat

Baldwin Saloon. 205 Court St.; (541) 296-5666; www.baldwinsaloon.com. Launched as a bar to serve workers of the railroad and the Columbia River, the Baldwin Saloon once did a booming business and even had a brothel attached to it. The building served over the years as a restaurant, a steamboat navigational office, a warehouse, a coffin storage site, a state employment office, and a saddle shop. In 1990, a year-long restoration process restored the building to its original purpose (excepting the brothel). The original brick walls and old fir floor were uncovered and given new life, and today mahogany and oak booths and tables, brass fixtures, and turn-of-the-century oil paintings mark the decor. An 18-foot long mahogany backbar made in the early 1900s holds an original mirror trimmed with stained glass panels and a big brass cash register. The menu offers fine dining by way of pastas, seafoods, and burgers. Open for lunch and dinner Mon through Sat. $$–$$$.

Cousins Country Inn and Restaurant. 2116 W 6th St.; (541) 298-5161; www.cousins countryinn.com. Northwest hospitality and homestyle cooking in one stop, sprinkled with a good dose of fun. The bright cheery restaurant offers microbrews, locally raised beefsteaks, giant cinnamon rolls, pot roast, and cousin Ed's chicken fried steak to weary travelers and locals. The hotel has 3 wings—the Coho, the Steelhead, and the Chinook, each with its own unique style and price range, though all rooms are very affordable. A heated outdoor swimming pool and a bottomless jar of cookies in the lobby round out your stay. Restaurant open 6 a.m. to 10 p.m. daily (until 9 p.m. in winter). $–$$.

Petite Provence of the Gorge. 408 E 2nd St.; (541) 506-0037; www.provence-portland .com. This spinoff of the popular Portland bakery and cafe Petite Provence offers delicious French pastries and yummy breakfast entrees like omelets, brie sausage scramble, and risotto cakes and eggs. For lunch, French onion soup, Monte Carlo sandwiches, and a goat cheese salad entice. There's an espresso bar, too. $.

Romul's Italian Ristorante. 312 Court St.; (541) 296-9771; www.romuls.com. One of the classier places in town, Romul's offers fine Italian dining in the historical district. A great wine list and lovely desserts round out the experience. Open 7 days a week for dinner and Mon through Sat for lunch. $$–$$$.

The Windseeker Restaurant. 1535 Bargeway Rd.; (541) 298-7171; www.windseeker restaurant.com. The Windseeker is perched alongside the Columbia River and offers stunning panoramic views of the gorge from indoor and outdoor patio dining. The food is lovely, too. Delicious dishes of the Pacific Northwest include poached salmon, stuffed halibut, homemade chicken and dumplings, and crab cakes. Don't miss the local wines, an appetizer known as the Tequila Guacamole Prawn Margarita, and the Sunday brunch. Surrounded by truly lovely gardens tended with as much love as the food. Open Mon through Fri 11 a.m. to 9 p.m., Sat and Sun 9 a.m. to 8 p.m. $$–$$$.

where to stay

Balch Hotel. 40 S Heimrich St., Dufur; (541) 467-2277; www.balchhotel.com. This vintage 1908 hotel 15 miles south of The Dalles on US 197 is a favorite for weddings and special occasions. The 3-story brick building has 20 bedrooms plus a magnificent suite on the third floor with a Mount Hood view and private bath with whirlpool tub. Each room is a little bit different, with period furnishings and decor. Some rooms have private baths, some share common baths. $–$$.

Celilo Inn. 3550 E 2nd St.; (541) 769-0001; www.celiloinn.com. Views of the Columbia River, Mt. Hood, and The Dalles Dam from remodeled rooms in a classic old hotel are the highlight here. Relax with a beverage by the pool after a cooling dip, and enjoy the view of boats going by on the river from the patio. The Celilo Inn offers a free glass of wine at check-in. If that only whets your appetite, try the room package that includes a great day tour of area wineries with an educated guide. Let them do the driving while you do the tasting. $–$$.

Columbia Windrider Inn. 200 W 4th St.; (541) 296-2607; www.windriderinn.com. This Dutch Colonial bed and breakfast is on the National Register of Historic Places. The

Windrider offers 4 guest rooms in downtown The Dalles and caters to windsurfers and sailboarders. The homelike atmosphere with sailboard storage, a pool, and a hot tub might make you feel like you are in college again. It's not fancy, but the location is great and it is very affordable. $.

The Dalles Inn. 112 W 2nd St.; (541) 296-9107; www.thedallesinn.com. This is the only hotel in the heart of downtown. Complimentary breakfast, fitness center, heated outdoor pool and Wi-Fi are all available in this older space that's been recently remodeled. Coffee makers, refrigerators, and microwaves are in every room, and this hotel is even dog friendly. $–$$.

worth more time

If you still have time, drive another 20 miles east on I-84 and cross the Columbia River to **Maryhill.** Samuel Hill, a successful road builder from the east who was the catalyst behind the Columbia Gorge Highway, purchased 5,300 acres of land along the Columbia River in 1907. Here he formed the Maryhill Land Company, named after his daughter. The location proved too remote, however, and the land company ultimately failed. On the suggestion of a friend, Hill took steps to turn the mansion into an art museum instead, a dream that was not fully realized until 1940, after Hill's death.

Today the gorgeous mansion perched on the hill over the Columbia Gorge holds a diverse collection, including exhibitions on Auguste Rodin, the Native People of North America, and International Chess Sets.

Even more interesting, perhaps, is the replica of Stonehenge that Samuel Hill built 3 miles east of the Maryhill Museum of Art. Hill duplicated, as nearly as possible, the original size and design of the ancient Neolithic ruin in England, Stonehenge. The Maryhill Stonehenge was dedicated in 1918 and stands today as Hill intended it, as a tribute to those who died in World War I.

From The Dalles, drive 20 miles east on I-84 E. At Biggs Junction, take the exit for US 97 N. Maryhill exits will appear just over the bridge.

southeast

day trip 01

southeast

the slopes of mt. hood:
sandy, zigzag & welches,
government camp

sandy

Sandy is located about halfway between Portland and Government Camp at an elevation of 1,000 feet in the Mt. Hood foothills. The town of 8,000 serves as not only the commercial hub of a rural area of over twice its size, but also as the gateway to Mt. Hood. Sandy is the last semi-major outpost before the string of villages that lead to the iconic mountain itself.

The city's beginnings are rooted in the 1850s, when the fledgling settlement served as a trading post on the Barlow Road, a popular pioneer route and part of the Oregon Trail. Sandy earned its name from travelers who came through here even earlier than that—Lewis and Clark. The explorers originally identified the nearby Sandy River as "Quicksand River." The name "Quicksand" eventually evolved into "Sandy."

Sandy mainly relies on tourism, but also supports many small farms and agricultural pursuits, like the several Christmas tree farms that surround it. This small city has an eclectic flavor—part mountain town, part agricultural town. With Portland only 28 miles away, there's still a touch of urbanity here, too.

getting there

Sandy is 28 miles southeast of Portland on OR 26/US 26 E. Mapquest and similar navigational tools may try to direct you east on Burnside Road from downtown Portland. While Burnside does eventually turn into OR 26, don't take this route! You'll spend your whole

southeast day trip 01

day trip going stoplight-to-stoplight. Take I-84 E out of Portland instead, and then take the 257th Drive exit (exit number 17/Kane Road). Follow signs for Mt. Hood/Sandy/Highway 26/US 26E.

where to go

Christmas Tree Farms. www.mthoodterritory.com. Oregon is the largest producer of Christmas trees in the US, and the Mt. Hood Territory is the largest producer in Oregon. Visiting a farm to choose and cut one's own tree during the holiday season is an Oregon tradition. These farms, in and near Sandy, are just two of many in the Mt. Hood region—see www.mthoodterritory.com for more suggestions. Most of these farms are open Thanksgiving to Christmas, but some also are open in the summer, when they offer produce, flowers, and a chance to visit your Christmas tree in advance. Call ahead for details.

Alder Creek Farms. 53895 E OR 26, Sandy; (503) 781-7707. Offers noble and grand fir. Open Nov 26 through Dec 24.

Dutcher's Tree Farm. 33755 SE Compton Rd., Boring; (503) 663-4127. Douglas fir, grand and noble fir, and un-sheared Douglas fir. Open Nov 28 through Dec 23.

Philip Foster Farm. 29912 SE OR 211, Eagle Creek (located 7 miles southwest of Sandy on Eagle Creek–Sandy Highway 172/OR 211); (503) 637-6324; www.philipfosterfarm.com. Pioneers didn't make it to Oregon without some help. One of the folks who did the helping was Philip Foster, who helped fund, build, and operate the Barlow Road. His work, along with others', paved the way for the thousands of covered wagons that would arrive in the Willamette Valley in the 1850s. Foster made a 640-acre land claim at Eagle Creek, south of Canby, in the late 1840s. The farm he created there served as a welcome sight for pioneers coming down the last hill into the Willamette Valley and the start of a new life. Today the Foster Farm still plays host to many. The farm offers tours and hands-on pioneer activities for the whole family. Walk through beautiful gardens, smell the flowers on the oldest lilac in Oregon, and visit the 1883 farmhouse and 1860 hay barn. Open Father's Day to Labor Day daily 11 a.m. to 4 p.m. and for special events in Sept and Dec.

Rainbow Trout Farm. 52560 E Sylvan Dr.; (503) 622-5223; www.rainbowtroutfarm.com. Ten ponds brimming with rainbow trout await you and your fishing pole. Actually, you don't even need to bring a pole—the folks at Rainbow Trout Farm will provide one for you, as well as clean and even cook your fish. Enjoy 30 acres of forested beauty, too. Cost is per fish, ranging from $0.50 to $25. Open 7 days a week, Mar 1 through Oct 15, 8 a.m. to dusk.

Sandy Farm Loop. Try this driving tour of the Sandy area to find farms producing everything from lavender to alpacas, free range eggs to sheep yarn, artisan soaps to pumpkins. Pick up a brochure at the Sandy Area Chamber of Commerce and Visitors Center at 38963 Pioneer Blvd. in downtown Sandy, (503) 668-4006, or print the PDF version from their website, www.ci.sandy.or.us.

Sandy Historical Museum. 39345 Pioneer Blvd. (next to the City Plaza, which is next to City Hall); (503) 668-3378; www.sandyhistorical.org. The Sandy Historical Museum's location borders a segment of the famous Barlow Road, which was the last leg of the Oregon Trail that brought thousands of pioneers in covered wagons over the Cascade Mountains to Western Oregon from the mid 1840s until the 1870s. The museum displays maps and information about the Barlow Road and a historical display of the logging industry. Open Mon through Sat 10 a.m. to 4 pm, Sun noon to 4 p.m. (subject to change).

where to eat

Joe's Donut Shop. 39230 Pioneer Blvd.; (503) 668-7215. What day trip isn't improved by a little sugar? At Joe's, a Sandy icon, fuel up on old-fashioned donuts in an old-fashioned atmosphere. Stop and grab a delectable donut—heck, why not get a dozen? This little shop with checkerboard paint will light up your whole day, and surely you're going to need snacks on the way home, too. Open daily 4 a.m. to 5 p.m. $.

where to stay

Sandy Salmon Bed and Breakfast Lodge. 61661 E US 26; (503) 622-6699; www.sandy salmon.com. Named for its location at the point where the Salmon and Sandy Rivers join, the Sandy Salmon is a gorgeous 6,000-square-foot log building and weekend retreat. Wildlife is frequently spotted, including chipmunks, squirrels, raccoons, deer, eagles, osprey, hawks, ducks, geese, herons, woodpeckers, and kingfishers. Fly-fishing opportunities are

a huckleberry end

*A decade ago, heading home from a honeymoon spent on the Oregon coast and Olympic Peninsula and reluctant to let the vacation end, my husband and I made a spontaneous stop at the **Mount Hood Huckleberry Festival and Barlow Trail Days** at Mt. Hood Village, near Brightwood between Sandy and Zigzag. We walked right into a party, complete with huckleberry pies and tarts, a Native American salmon bake, Native American storytelling, and live music. Turns out the celebration had been going on since the late 1800s. Well, not continuously. The festival was founded by Oregon Trail emigrant Samuel Welch, namesake of the village of Welches, to celebrate the birth of tourism on the mountain. That's something that's still worth celebrating. We went home toting huckleberry jam. The Mt. Hood Huckleberry Festival is held annually the weekend before Labor Day Weekend. For more information, visit www.cgs-mthood.tripod.com/huck_festival.*

right out the front door, and simply relaxing in the fresh mountain air is always an option, too. $$$.

zigzag & welches

A string of unincorporated communities stretches between Sandy and Government Camp, the high point of the Mt. Hood pass on US 26 E. These little towns are locally called villages, and collectively known as the Villages at Mt. Hood.

As one drives up the mountain through the villages, the highway becomes increasingly narrow, the fir-dominated forest denser, and the side-of-the-road attractions more intriguing. Little log cabins and colorful pieced-together buildings—brightly painted and puffing smoke out of their oversized chimneys—house restaurants, bars, and lodging. Depending on the time of year, brilliant sunshine filters through leaves, a permeating fog hangs in the trees, or snow buries the rhododendron at roadside. All the while, Mt. Hood, Oregon's tallest mountain, beckons travelers along through a forested corridor.

Zigzag and Welches are two of the Villages at Mt. Hood, located adjacent to each other on US 26 E, the former Barlow Road. Zigzag was named after the nearby Zigzag River, a tributary of the Sandy River. Welches was named after Samuel Welch, a homesteader who settled near Welches Creek in 1882. Both offer respite and refueling along the way up the mountain, and Welches is home to one of Oregon's most popular resorts.

getting there

Follow US 26 W from Sandy 17 miles to Zigzag, which is right on the highway. Welches is just south of Zigzag, less than a mile, also just off US 26 W.

where to go

Bald Mountain. E Lolo Pass Road, approximately 15 miles north out of Zigzag. Anybody can drive by Mt. Hood, but hiking to Bald Mountain provides a fabulous view of the mountain that not many people see. Even better—it's an easy hike. After the 0.8-mile amble, you hardly feel worthy of the acres of wildflowers and drop-dead-gorgeous view of Oregon's highest mountain that lays before you. Bring your out-of-town friends here to show them what the beauty of Oregon is all about, but don't forget to take a map. You wouldn't want to get your friends lost and become the cause of one of Mt. Hood's infamous recues.

Cascade Streamwatch/Wildwood Recreation Site. 65670 E US 26 E, Welches (on the south side of US 26 between mile posts 39 and 40); (503) 622-3696; www.blm.org/or. The Bureau of Land Management runs this park, trail, and recreation site, which invites visitors to explore natural streams and wetlands from boardwalks and interpretive trails. Still not sure what the difference is between a salmon and a steelhead? See young examples of both fish through a unique underwater fish-viewing chamber in a stream. Itching to get your toes wet? Wade the waters of the wild and scenic Salmon River. The site is a day use area and home to family picnic units, several group shelters, playing fields, and access to the Salmon Huckleberry Wilderness. In September, the Festival of the Forest offers food, art, music, entertainment, and the joy of nature. Park open Mar 15 through Nov 30; $5 per passenger car.

Zigzag Ranger Station. 70220 E Hwy. 26, Zigzag; (503) 622-3191. On the National Register of Historic Places since 1986, 19 of 20 buildings at this forest service compound are historically significant. Many of the buildings were constructed by the Civilian Conservation Corps in the 1930s and 1940s, when the slopes of Mt. Hood were much more remote than they are today. The Forest Service still uses the ranger station as the Zigzag Ranger District headquarters. Also on the grounds you'll find the Wy'East Rhododendron Gardens. Conceived in 1952 as a roadside beautification project, the gardens contain more than 50 types of gorgeous rhododendron plants and many shrubs and trees, including the rare dawn redwood. The grounds are open year-round for self-guided tours. A garden map is available at the Zigzag district office.

where to eat

Altitude Restaurant. The Resort at the Mountain, 68010 E Fairway Ave., Welches; (503) 622-2214; www.altituderestaurant.com. If you're after swanky upscale dining outside of the city, Altitude is your place. Fresh farm-to-table cuisine with Northwest flair served in a non-stuffy environment is this restaurant's specialty. With 100 wine varietals and a full bar with innovative cocktail menu, Altitude is a great place just to go and have a drink, as well. Open daily for breakfast, lunch, and dinner. $$–$$$.

Rendezvous. 67149 E US 26, Welches; (503) 622-6837; www.rendezvousgrill.net. Chef/co-owner Kathryn Bliss designs innovative, seasonal menus using many local products, including chanterelle mushrooms and huckleberries. The Rendezvous has developed a reputation for devastating desserts, all prepared freshly in-house. Open daily for lunch and dinner. $$$.

Skyway Bar and Grill. 71545 E US 26, Zigzag; (503) 622-3775; www.skywaybarandgrill .com. The Skyway looks from the outside as if it's holding its own contest for bold design, and winning. The bright red building with blue accents and a gigantic "Enter" sign will surely catch your attention. Inside, a roadhouse-style interior is home to classic American barbeque food with an Oregon spin. Service and atmosphere are friendly, and live music, karaoke, pool, horseshoes, and a campfire out back make things even more fun. Open Thurs through Sun, dinner only. $–$$.

The Zigzag Inn. 70162 E US 26, Zigzag; (503) 622-4779; www.zigzaginn.com. The historic Zigzag Inn was built of hand-cut logs in the late 1920s by William John "Bill" Lenz, who also was responsible for many other notable structures in the area. The inn has pleased guests as a family run restaurant ever since, offering casual, affordable family dining in a lodge-like atmosphere with authentic touches like antler chandeliers. Open 7 days a week for lunch and dinner, plus breakfast on Sat and Sun. $–$$.

where to stay

The Cabins Creekside at Welches. 25086 E Welches Rd., Welches; (503) 622-4275; www.mthoodcabins.com. These creek-side cabins with vaulted wood ceilings are a cozy place to stay for up to 4 people. Hot tub spa sits over the creek and offers a spectacular view of the forest. $$.

The Resort at The Mountain. 68010 E Fairway Ave., Welches; (503) 622-3101; www.theresort.com. Luxury tucked away amongst rural mountain towns is this full resort with golfing, spa, restaurants, and more. There are 157 guest rooms and suites on 300 acres of evergreen forest and lush mountain flora. $–$$$.

government camp

Government Camp was given its name by settlers traveling the Barlow Road, who discovered several wagons at the location, abandoned by the Regiment of Mounted Riflemen. Today the unincorporated community thrives by way of its location on the south slope on Mt. Hood, where it serves as base camp for a wide range of outdoor activities and adventures. Hikers, mountain bikers, skiers, climbers, campers, birders, snowboarders, and tourists come to Government Camp year-round.

At an elevation of 4,000 feet and with an average snowfall close to 300 inches, Government Camp is as lovely as it is remote and alpine. It's also an old-school skiers kind of hangout, with its own rugged culture.

getting there

From Zigzag, Government Camp is 10 miles east directly on US 26 W.

where to go

Mt. Hood Adventure. 88335 E Government Camp Loop; (503) 715-2175; www.mthoodadventure.com. This purveyor of recreation tours, outfitting, and rentals truly provides every adventure possible in the Mt. Hood area. Whether you are set on trying your hand at rock climbing or bird watching, kayaking or inner-tubing, hiking or sleigh rides, these folks can hook you up. Prices vary.

Mt. Hood Cultural Center and Museum. 88900 E US 26; (503) 272-3301; www.mthoodmuseum.org. Six galleries interpret natural history, fine arts, the evolution of skiing on Mt. Hood, mountain climbing, and the Forest Service and Mt. Hood. Located on the old Barlow

wy'east

The Multnomah Indian tribe called Mt. Hood Wy'east. In one version of the legend, two sons of the Great Spirit Sahale fell in love with the beautiful maiden Loowit. But she couldn't decide who to choose. The two braves, Wy'east and Klickitat, burned forests and villages in their battle over her. Sahale became enraged and destroyed the three lovers. He erected three mountain peaks to mark where each fell—Mt. St. Helens for Loowit, Mt. Hood for Wy'east, and Mount Adams for the mourning Klickitat.

Road. Museum bookstore, art sales gallery, visitor information services, and Internet access on site. Open daily 10 a.m. to 5 p.m., except holidays. Free.

Mt. Hood Skibowl Summer Adventure Park & Alpine Slide. 87000 E US 26; (503) 222-BOWL; www.skibowl.com. During winter months, take the kids to the slopes of Portland's closest ski resort, which boasts more night skiing than any other resort in the country, a nearby tubing hill, and hundreds of miles of family-friendly cross-country Nordic trails in the Mt. Hood National Forest. When the snow melts, SkiBowl turns into a Summer Adventure Park with more than 20 attractions including a half-mile dual alpine slide, mountain bike park with more than 40 miles of trails, bike rentals and tours, automated batting cages, frisbee,18-hole mini golf, and horseback riding. Prices vary.

where to eat

Charlie's Mountain View. Government Camp Loop Rd.; (503) 272-3333; www.charlies mountainview.com. Here's where to find an old-school Government Camp experience. Classic ski town cuisine meets fresh produce and high-quality meats at Charlie's, where après-ski means an Original Mountain cheeseburger, waffle fries, prime rib, or a Caesar salad. Charlie's is known for nightlife and offers live music on weekends. Extensive beer and wine list, too. $–$$.

where to stay

Collins Lake Resort. 88149 E Creek Ridge Rd.; (503) 928-3498; www.collinslakeresort .com. The comfort and luxury of a small resort in the heart of ski paradise. Collins Lake Resort offers chalets with 2 to 3 bedrooms, 2.5 baths, well-equipped gas kitchens, and an open great room with a stone fireplace. Many units also have gas barbecues on the private outdoor deck. Chalets have a mountain view, creek view, or forest view, each with tall windows to allow you to take advantage of beautiful views. $$$.

picture perfect

Trillium Lake is the quintessential alpine lake—crystal blue water, enchanting forested perimeter, incredible volcanic peak as backdrop—which is probably why it's been photographed so very much. Even if you've never been here, you've likely seen the lake on a postcard. Trillium Lake is popular for fishing and picnicking, but the last time my family visited, my daughters spent an entire afternoon playing in the mud. The grown-ups weren't so interested in the mud, but with Mt. Hood to gaze upon and the sun overhead on a leisurely summer day, no one was complaining. Three miles past Government Camp, take a right off US 26 onto Trillium Lake Road. There is also a campground here. In the winter, a popular cross-country ski and snowshoe trail passes through here. Just don't forget the camera.

Huckleberry Inn. 88611 E Government Camp Loop; (503) 272-3325; www.huckleberry-inn.com. Huckleberry Inn offers easy access to ski areas, cross country paths, and in the summer, hiking trails and mountain lakes. Sixteen lodging rooms as well as dorm-style facilities for ski or tour groups make this a convenient place to stay; the steakhouse (open during the holiday week and ski season weekends) and the 24-hour family-style restaurant are very popular. Cafe: $. Steakhouse: $$. Lodging: $–$$.

Timberline Lodge. 27500 E Timberline Rd.; (503) 231-7979; www.timberlinelodge.com. Mt. Hood's Timberline Lodge, which sits at an elevation of 6,000 feet on the flanks of Mt. Hood, is legendary. The massive, imposing wood structure was built in 1937 and immediately became a Pacific Northwest icon. Even if you've somehow missed hearing about Timberline or seeing a picture, you'll still recognize the exterior if you've seen the movie *The Shining*. Don't worry—the inside isn't haunted by the spirit of Jack Nicholson's character, Jack Torrance, a troubled writer who snaps during a winter at an isolated hotel. Your stay promises to be much more pleasant. The National Historic Landmark is warm and spacious, with a stone and wood interior that's steeped in rich Pacific Northwest history. From the Ram's Head Bar, watch skiers take to the slopes and climbers set out for the summit—Mt. Hood is one of the most popular mountains to climb in the Pacific Northwest. The rooms can be small but have been renovated and are charming. You don't need to be a guest to enjoy Timberline—25-minute tours are offered by US Forest Service rangers for free and available to everyone Thurs through Sun at 11 a.m., 1 p.m., and 2 p.m. Dining: $–$$$. Lodging: $$–$$$.

day trip 02

southeast

columbia river basalt country:
maupin

maupin

Maupin is a little outpost in the rolling high desert hills of the lower Columbia River basin that might have been left to a few lonely ranchers if it weren't for the lively river that flows through town. The section of the Deschutes River that passes through here is one of the most popular waterways in the state of Oregon for rafters and kayakers. The climate, access to great rapids, and predictable water flows make the Deschutes ideal for river rats, and thousands flock here each summer to get a taste of Boxcar and Elevator rapids. Beginning in May and continuing through the warmer months, this place bustles with activity.

In the winter, it's pretty quiet around here. But the ranchers are still around. In fact, many of the ranches in these parts have been worked by the same family for generations. If there is one thing anyone who has ever run or worked a ranch knows, farm country is never boring. Nor is it unattractive. The skies are wide open and blue here most of the year, and the rolling sage and rabbit brush plains allow for picturesque and sweeping views.

The weather is nice, too. A little known secret about this part of the state is that when it's raining in Portland, it's often sunny and hot in Maupin. Because of the high desert weather in Maupin, summers start earlier and end later. The busiest time of the year for rafting is July and August, but savvy river rats know that the best time of year to go rafting is September and October. During the fall, there are fewer folks on the river and the experience with the environment and the guide is much more personal.

southeast day trip 02

shaped by molten rock

The topography in this region and to the north and east was formed by the Columbia River basalt flows—great lava floods of 17 to 14 million years ago. As you look at the horizon, think about flowing liquid rock and how it shaped the rolling hills around you. Later, over millennia, the Deschutes River cut through the basalt, exposing layers of rock. Rimrock, or columnar basalt, is the vertical spires you see comprising some cliff-sides in this country. Rimrock is beautiful, as well as indicative of the high desert, the Columbia basin, and Columbia River basalt flow country.

Some of the locations in this day trip are located (as noted) in Tygh Valley, a little town in a gorgeous valley just 10 miles north of Maupin on US 197. Climb out of the Deschutes River canyon through wheat fields to this forested, mountainous community.

getting there

Take I-84 E out of Portland to the Kane Road exit, exit 17, 257th Drive. Follow 257th and follow signs for US 26 E. Drive 55 miles on US 26 W. Turn left onto OR 216 E. Drive 26 miles. Turn right onto US 197/The Dalles-California Highway. Drive 3 miles to Maupin.

where to go

Rafting. Whitewater rafting can be a very awakening experience, placing a person in a vulnerable state and allowing for an awesome adrenaline rush. The Deschutes River attracts hundreds of thousands of people in search of this experience from all over the country and beyond each year.

The Deschutes River originates high in the Cascade Mountains, south of Maupin 100 miles. The river carves its path through 250 miles of high desert before flowing into the Columbia River to the north. The section of the Deschutes River known as the Lower Deschutes is the 100-mile section from Pelton Dam (near Lake Billy Chinook) to the mouth of the Deschutes. The lower river offers a beautiful desert canyon filled with sage brush, osprey, incredible basalt rock formations, and plenty of exciting rapids.

Rafting season takes off in late May/early June and continues until October. The most common raft trip is the day trip, a 13-mile stretch from Harpham Flat to Sandy Beach. This trip takes about 3.5 hours (or longer if you pull over to swim, have lunch, and explore river rock slides). Floaters on this stretch of the river will experience Class III and IV rapids. Several companies exist to get tourists out on the water. Some only offer guided trips and others offer do-it-yourself trips. The Deschutes River is relatively easy to raft or kayak if one isn't an expert, but a guide is always a good way to go if you've never rafted before. Guided day trips typically run about $75 to $95 per person.

Here are a few outfitters and guide services to help you experience the Deschutes:

Deschutes River Adventures. 602 Deschutes Ave.; (541) 395-2238; www.800-rafting.com. Deschutes River Adventures is one of the pioneer raft shops in Maupin, launched 30 years ago to rent rafts to people coming over for day trips from Portland. DRA offers guided day trips, as well as day and overnight do-it-yourself raft rentals (with no guide).

Deschutes U-Boat. 501 Hwy. 197 S; (541) 395-2503; www.deschutesuboat.com. This is another long-time family-run raft business that has been in Maupin since the rafting phenomenon began. Deschutes U-Boat offers raft and kayak rentals and guided day trips.

River Drifters. 405 Deschutes Ave.; (800) 972-0430; www.riverdrifters.net. River Drifters offers a number of trips on the Lower Deschutes, from half-day journeys to 5-day vacations. One of the more popular trips is the full-day trip, which covers more than 14 river miles and takes between 5 and 6 hours to complete.

Sage Canyon Raft Company. 502 Deschutes Ave.; (800) 538-RAFT; www.sage canyonriverco.com. Sage Canyon offers the regular gamut of Deschutes trips—half-day, full-day, etc. This outfitter is particularly good for overnight rafting trips. Trips can be anywhere from 2 nights to 5 nights, and include food, site preparation, river history, and fishing guiding along the way. Overnight trips run $250 to $375 per person.

Fishing. The Deschutes River is as rewarding for fishing as it is for whitewater rafting and kayaking. Salmon and steelhead have always been a huge life source for Maupin and South Wasco County residents. Salmon runs hit in the spring and fall, and attract eager fishermen ready to test their skill and luck. With a limit of 2 salmon per day, a fortuitous fisherman can go home with 30 pounds of fish and feed a lot of happy friends and family. The Steelhead run hits September to November, also attracting droves of people. Both fly and spinner fishing are world class on the Deschutes River.

Deschutes Angler. 504 Deschutes Ave.; (541) 395-0995; www.deschutesangler .com. This shop and guide service provides fly-fishing retail products and services, Deschutes River fishing trips, and private lake guided fly-fishing trips.

Deschutes Canyon Fly Shop. 599 S Hwy. 197; (541) 395-2565; www.flyfishing deschutes.com. Since 1985, the folks at Deschutes Canyon Fly Shop have aimed to provide the best products, guided trips, and accurate information about river and fishing conditions possible. Customized fly-fishing guided services are available to help you decipher the river, improve technique, and increase effective fishing time. Deschutes Canyon has a private trophy lake, too. Guided trips run $250 to $595. Call for details.

Hunting. While not for everyone, hunting has a long history in this region and continues to be a very popular and productive activity in the Maupin and Tygh Valley area. Upland bird hunting season begins in the fall and runs through January. Deer, elk, antelope, bighorn sheep, bear, and bird are just some of the game available for tag holders in this area. While hunters need not employ a guide, it is crucial to understand the regulations and safety requirements of hunting. Contact the Oregon Department of Fish and Wildlife, www.dfw .state.or.us, or hire one of these guides for your hunting adventure.

River Runner Outfitters. (541) 978-0152; www.fishdeschutes.com. These guides specialize in upland bird hunts. Or try a "cast and blast"—a local's favorite that involves hiking the canyon for wild chukar and walking the river's banks for pheasant, intermingled with fishing the river.

White River Hunt Club. 84060 Fred Ashley Rd., Tygh Valley; (541) 483-2115; www .whiteriverhunt.com. This family-owned ranch consists of more than 1,200 acres of varying terrain on which to hunt. More than 3 miles of White River frontage make this place very beautiful, as well.

buckin' broncos

*There are rodeos, and then there are authentic, down home, small town, truly West-ern rodeos. The **Wasco County Fair and Rodeo** is one of the latter. Held the third weekend in August in Tygh Valley, this event is an honest hometown rodeo com-plete with clowns, cows, and plenty of action. The fair offers up all that county fairs should—4-H exhibits, livestock, carnival rides, entertainment, and food. The corol-lary event—a demolition derby—adds to the wild and crazy good times. The entire affair is a highlight of the year in this part of the state, for locals and tourists alike. Bring some boots because there are fences to hop and cow pies to traverse. Don't miss the funnel cakes—they are beyond compare. See www.wascofair.com or call (541) 483-2288; 81849 Fairgrounds Rd. in Tygh Valley.*

where to eat

Anglers Restaurant and Lounge. 34 N Mariposa Dr., Tygh Valley; (541) 544-2299; www .anglersrestaurantandlounge.com. Comfort food and drink is served here alongside spectacular views of Mt. Hood and Pine Hollow Reservoir. Steak, seafood, pasta, pizza, and nightly specials keep the crowds happy, and lunch boxes to go are available for fishermen. There's nothing too fancy about Anglers—just homestyle food and a great Western bar experience. Open for breakfast, lunch, and dinner 7 days a week. $.

The Rainbow Tavern. 411 Deschutes Ave.; (541) 395-2497. The Rainbow, or "The Bow," as locals call it, is a Maupin icon. If you are in the mood for cheap drinks, a juke box, Hamm's on tap, a dance floor, pool tables, and real-life cowboy sightings, this is your spot. And anyway, it's really the only spot to go for any sort of nightlife in Maupin. This authentic cowboy bar offers up live music in the summer every Fri and Sat night. Weekends are usually packed during the summer, but with a stimulating mix of folks from guides to tourists to locals to rafters. Homestyle country food is at the ready. The Bow is not swanky but it can be a whole lot of fun. $$.

Sportsman's Pub and Grub. 56826 Wamic Market Rd., Tygh Valley; (541) 544-3011. Authentic cowboy bars are a dime a dozen around here, apparently. This one, past Tygh Valley on OR 48/Wamic Market Road, offers a full-service bar, a pool table, and all Oregon Lottery games. If you like to sing, come here for karaoke every Fri and Sat night starting at 8 p.m. The Sportsman's Pub and Grub also offers breakfast, lunch, dinner, pizza, catering, and orders to go. $–$$.

where to stay

Camping. Maupin is the sort of place that simply calls out for camping. There's nothing much better than hearing the river roll by as you gaze into a sky full of stars and stay up late around a campfire in the high desert. Here are a few options.

> **BLM.** (503) 808-6002; www.blm.gov/or. The Bureau of Land Management offers several first-come, first-served camp sites along the Deschutes River in the Maupin area. Oasis, Blue Hole, and Oak Springs are a few popular sites. There are several more, too: see the web for details. Prices range from $8 to $35. $.

> **Hunt Park.** 81849 Fairgrounds Rd., Tygh Valley; (541) 483-2288. Near the fairgrounds, this park can accommodate up to 1,000 overnight campers. The park has 120 RV hookups with power, water, high-speed Internet, and a shared dump station. Tent campers can choose from multiple camping locations with convenient bathrooms and showers. Sites are $15 to $20. $.

> **Maupin City Park.** 206 Bakeoven Rd. (541) 395-2252; www.cityofmaupin.com. Pitch a tent or park an RV right in town. On-site amenities include restrooms with

showers, full hookups for RV sites, an on-site park supervisor, free Wi-Fi, and a community building available to rent with a kitchen. Make a reservation in advance if you'd like. Sites cost $15 to $35. $.

Imperial River Company. 304 Bakeoven Rd.; (800) 395-3903; www.deschutesriver .com. Located right on the Deschutes River, the Imperial River Company is arguably the most luxurious lodging in Maupin. There are 25 Oregon history-themed guest rooms, each with scenic views of the river, that provide a comfortable and interesting place to lay your head. Choose a river-view room with a private balcony and a jet tub, or take a ground-level room for easy access to and from the Deschutes. Many rooms have private decks; the lodge lobby has a communal fireplace to hunker near. The restaurant is a popular spot, too. The dining room provides delicious and hearty meals like fresh cut steak and baby back ribs. Their all-natural, range-grown Angus beef comes from the Imperial Stock Ranch, nearby in Shaniko. Imperial River Company also organizes rafting, hunting, and fishing trips for guests. $–$$.

The Oasis Resort. 609 US 197 S; (541) 395-2611; www.deschutesriveroasis.com. The Oasis Resort offers overnight lodging, Deschutes River fly-fishing for trout and steelhead, and cozy, comfortable accommodations. Private cottages are circled around a lush, green lawn and are very affordable to rent. The restaurant serves up delicious breakfast, lunch, and dinner. Most famous for old-fashioned, hard ice cream milk shakes, terrific burgers, and ribs, the Oasis Café offers a diverse menu ranging from large farm-style breakfasts to full dinners. An extensive selection of microbrews and Northwest wines accents your meal. Browse the historic photos and memorabilia (including Mike's "world's smallest fly-fishing museum") and see why the Oasis has been the favorite of fly-fishers since 1928. A fly-fishing package offers lodging, food, and a guided fishing trip. The Oasis also runs a campground, just ⅛ mile upriver, with grassy tent and RV spaces. $.

The River Run Lodge. 1210 Hartman Ave.; (877) 335-8867; www.riverrunlodge.net. This casual, country-styled lodge offers 6 simply decorated rooms, each with fish-printed bed-spreads, wall art, and decor. Located in the heart of Maupin's recreation district, River Run Lodge offers easy access to the river, restaurants, and other local amenities. $.

worth more time

Shaniko. At its heyday, the city of Shaniko was a transportation hub and considered the "Wool Capital of the World." Located at the center of 20,000 square miles of wool, wheat, cattle, and sheep production, 150 years ago Shaniko was a boom town. Today, it's a vir-tual ghost town. The last census turned up a population of less than 30 people. But that doesn't mean there isn't anything to see here. Preservation of this historic town has been spearheaded by investments from Robert B. Pamplin, Jr., a businessman and owner of the *Portland Tribune* and Columbia Empire Farms. The **Shaniko Historic District** includes the

Shaniko Schoolhouse, the **Shaniko Jailhouse,** and the **Shaniko Historic Center,** all of which have been restored.

Nearby, the **Imperial Stock Ranch Headquarters** (www.imperialstockranch.com/ranch /history) has been a working ranch since before 1900. The owners have taken pains to preserve the ranch and sheep ranching. Most folks just drive through Shaniko these days, but it's worth getting out and taking a stroll around, looking at the old buildings and pondering change. To reach Shaniko from Maupin, head south 21 miles on US 197 to the intersection with US 97. Turn left onto US 97 and continue another 12 miles to Shaniko.

day trip 03

southeast

crags, ag & native culture:
warm springs, terrebonne

warm springs

Warm Springs is the primary residential hub of the Warm Springs Indian Reservation. The reservation was established by the Treaty of 1855 on a small reserve of land in north-central Oregon where several tribes had lived for thousands of years. In 1937, the Wasco, Paiute, and Warm Springs Tribes organized as the Confederated Tribes of Warm Springs and became a sovereign, self-governing nation.

The 1,000-square-mile reservation descends from the alpine, fir-laden slopes of Mt. Hood to the sagebrush, rabbit brush, and ponderosa pine ecosystem of the high desert. The Deschutes River runs north through the reservation, past Warm Springs and continuing to the Columbia River. Whitewater rafting and fishing are very popular activities on this stretch of the river. Rimrock winds its way through many sections of the reservation, visible from the highway or from the water.

The reservation is a beautiful, serene place with much to explore. However, as an official Indian reservation, the majority of the acreage of the Warm Springs is reserved for tribal members. With the exception of the campgrounds, Kah-Ne-Ta resort, and state roads and the services that lie on them, the reservation is closed. Be sure to honor these rules. There's plenty to see and do along the reservation's main thoroughfares.

southeast day trip 03

getting there

From Portland, Warm Springs is beyond Mt. Hood to the south and east. Take I-84 E out of Portland to the 257th Drive exit (exit number 17/Kane Road). Follow signs for OR 26/US 26 E/Mt. Hood. Continue past Mt. Hood on US 26, for a total of 87 miles from the beginning of US 26, 104 miles total.

where to go

The Museum at Warm Springs. 2189 US 26; (541) 553-3331; www.museumatwarm springs.org. The Museum at Warm Springs was created by the Confederated Tribes of the Warm Springs Reservation to preserve their traditions and to keep their legacy alive. Tribal-inspired architecture created this 25,000-square-foot, award-winning museum located along Shitike Creek. Explore traditional dwellings including a tule mat lodge, wickiup, and plankhouse that have been meticulously constructed to show life in this landscape long ago. There's a great basket collection, and many lovely beaded objects. You may listen to ceremonial songs and traditional languages, witness a Wasco wedding exchange, or watch yourself on camera as you try the hoop dance. Open from 9 a.m. to 5 p.m. daily from Mar to Nov; the museum is closed on Mon and Tues from Nov through Feb.

where to eat

The Teepee Deli. 3240 Walsey Lane, Suite 2; (541) 553-2568; www.teepeedeli.com. Classic deli counter meets modern convenience at this little spot on the reservation. Build-your-own-style cold-cut sandwiches, whole fruit, soft drinks, and an operational tech center with free Wi-Fi all co-exist happily at the Teepee Deli. Open Mon through Fri 10 a.m. to 3 p.m. $.

where to stay

Kah-Nee-Ta High Desert Resort and Casino. 6823 Hwy. 8; (800) 554-4SUN; www.kah neeta.com. Kah-Nee-Ta Village has been around since 1964, named for the Indian Xnitla, or "Root Digger." Xnitla was a scout and spiritual leader who lived on the property, using the on-site natural hot springs and indigenous plants for medicinal purposes and religious ceremonies. Today, Kah-Nee-Ta is still a great place to boost one's spirit in the arid high desert. The full-scale resort offers a variety of accommodations from suites and private view balcony rooms to lodging in actual teepees, and even a full-service RV park. The casino offers many opportunities to win (or lose), from slots to blackjack. The hot springs still runs through Kah-Nee-Ta, and one of the pools is a naturally heated mineral pool perfect for soothing one's tired bones. Kah-Nee-Ta has a full spa, which includes mineral soaks in its services. A par-72 championship golf course is consistently highly rated, volleyball and tennis are available, year-round stables offer pony rides and trail rides, and several restaurants from fine dining to casual dining tempt the taste buds. For a true taste of native culture, don't miss Kah-Nee-Ta's famous traditional salmon bake buffet, offered Saturday nights in the summer. Salmon fillets are skewered on cedar sticks and baked over alder-wood coals by tribal members, and the fish is served with Indian fry bread while Warm Springs people show off traditional Indian dancing styles. Tip—a free "Fun Bus" runs to Kah-Nee-Ta from Hood River, Bend, Portland, Tygh Valley, Terrebonne, and more locations a few times a month. See website for details. $–$$.

Pelton Park Campground. The access road to Lake Simtustus is off of US 26 approximately 2 miles south of Warm Springs; (541) 325-5292; www.peltonpark.com. Pelton Park is a pocket of high desert camping and recreational paradise. Visitors boat, camp, fish, view wildlife, and just relax. Located on the shore of Lake Simtustus, the reservoir behind Pelton Dam, Pelton Park has 71 campsites, a picnic area, a boat launch and moorage, and a park store with groceries, ice, fishing tackle, boat rental, and fuel. The lake has a small waterskiing area, but most of the lake has a speed limit of 10 miles per hour. Best to stick to fishing, canoeing, and kayaking. Nearby at the Pelton Wildlife Overlook, located just north of Pelton Park, short trails lead to viewing platforms where you can view ducks, geese, great blue herons, shorebirds, eagles, and other raptors.

The Inn at Cross Keys Station. 66 NW Cedar St., Madras; (541) 475-5800; www.innat crosskeysstation.com. Once upon a time, the area known as Cross Keys just north of here was a stagecoach stop for the line linking Shaniko to Bend. A century later, this brand-new 3-story hotel also acts as a traveler's oasis in the desert. Memorabilia reminiscent of the early 1900s, when residents made a living here growing alfalfa, raising cattle, and shepherding sheep, decorates the lobby. But the rest of the hotel is thoroughly modern and includes a pool, fitness center, and complimentary breakfast. Pretty standard lodging, but the best you'll find around here. $–$$.

the nose knows

Madras, the community that sits between Warm Springs and Terrebonne, is one of the richest agricultural areas east of the Cascade Range in Oregon. Jefferson County leads the world in carrot seed production, and other commercial crops include vegetable, grass, and flower seeds; garlic; mint; and sugar beets. As you pass through this part of the state, roll down your window—often the smell of garlic or mint is in the air, and guessing which can be a fun road trip game. In the spring, keep an eye out for wild asparagus growing in the roadside ditches. Fruit stands and roadside veggie vendors pop up seasonally, too.

terrebonne

Terrebonne is hard to define. At first glance the area north of Redmond looks like just another stretch of arid high desert, a blip on the map in a sea of sagebrush. But there's more going on here than meets the eye. Terrebonne serves as paradise on earth to an eclectic group of visitors and residents, from world-class athletes to ranchers to wealthy retirees to vintners.

Some are drawn to the incredible rock formation Smith Rock, which is hard to miss even from the highway. Some come for the good soil. All, probably, love the killer views of the Cascade Range. There's something special about the climate here, too. During the time of the year when the rest of Central Oregon has frost nipping at its heels and is getting snowed upon, Terrebonne seems to stay a little bit warmer and drier. On those wet, cold spring days when everyone is dying to dry out and warm up, Smith Rock is a great place to be.

Get off the highway and you'll see Terrebonne's diversity and charms. Next to brand new multimillion-dollar homes are century-old farms selling pumpkins and free-range beef. Socioeconomic and cultural differences abound, but everyone who lives and visits here agrees that Terrebonne (which means "good earth" in French) is a little slice of heaven.

Terrebonne is still rural, and you won't find many services, but there are a few gems tucked away here and there.

getting there

From Warm Springs, continue southeast on US 26 until it merges with OR 97/US 97 at Madras, 14 miles south of Warm Springs. Continue south on US 97 another 21 miles to Terrebonne.

where to go

Crooked River Ranch Golf Course. 5195 Club House Rd.; (800) 833-6343; www .crookedriverranch.com. The fifth hole at this fabulous golf course has been recognized as the most beautiful golf hole in Oregon. There are fabulous canyon, rimrock, mountain, and river views, not to mention the wildlife. You'll have a hard time keeping your eye on the ball.

Lake Billy Chinook. Located about 20 miles west of Culver off of the Culver Highway; www.lakebillychinook.com. Lake Billy Chinook is a spectacular lake created by the nexus of three rivers—the Metolius, the Deschutes, and the Crooked—put in place by the Round Butte Dam. With 72 miles of shoreline and 6 square miles of water, the lake is a popular destination for many recreational activities, including fishing, hiking, waterskiing, camping, and more. For the truly passionate, rent a houseboat and spend several days on the lake. Day-use permits are required and can be purchased at the Cove Palisades State Park office, campground registration booths (summer only), and local sporting goods and convenience stores. See website for details.

Maragas Winery. 15523 SW US 97, Culver; (541) 546-5464; www.maragaswinery.com. People said you couldn't grow wine grapes in Central Oregon. Doug Maragas proved them wrong. This boutique winery produces hearty Bordeaux-style reds and southern European-style muscats, German-style pinot gris, and a new-age style of chardonnay. Since planting Jefferson County's first vineyard in 2007, the Maragas family has hosted several events a year in their big red barn, celebrating good wine and good people. Tours, tasting, and patio open Tues through Sun 11 a.m. to 5 p.m. See website for special events.

Peter Skene Ogden Scenic Viewpoint. Three miles north of Terrebonne on US 97; (800) 551-6949. If you enjoy vertical basalt cliffs and scenic river canyons, the Ogden Wayside is for you. The park is perched at the top of a striking canyon. Bring a camera!

Pumpkin Patches. Terrebonne is one of the most amazing places in Oregon to visit a pumpkin patch, if only for the views and the sun. These two farms both have Smith Rock as epic backdrop, and there's something about the wide-open sky that makes the light here picture-perfect. Bring a camera—this is the spot to take your annual family photo. Oh, yes, and you surely can pick the perfect jack-o-lantern pumpkin here, too.

> **Central Oregon Pumpkin Co.** 1250 NE Wilcox Ave.; (541) 504-1414; www.the maize.com. Pumpkin patch and so much more, including zoo rides, a pumpkin cannon, hay fort, harvest market, wagon rides, pumpkin launcher, and more. The best part is "the maize"—a maze made of corn that's a different design every year. Open 7 days a week in Oct. Free entry, fees for maize and pumpkin purchase.

> **DD Ranch.** 3836 NE Smith Rock Way; (541) 548-1432. The DD Ranch is a family-owned venture. What was all about the pumpkins has expanded over the years. You can still come here for a fabulous pumpkin patch outing every October—there's a petting zoo, hayrides, and a harvest market, as well as rows and rows of the big round gourds we love to carve. But DD has started hosting a Christmas event, too, with trees for sale and Santa hanging around offering up "ho ho hos." The DD is also a great place to buy free-range, hormone-free pork and beef, and rumor has it they've started a community-supported-agriculture produce-buying program, too. Free entry, fees for pumpkins and some activities. Open the entire month of October; call for seasonal hours.

Rockhard/Juniper Junction. 9297 NE Crooked River Dr.; (541) 548-4786. Only in Terrebonne would climbing and mountaineering equipment coexist with world-famous fresh wild huckleberry ice cream in a ramshackle wood-shingled building. But don't miss the chance to stop in—ice cream this good is never a bad idea, even if it's 10 a.m. Hours vary seasonally.

Smith Rock State Park. 9241 NE Crooked River Dr. (off US 97, 14 miles south of Warm Springs); (800) 551-6949; www.oregonstateparks.org. Smith Rock is something everyone should witness at least once. It's true that you can see the wondrous multicolored majesty of welded tuff volcanic rock from US 97, but Smith Rock is best experienced close up. Most people come here for the rock climbing, which is world famous. There are hundreds of routes, some that are extremely difficult, and climbers from literally everywhere on earth have been summoned here to prove their mettle. If you're a newbie, consider taking a private or group lesson with Chockstone Climbing Guides (541-318-7170; www.chockstone climbing.com). But, if scaling a rock wall is not your cup of tea, come to hike, picnic, view wildlife like deer, beavers, and eagles along the Crooked River, or summit the trail known as Misery Ridge. It's steep, but entirely walkable, requiring no ropes or any of the skill the rock climbers you'll see on the way need. At the top, take in a stunning view of the Cascade Range, the river below, and surrounding ranches and farms. It will blow your mind. Oregon State Parks charge a fee to park—purchase a day-use, 12- or 24-month pass.

where to eat

La Siesta Cafe and Cantina. 8320 N US 97; (541) 548-4848. Darn good Mexican food in a simple, homey establishment, with a motley collection of art on the walls and all the chips and salsa you can eat. The margaritas are dandy and there are several local brews on tap, too. $.

Pump House Bar and Grill. 8320 US 97; (541) 548-4990. Traditional saloon with steaks, ribs, chicken fried steak, pasta, seafood, burgers, and more. Open for lunch and dinner 7 days a week. Live music some weekend nights. $–$$.

Terrebonne Railroad Depot. 400 NW Smith Rock Way; (541) 548-5030; www.terre bonnedepot.com. Constructed in 1911 for the Oregon Trunk Railroad, the Terrebonne Oregon Trunk Passenger Depot was left abandoned for much of the latter half of the 20th century. A total renovation in 2005 restored the historic structure and transformed it into a lovely restaurant serving steaks, pastas, pizza, sandwiches, and burgers. New American cuisine is prepared according to season and showcases the wonderful variety of flavors found in the Cascade region. The spacious, well-lit space includes a massive, elegant bar carved by local artisans from old-growth fir blocks that once supported the depot's floor. Open Wed through Sun for lunch and dinner. $$.

where to stay

Sunview Motel and Resort. 5010 SW Clubhouse Rd.; (800) 282-0944; www.sunview motelandresort.com. Next door to the Crooked River Golf Course is this little motel. Clean, standard rooms have great views of the high desert landscape and the rimrock canyon of the Crooked River. There's a volleyball court, tetherball, and a horseshoe pit on site. A tennis court, basketball court, and free outdoor swimming pool are nearby. $–$$.

day trip 04

southeast

high & dry:
bend

bend

Bend is a bit of a stretch distance-wise as a day trip from Portland, but don't tell that to all of the people who day trip to this high desert town every year. The charms of Central Oregon are just too powerful to resist for many Portlanders, never mind the 3-hour drive each way. Wide open, sunshiny skies and unlimited recreational opportunities lure thousands of visitors to Bend each year, no matter how much time they can spare.

Bend was born a logging town over a century ago and remained small, rural, and fairly isolated until the 1990s. Then word got out. Oregon might be known for rain, but that weather phenomenon mostly stays clear of the state's "dry side"—the area east of the Cascade Range that includes Central Oregon. Bend gets about 12 inches of precipitation a year, compared to the nearly 40 annual inches that fall on Portland. Tourists and fans of Mt. Bachelor ski resort from around the Pacific Northwest had been hip to Bend's charisma for a long time, but a decade ago, word traveled to the rest of the nation. The population boomed. Culture and amenities multiplied. Bend was reborn as a classy, happening destination—which still offers a lion's share of the best recreational options in the state.

As a day tripper, your primary challenge will be figuring out what to do first. You'll have no shortage of options. World-class skiing, hiking, cycling, golf, fishing, mountaineering, paddling, shopping, dining, and festival-going are all at your fingertips.

southeast day trip 04

getting there

There are two primary routes to choose from between Portland and Bend, and folks tend to be loyalists about which path is best. Either way you need to cross the Cascade Range—you can choose to do so via Mt. Hood and Blue Box pass or via Salem and the Santiam Pass. I personally prefer the latter, to avoid the suburbs of Gresham and busy ski traffic on Mt. Hood. In the winter, it's a good idea to check www.tripcheck.com to see if one route or the other is clearer of weather challenges.

From Portland via Salem, head south out of Portland on I-5. Just south of Salem, watch for the OR 22 exit, exit 253, towards Detroit Lake/Bend. Turn left (east) onto OR 22. OR 22 becomes North Santiam Highway. Continue to follow this route east until it merges into US 20 E. Travel through Sisters and another 20 miles to Bend. Total mileage from Portland is 175 miles.

where to go

Breweries. Bend is a microbrew-lovers' dream. In fact, while the microbrewery phenomenon didn't exactly begin here, it sure sunk its teeth in. Since Deschutes Brewery was founded in 1988, seven more breweries have opened in Central Oregon, with a couple more rumored to be opening soon. Beer and Bend are so intertwined that there's a new activity in town, called the Bend Ale Trail. See www.visitbend.com for a map and passport that will guide you on a journey through Bend's seven breweries. For extra credit, visit the brewery in Sisters. Then return to the Visit Bend Welcome Center (917 NW Harriman St.) to receive a free silipint (a silicone pint glass for people on the go).

Or simply pick and choose from this list, no overachieving necessary. All but one of these establishments are also restaurants; each serves a variation on pub-style comfort food.

Bend Brewing Company. 1019 NW Brooks St.; (541) 383-1599; www.bendbrewing .com. Bend's second-oldest brewery and brewpub sits on the Deschutes River downtown and offers outdoor seating in the summertime. Brewer Tonya Cornett was the first woman to win Small Brewpub Brewer of the Year at the World Beer Cup a few years' back. The beers here are little delicious platforms for her talent. Brewery tours by appointment. Open daily for lunch and dinner.

Boneyard Beer Co. 37 NW Lake Place; (541) 323-2325; www.boneyardbeer.com. Bend's newest brewery operates out of an old warehouse tucked away in a little neighborhood near downtown. Their facility only offers tastings and beer sales—no food. Still, Boneyard has already nurtured a growing reputation for themselves as purveyors of great beer. Call for hours.

Cascade Lakes Brewery. 1441 SW Chandler Ave.; (541) 388-4998; www.cascade lakes.com. This popular lodge-like restaurant serves Cascade Lakes' range of microbrews, which include cleverly named gems like Bombshell Blonde. A full bar and outdoor seating complement this establishment. Tours by appointment. Open daily for lunch and dinner.

Deschutes Brewery. Brewery: 901 SW Simpson Ave.; (541) 385-8606; Public House: 1044 Bond St.; www.deschutesbrewery.com. The granddaddy of Bend breweries distributes today all over the country, but the magic still happens here at the brewery on Bend's Westside. Tours are offered Mon through Sun at 1, 2, 3, and 4 p.m. and will leave you wiser and more appreciative of beer—especially after you've tried the free samples. There is also a tasting room here, open 7 days a week from noon to 5 p.m. The Public House and restaurant is located downtown and serves up all of Deschutes' beers as well as lots of food. Open daily for lunch and dinner.

McMenamins Old St. Francis School. 700 NW Bond St.; (541) 382-5174; www .mcmenamins.com. The McMenamin brothers strike again with this converted Catholic school in downtown Bend. The brewery is in the basement and sports some fun and funky murals on the walls and tanks. Beers on tap vary by season, but there's always something great flowing. Tours by appointment. Open daily for breakfast, lunch, and dinner.

Silver Moon Brewing. 24 NW Greenwood Ave.; (541) 388-8331; www.silvermoon brewing.com. Award-winning signature beers and seasonal specials are served at this brewpub and restaurant, also a popular spot for live music and entertainment. The decor here is eclectic, the vibe laid back and old school—play a game of pool or kick back in mismatched chairs and hang out as long as you like. Ten-person tours of the brewery are available by appointment, and end with a half-hour tasting of a 7-beer flight. Open 7 days a week for lunch and dinner.

10 Barrel Brewing Co. 1135 NW Galveston Ave.; (541) 678-5228; www.10barrel .com. The 10 Barrel brewpub is the new cool kid on the brewery scene, offering up really fabulous beers in a totally renovated restaurant space on Bend's Westside. The outdoor fire pit is the center of the action summer or winter; indoors, imperial pints are served with pizza, burgers, and more. Open for lunch and dinner 7 days a week.

Three Creeks Brewing. 721 Desperado Court, Sisters; (541) 549-1963; www.three creeksbrewing.com. Sisters' singular brewery makes good microbrews with Western flair, including the aptly named Anvil Amber and Old Prospector. Located in the Five Pine campus, near the movie theater, resort, and spa. Open for lunch and dinner 7 days a week.

Deschutes River Trail. Bend Parks and Recreation District, 799 SW Columbia St.; (541) 389-7275; www.bendparksandrec.org. This trail is the crowning jewel in a local parks system that consists of dozens of gorgeous, well-planned parks. The River Trail consists of almost 19 miles of paved and dirt trail, and provides nearly uninterrupted access to the Deschutes River, which runs through the heart of Bend. Pick up a map at parks headquarters (address listed here) or simply head for the river, pick up the trail, and walk as far as you'd like.

Golf. Bend is home to more golf courses per capita than any other Oregon region. The good news is that many of them are open nearly all year. The bad news is that they aren't all open to the public. Here are three that are:

Rivers Edge Golf Course. 400 NW Pro Shop Dr.; (541) 389-2828; www.riverhouse .com.

Tetherow. 61240 Skyline Ranch Rd.; (541) 388-2582; www.tetherow.com.

Widgi Creek Golf Club. 18707 Century Dr.; (541) 382-4449; www.widgi.com.

The High Desert Museum. 59800 S US 97; (541) 382-4754; www.highdesertmuseum .org. Since it opened in 1982, The High Desert Museum has been introducing people to the history, natural history, and culture of the high desert region. This sprawling museum has exhibits indoors and out that include live animals throughout, from lizards to sturgeon, porcupines to burrowing owls, lynxes to black widow spiders. Exhibits interpret the history of the West, Native American culture, the forest, birds of prey, and more. There is a cafe and really fabulous gift shop, too. Open every day except Thanksgiving, Christmas, and New Year's Day. Open 9 a.m. to 5 p.m. May 1 through Oct 31; 10 a.m. to 4 p.m. daily, Nov 1 through Apr 30. Admission is $15 for adults, $12 for seniors, and $9 for youth.

Mt. Bachelor. SW Century Drive, 21 miles west of Bend; (541) 382-2442; www.mtbachelor .com. Skiers, snowboarders, and Nordic skiers flock here each winter, but that's not the only reason to visit Central Oregon's most popular volcano. In the summer, lifts run to the summit and give an inimitable view of the Cascade Range. The Cascade Lakes Highway, also called SW Century Drive, along which Mt. Bachelor is located, is one of the most beautiful drives in the state and passes by a handful of alpine lakes, many of which have beaches and campgrounds; Elk Lake has a lodge and restaurant, too. In the winter, Century Drive closes just past Mt. Bachelor; stay at the mountain and enjoy 3,000 acres of lift-served terrain, 71 runs, and 56 kilometers of groomed Nordic trail, all covered in plenty of ski-able, board-able, sled-able snow.

Pilot Butte. OR 20/Greenwood Avenue just east of NE 12th Street. This cinder cone stands 500 feet over the middle of town and serves as equal parts landmark and destination. It served as a beacon in the high desert 100 to 200 years ago, guiding travelers working their way to Bend or further west. Today there is both a trail and a road to the top; millions of visitors ascend each every year. From the top the entire city of Bend is visible as well as many mountains in the Cascade Range. Fireworks are launched from the top each Fourth of July. The road closes seasonally, but the trail is always open. It's steep but worth the climb.

where to shop

Bend has two primary, distinct shopping districts, each with its own style and more shops than we can list here.

Downtown. (541) 788-3628; www.downtownbend.org. Bend's downtown has transformed in 20 years from quiet and sedated to booming and happening. All varieties of wonderful shopping opportunities are here, from fresh flowers to haute couture to antiques to books. Make sure to visit **Lulu's** (150 NW Minnesota Ave.) for fabulous women's clothing, **Dudley's** (135 NW Minnesota Ave.) for new and used books as well as coffee and snacks, **John Paul Design** (1006 NW Bond St.) for original world-class jewelry, and **Patagonia by Pandora's Backpack** (920 NW Bond St., Suite 101) for fine outdoor clothing. The first Friday of each month, downtown hosts an art walk—the streets are packed with activity.

The Old Mill District. 520 SW Powerhouse Dr.; www.theoldmill.com. Formerly just what it sounds like—the site of Bend's original lumber mills—The Old Mill District is located on the Deschutes River and is a beautiful, upscale outdoor mall. There are many chain stores here as well as local shops and restaurants. The Gap and Banana Republic are here, and don't miss the Oregon Duck Store and Strictly Organic Coffee. A cinema and walking trail are here, too; across the river on a footbridge is the Les Schwab Amphitheater, which books great music acts all summer season. Minimum store hours for the Old Mill District are Mon through Sat 10 a.m. to 8 p.m. and Sun 11 a.m. to 6 p.m. Longer hours during the holidays.

where to eat

Anthony's Home Port. 475 SW Powerhouse Dr.; (541) 389-8998; www.anthonys.com. The menu here features delicious fresh Northwest seafood flown in directly from the ocean, but the real attraction is this restaurant's location. The spectacular view of the Deschutes River as well as Mt. Bachelor and the Three Sisters Mountains provides such a stunning backdrop you'll hardly care what you eat (and it's all fabulous anyway). Make a reservation for sunset; in the summer, sit outdoors and watch the reflection off the river. Open for lunch and dinner 7 days a week; brunch on Sunday. $$–$$$.

The Blacksmith Steakhouse, Bar and Lounge. (541) 318-0588; www.bendblacksmith .com. Several years ago, this place was getting national recognition for its "new ranch cuisine"—Western-style comfort food like trout, meatloaf, mac and cheese, and lots of steaks done up fancy and served in subdued comfort in this old blacksmith shop in downtown Bend. The food is still pretty great, but recently the Blacksmith has become known for its happy hour and nightlife, too. Come here after hours on weekends for dancing and late-night food specials. Open 7 days a week from 4:30 p.m. to close. $$–$$$.

Chow. 1110 NW Newport Ave.; (541) 728-0256; www.chowbend.com. This converted bungalow house serves up complicated, delicious, entirely homemade breakfasts and lunches that include lots of locally sourced products. The menu offers everything from ginger pancakes to smoked salmon and bacon hash to a corned beef and kraut sandwich, all of which you can wash down with a mean Bloody Mary. Open 7 a.m. to close (after lunch) 7 days a week. $–$$.

Hola! Old Mill District; (541) 647-2711; www.holabend.com. The very best Peruvian Mexican food you will ever eat, including ceviche, mole, chile relleno, and amazing seafood enchiladas, all with fabulous flavor and freshness. The full bar provides amazing margaritas, the space is colorful and vibrant, the service really friendly. This place gets the food right clear down to the desserts—the pièce de résistance is bananas flameadas, which consists of sliced bananas pan fried with butter, brown sugar, and cinnamon, fired up with rum, and served on top of vanilla ice cream. It's made right at your table. Open 7 days a week for lunch and dinner. $$.

Jackson's Corner. 845 NW Delaware Ave.; (541) 647-2198. This is the place to go if you want to feel like a local. This old market in a residential neighborhood near Bend's downtown does many things, and does them all well. There is a small deli and grocery section that stocks great beers, prepackaged foods, and a few staples. In the back, an espresso stand serves up truly excellent coffee all day. At the counter, order meals that defy expectations of counter service. The kitchen here produces excellent food, often prepared from local and organic products. Seating is casual and sometimes communal. There is some outside seating in the summer. Hang out here as long as you want—everyone feels at home at Jackson's Corner. Open 7 days a week for breakfast, lunch, and dinner. $–$$.

Pine Tavern. 967 NW Brooks St.; (541) 382-5581; www.pinetavern.com. The Pine Tavern may have the reputation of being a bit antiquated, but it's earned it. This restaurant has anchored downtown Bend on the Deschutes River since 1936. Known for the Ponderosa pine tree growing through the center of the dining room, sourdough scones with honey butter served before every meal, and the most picturesque patio in town, the Pine Tavern serves Pacific Northwest food like smoked salmon salad with pears and crumbled blue cheese and pork tenderloin. The food and service are simple, rooted in the past, and excellent. Open for lunch Mon through Sat and dinner 7 nights a week. $$.

Sparrow Bakery. 50 SE Scott St., #22; (541) 330-6321; www.thesparrowbakery.com. This little French bakery is a bit off the beaten path, but finding it will make your taste buds happy. The pastries here are divine—don't miss the Ocean Roll, which is like a cinnamon roll only much better, and the hand-folded croissants. Grilled sandwiches and salads are served at lunchtime, and often include local produce and products as ingredients. Open Tues through Sat 7 a.m. to 2 p.m. $.

Typhoon! 550 NW Franklin Ave., #148; (541) 322-8889; www.typhoonrestaurants.com. This branch of the Portland Thai restaurant with the same name is equally delicious and possibly even more fabulous inside. Long gauzy curtains separate diners from one another and the atmosphere is dark, moody, and romantic. Each dish is impeccably prepared with fresh veggies, seafood, and meat. The lunch combination plates are the best deal. $$–$$$.

> ## festival heaven

One thing that Bend's population and culture boom spawned is a flurry of festivals. Between May and November, there's something fabulous happening every week-end—often more than one thing simultaneously. The first Friday of every month brings a hoppin' art walk to downtown (www.downtownbend.org). In the summer, free concerts are held every Sunday afternoon at Les Schwab Amphitheater (www .theoldmill.com). There are children's festivals, literary festivals, hot air balloon festivals, cycling festivals, beer festivals, live music festivals, antiques festivals, car festivals, and Oktoberfests. My very favorite festival by far is the **Bend Film Fest,** *held the first weekend of October each year. Four days of independent films, parties, workshops, lectures, and the camaraderie of festival become more than the sum of their parts. This event brings people together to talk about the things great films can urge us to consider—the mysteries and joys of life, pain and joy and happiness, and the ways we are all alike and yet unique. Like all forms of great art, independent films can make us see anew the beauty and connection that is around us already. See www.bendfilm.org for more information on the Bend Film Fest. For a complete listing of Bend's festivals, see the appendix in this book.*

Victorian Café. 1404 Northwest Galveston Ave.; (541) 382-6411. With something like 9 different kinds of eggs Benedict on the menu, the Victorian has earned itself the title of best Bend breakfast many times over. There's often a line outside this old house on Bend's Westside, but the wait is made more tolerable by a fire pit and the availability of Bloody Marys. Beyond poached eggs topped with everything from smoked salmon to mangos, choose from pancakes, omelets, and all the usual breakfast fare. Lunch brings fabulous sandwiches and salads, but breakfast is served all day and is really how this place shines. The menu is pretty expensive, but it's worth it. In the summer, sit outside on the patio. $$.

Zydeco. 919 Bond St.; (541) 312-2899; www.zydecokitchen.com. Cajun cooking with a Pacific Northwest flair is served at this cool downtown restaurant. The scene is modern and hip, the food spicy and scrumptious. The blackened catfish with Zydeco sauce, Dungeness crabmeat, sautéed spinach, and mashed potatoes will melt in your mouth. Open for lunch Mon through Fri 11 a.m. to 2 p.m. and dinner 7 days a week from 5 pm. to close. $$–$$$.

where to stay

Lara House Lodge. 640 NW Congress St.; (800) 766-4064; www.larahouse.com. If romance and a prime location across from Bend's Drake Park are what you are after, this bed and breakfast will suit your needs. Six guest rooms have attractive mission-style furnishings, exquisite linens, and down comforters, all with private baths. Guests relax by the cozy fireplace, beautiful sunroom, and candlelit front porch. Every evening, there is a wine hour featuring Pacific Northwest wines paired nicely with delicious hors d'oeuvres and gourmet cheeses. In the morning, a sumptuous multi-course breakfast will get your day started right. It's all fairly expensive here, great for a special occasion. $$$.

McMenamins Old St. Francis School. 700 NW Bond St.; (541) 382-5174; www .mcmenamins.com. What was once a private Catholic school is now a whimsical, fun hotel, restaurant, bar, theater, and music venue. These brick buildings in downtown Bend are full of old memorabilia, murals, and 19 richly appointed guest rooms that used to be classrooms. There are also 4 individual rental cottages on site, as well as a fabulous soaking pool that's open to the outdoors through a hole in the ceiling and tiled beautifully by a local artist. Don't miss O'Kane's Pub, a stand-alone building studded with gorgeous stained glass and surrounded by a courtyard, specializing in scotch. There is often live music on weekends and for special celebrations. Don't worry about the nuns—they are all gone. $$.

Mt. Bachelor Village Resort. 19717 Mount Bachelor Dr.; (800) 547-5204; www.mtbachelor village.com. This resort combines the convenience of being in town with the peace and quiet of a forested, riverfront location. Spectacular Deschutes River views are available from the River Ridge suites, which also have gas fireplaces and private hot tubs on a deck overlooking all of that spectacular river and forest. The Ski House condominiums are less expensive but not nearly as nice—spring for the River Ridge suite. You won't regret it. Tennis and a swimming pool on site, too. $$$.

The Oxford Hotel and 10 Below. 10 NW Minnesota Ave.; (877) 440-8436, (541) 382-1010; www.oxfordhotelbend.com. The restaurant in the new Oxford Hotel, Bend's only four-star boutique lodging, is tucked away in the basement. But that secluded location only makes this bright space feel all the more singular from the rest of the world. The chic urban restaurant put itself out on a limb in terms of decor—and you might feel like you are out on a limb surrounded by tree cross-sections on the wall, tree motifs on the curtains, and shades of green all around. The food is top-notch, as well. If you're here for lunch, don't miss the BLTA. The grilled rustic toast, thick-cut bacon, tomato, avocado, and smear of maple aioli is a perfect example of why sweet, fat, and salt have always been some of our favorite things. Open for breakfast, lunch, and dinner daily (even holidays). The hotel rooms are also absolutely metropolitan, done up in rich earth tones with flashes of white and silver, with touches like opaque etched-glass screens and local French presses and fresh coffee in the rooms, and organic bath and body products in the bath. The beds are divine. The Oxford prides itself on its sustainable practices, and is one of the only hotels in the state to use non-chemical-based cleaning products. $$–$$$.

south

day trip 01

south

oregon's beginnings:
oregon city

oregon city

Oregon City is located 13 miles southeast of Portland on the east side of the Willamette River, just below Willamette Falls. The town is part of the Portland Metro Area, and there is no obvious division between Oregon City and the other suburbs that surround Portland. But don't dare suggest to an Oregon City resident that they live in Portland. Residents of this town take their distinction seriously. That might be in part because of Oregon City's history.

The city played a significant role in Oregon's beginnings. Established by Dr. John McLoughlin of the Hudson Bay Company in 1829, Oregon City was the first city in the US west of the Rocky Mountains to be incorporated. Oregon Territory was officially created in 1848 and Oregon City was designated as the territory's first capital, an honor it held until the capital was moved to Salem in 1852.

Oregon City remained a vibrant community, if a little quieter, after Oregon was granted statehood in 1859. In later years, Oregon City's economy rested on the forest industry, until harvest dried up in the 1980s.

Today, Oregon City's appeal resides in history—the center of the city retains part of its historic character through the preservation of houses and other buildings from the era of the city's founding. Oregon City residents are very proud of their gritty, authentic downtown revival. Appeal also rests in Oregon City's unique geographical placement at the confluence of the Clackamas River and the Willamette River. This unique topography includes three

N

Scappoose

Columbia River

Sturgeon Lake

502

Battle Ground

5

503

WASHINGTON

30

500

5

Vancouver

Camas

OREGON

26

84

Fairview

Portland

Hillsboro

Gresham

8

26

Beaverton

205

Willamette River

Milwaukie

Damascus

Tigard

99W

99E

212

219

224

Sherwood

205

Gladstone

Oregon City

5

219

Newberg

Wilsonville

Canby

213

99E

Aurora

St. Paul

0   5   10 miles

Hubbard

211

speed with a view

Want to see Oregon City and Willamette Falls from a totally unique perspective? Try a **Willamette Jet Boat tour.** *The history, wildlife, and Willamette Falls tour leaves from Portland, near OMSI (Oregon Museum of Science and Industry), and jets upriver to Willamette Falls and back, offering views you'd never get from land. May through September. Call (888) JETBOAT; www.willamettejet.com. Another river-tour option is to take a cruise on the* **Portland Spirit,** *a 98-foot custom-built yacht. See www.portlandspirit.com.*

terraces that rise above the river, creating an elevation range from about 50 feet above sea level at the riverbank to more than 250 feet above sea level on the upper terrace. The lowest terrace, on which the earliest development occurred, is only 2 blocks or 3 streets wide, but stretches northward from the falls for several blocks. This is where you'll want to begin your day of exploration, though Oregon City offers many other pleasures, too.

getting there

Oregon City is located 13 miles south of Portland. Take exit 9 off of I-205 from the north or south, or take OR 99 E/McLoughlin Boulevard south from Milwaukie. McLoughlin Boulevard can be very slow going during high volume traffic hours—avoid at these times.

where to go

Dream Ridge Stables. 20524 S Ridge Rd.; (503) 631-8466; www.dreamridgestable.com. Need a horse fix? Horse rides at Dream Ridge begin with basic instruction in an indoor riding arena and then move to an outdoor field filled with barrels, cones, poles, small jumps, and wide open spaces. Owner Karen Bower then leads the way through beautiful trails with views of the Viola valley and the lower Cascade Mountains. Prices vary.

Ermatinger House and Living History Tea Textile Museum. 619 6th St.; (503) 650-1851. Built in 1845, the Ermatinger House is the oldest house in Clackamas County. Asa Lovejoy and Francis W. Pettygrove flipped a coin here to decide the name of the city that is now Portland. In 1910, the Ermatinger House was among many Oregon City historic homes that were moved to save them from destruction as a result of encroaching development around Willamette Falls. Living history teas and tours available. Tip: You must call to schedule a visit of the interior, but of course you can check out the exterior anytime.

First City Walking Tours. (503) 880-3439; www.therealoc.net/tours. Take a walking tour of downtown or the historic McLoughlin Neighborhood with an expert on the secrets of

Oregon City past and present. Most tours meet in the observation deck of the Oregon City municipal elevator. See website or call for dates and times. Tours run about $10 per person.

John McLoughlin House. 713 Center St.; (503) 656-5146. The Canadian-born Dr. John McLoughlin has been called the Father of Oregon, and he was certainly the father of Oregon City. The fur trade was booming in 1824 when Dr. McLoughlin crossed the Rockies, establishing Ft. Vancouver on the Columbia River a year later. Beaver fur hats had become a popular item the world over, and British, French, and American trappers descended on the west. McLoughlin served as chief factor, or superintendent, of the British Hudson's Bay Company at the fort for many years, befriending Native Americans and lending a hand to pioneers. Though it was miles south of the fort, McLoughlin took to the Oregon City site, founding a city here and eventually retiring in this house. In 1941, the McLoughlin House was designated by Congress as the first National Historic Site in the West. Open for tours Wed through Sun. Free admission.

Oregon City Municipal Elevator. 300 7th St. (Official address is 610 Bluff St., but main street entrance is on 7th St.); (503) 657-0891. Oregon City is divided into upper and lower areas; the lower area is on a bench next to the Willamette River, and the upper area sits atop a bluff. Trails connected the two before stairs were built in the 1800s. In 1915, modernity came to town and the city built the Oregon City Municipal Elevator to ferry residents between their town's two tiers. The elevator continues to operate as one of only four municipal elevators in the world and "Elevator Street" remains the only vertical street in North America. Open to the public 7 days a week; no charge.

Oregon City Farmers Market. Downtown, 2051 Kaen Rd. off Beavercreek Road; www.orcityfarmersmarket.com. From May through Oct on Sat and Wed, 9 a.m. to 2 p.m., visit Oregon City's historic downtown for fresh and local produce, pastured meats, farm eggs, wines, honey, preserves, breads, flowers, plants, goat's milk soaps, and gelato from local farmers and vendors. Chefs from local restaurants offer demonstrations; live music lifts spirits. Park and ride the Historic Trolley to the Market.

Oregon City Trolley. Downtown; (503) 496-1571. Oregon City has three cheery red trolleys—*Helen, Josephine,* and *Marguerite,* each named after people in Oregon City history. The free trolleys travel throughout Oregon City's Historic District with many stops along the route, including museums, points of interests, and shops. Summer season only!

The Oregon Lavender Farm. 20949 S Harris Rd.; (800) 289-8427; www.libertynatural.com, www.oregonlavenderfestival.com. The Oregon Lavender Farm hosts the Annual Clackamas County Lavender Festival the last Saturday and Sunday in June each year. Wine tasting, food, music, distillation demonstration, and much more occur on the farm's 10 acres of lavender angustifolia "Buena Vista," developed for its super blue color and superior fragrance. The farm is the home of Liberty Natural Products, Inc. a primary supplier of more than 1,000 botanical extracts, and also participates in the Oregon Lavender Festival—an event with multiple locations—every July.

Spirits of Oregon City Walking Tour. (503) 679-4464; www.nwghosttours.com. Pass by some of Oregon City's most spirited places and hear their ghost stories. Who knows—maybe you'll meet your very own ghost. Two different tours in Oregon City: McLoughlin Neighborhood and Downtown Oregon City.

Stevens-Crawford Heritage House. 603 6th St.; (503) 655-2866. Wagon master Medorem Crawford, who brought pioneers across the Oregon Trail, built this house in 1907–08. A classic example of Foursquare architecture, this house, amazingly, contains all of its original furniture. Open Thurs through Sat for tours.

Willamette Falls/McLoughlin Promenade. Runs along McLoughlin Boulevard; access at 7th and Center Streets. This 7.8-acre linear park on the bluff above downtown provides spectacular views of the Willamette River, Willamette Falls, and downtown Oregon City. The charming concrete walkway was originally constructed in 1937 as a Works Progress Administration project and was recently restored. Seating, picnic areas, and historical markers along the way are lovely and helpful, but the real attraction is the view of the second-largest waterfall in the United States, former gathering place of Native American tribes and Oregon's early pioneers.

where to shop

Bob's Red Mill Whole Grain Store and Visitors Center. 5000 SE International Way, Milwaukie; (503) 607-6455; www.bobsredmill.com. Bob Moore reopened a historic flour mill near Oregon City 25 years ago with hopes to preserve the ancient craft of stone milling and to grind whole grains for the local community. Today, Bob's Red Mill produces more than 400 flours, cereals, and baking mixes, including certified gluten-free and certified organic products. Their newly opened Bob's Red Mill Whole Grain Store and Visitors Center features a bakery, deli, cafe, 18-foot operating waterwheel, and historic milling equipment. Store and visitors center open Mon through Sat; factory tours conducted Mon through Fri.

Dave's Killer Bread. 5209 SE International Way, Milwaukie; (503) 335-8077; www.daves killerbread.com. Right across the street from Bob's Red Mill is Dave's Killer Bread Outlet Store, where you can get Dave's truly killer, delicious, organic whole grain breads at a discount. Dave says he used to get into lots of trouble, and you can hear that story if you want, too. But now he just makes fabulous bread. Yum.

Pendleton Woolen Mills. 8550 SE McLoughlin Blvd., Portland; (503) 535-5786; www .pendleton-usa.com. Pendleton Woolen Mills has been making fine blankets in classic designs for 140 years. On McLoughlin Boulevard north of Oregon City is the Pendleton Woolen Mill Store, your source for first quality Pendleton fabrics, remnants, yarn, buttons, notions, and patterns at unbelievable prices. Weekly deliveries from Pendleton's mills bring multicolored selvage and blanket trimmings (worms) to incorporate into a rug or other creative sewing project.

where to eat

Highland Still House Pub. 201 S 2nd St.; (503) 723-6789; www.highlandstillhouse.com. Looking for Portland's widest selection of single-malt scotch? Here's your spot. This friendly Scottish-style pub features a cozy old-world atmosphere with antique furnishings from England and Scotland, and cooks up traditional Scottish fare with a Northwest influence for lunch and dinner 6 days a week. Outdoor seating with views of the Willamette Falls is significant perk. Closed Monday. $$.

Singer Hill Café. 623 7th St.; (503) 656-5252; www.singerhill.com. Cafe, bakery, and community hub, with innovative demonstration garden out back and live music some Sundays. This place is a real local's favorite. Open 7 a.m. to 6 p.m. Mon through Sat, 9 a.m. to 5 p.m. Sun. $.

The Stone Cliff Inn. 17900 S Clackamas River Dr.; (503) 631-7900; www.stonecliffinn .com. Located on the historic Baker Rock Quarry site, this fine dining establishment and log structure is nestled amid old growth trees on cliffs overlooking the Clackamas River, with stunning views from the outside deck. Northwest cuisine pleases all. Claim to fame: The Stone Cliff Inn was one filming site of the *Twilight* movie. Lunch and dinner 7 days a week. Reservations recommended. $$$.

Weatherford's Grand Lodge. 602 7th St.; (503) 723-9253; www.weatherfordsgrand lodge.com. This historic Odd Fellows Lodge houses a restaurant and upstairs ballroom. The menu features a strong passion for fine foods, especially local and organic produce. Specialty kids menu and happy hour specials. Open 7 days a week for 3 meals a day at 11:30 a.m.; Sun at 9:30 a.m. $$$.

where to stay

Sandes of Time Bed and Breakfast. 16022 SE River Rd., Portland; (503) 654-8813; www.sandesoftime.com. If driving all the way back to Portland is just too much to bear after a day spent slowing down to the pace of lovely Oregon City, book a room at the Sandes of Time Bed and Breakfast in Milwaukie, halfway between Oregon City and Portland. This wonderful old home was completed in 1907 atop a rocky knoll on 3 park-like acres. Recently restored and renovated, it now includes 4 downright lovely guest rooms and 3 covered porches with porch swings—the perfect place to while away the evening. $$.

day trip 02

south

treasure hunting:
woodburn, aurora

woodburn

Woodburn earned its name literally. A slash burn, set after the railroad line had been laid in the 1880s, burned out of control and destroyed a woodlot here. Voilà—a city was named.

Today, however, that which was once burned black is green. Nurseries and farms abound in this part of the Willamette Valley, many of which you can visit. Everything from pumpkins to lawn seed to fruit trees to strawberries is cultivated here, and buying it from the source always a fun, rewarding option.

Aside from flora, Woodburn is known for shopping. The Woodburn Company Stores is Oregon's number one tourist attraction, with 4 million visitors per year to its more than 100 outlet shops. While the stores are located right on Oregon's busiest thoroughfare, I-5, and represent the height of modern commerce and style, venture into Woodburn proper and you might see a glimpse of the past. Woodburn has been home to a sizable community of Russian Orthodox Old Believers since the 1950s, when this Christian reformed church escaped persecution from the official Russian Orthodox Church and moved to the United States from Turkey. On the streets of Woodburn, one might see women in long skirts and scarves and men with beards.

getting there

Take I-5 south from Portland for 29 miles. Take the OR 214 exit, exit 271, toward Wood-burn/Silverton. Turn left onto OR 214 and proceed directly into Woodburn.

where to go

Al's Garden Center. 1220 N Pacific Hwy.; (503) 981-1245; www.als-gardencenter.com. Awarded Garden Center of the Year in 2006 by Garden Centers of America, Al's produces 6 million plants a year. The Garden Center also offers several seminars and special events a year, like Kid's Bulb Day. Check the website for details. Open Mon through Fri 10 a.m. to 6 p.m., Sat 9 a.m. to 6 p.m., Sun 10 a.m. to 5 p.m.

Bauman Farms. 12989 Howell Prairie Rd. (off OR 99 E south of Woodburn); (503) 792-3524; www.baumanfarms.com. Bauman family matriarch Great Grandmother Elizabeth Bauman started farming here in 1894, but things didn't really take off commerce-wise for this small farm for nearly 100 years. Today Bauman Farms is home to a nursery, bakery, and vegetable farm that attract hundreds of visitors a year. Host to many seasonal events, including an Easter egg hunt and a pumpkin patch in the fall, Bauman Farms also offers homemade zucchini bread, donuts, and pie. Hours vary annually.

Garden World. 10506 Broadacres Rd.; (503) 982-2380; www.gardenworldonline.com. A big sign on I-5 alerts passers-by to this amazing garden store's existence, but the freeway view has nothing on an up-close-and-personal visit. Whether you are after a one-stop plant shopping trip, a tour with your designer or contractor, or field trip with the kids or garden club, Garden World is your destination. Ten acres and 1,000 varieties of locally grown plant material including 100 different Japanese maples, rare and unusual conifers, and many sizes of shade and flowering trees make this place pretty as well as productive.

Settlemier House. 355 N Settlemier Ave.; (503) 982-1897; www.settlemierhouse.com. This Victorian/Craftsman house was built in 1892 and sits on nearly 3 acres of beautifully landscaped grounds. A very popular spot to host private events, and tours are offered to the public on the first Sunday of each month.

Wooden Shoe Tulip Farm. 33814 S Meridian Rd.; (503) 634-2243; www.woodenshoe .com. The Wooden Shoe Tulip Farm has been around since 1986, but the Iverson family has been growing tulips even longer than that. Why not, when they are so beautiful? Today the operation includes bulbs, cut flowers, potted tulips, a gift shop, other plants, and all sorts of food and activities on weekends. In April, Wooden Shoe opens their 40 acres of tulips and daffodils for an entire month for the Tulip Fest. In October, it's all about the Pumpkin Fest. See the website for details.

where to shop

Woodburn Company Stores. 1001 Arney Rd.; (503) 981-1900; www.shop-woodburn
.com. Here, it is entirely possible—possibly even inevitable—to shop until you drop. More
than 100 outlet stores are here in one enormous complex, including Adidas, Banana
Republic, Liz Claiborne, Nautica, Carter's, Levi, and more and more and more. When
you can't take it anymore, grab some refreshment at Cold Stone Creamery or Pan Asian
Express, and then get back at it. Around Christmastime, this place is jamming, but given
that it's the most popular tourist destination in the state, you can count on it being pretty
busy all year long, especially weekends. The parking lot can be a zoo, but that's just the
price to pay for great prices. If you apply yourself, you can take care of your entire holiday
list in one powerful day. Open Mon through Sat 10 a.m. to 8 p.m., Sun 10 a.m. to 7 p.m.

where to eat

Orchards Grille at OGA Golf Course. 2850 Hazelnut Dr.; (503) 981-4653; www.ogagolf
course.com. Good food, gracious service, and one of the best picturesque settings in the
North Willamette Valley. Restaurant serves American food with Italian influences 7 days a
week for lunch; lounge and deli selections offered from dawn until dusk. By the way, the
golf course is great to play as well. $–$$.

Vitality Food and Spirits. 1475 Mt. Hood Ave.; (971) 983-5280; www.iamvitality.com.
Located at the Spa at Wellspring, this restaurant offers delicious foods and an extensive
menu, including heart-healthy, organic, and gluten-free dishes. Open for breakfast, lunch,
and dinner Mon through Sat. $–$$$.

aurora

Visiting Aurora is a little bit like taking a time machine 150 years into the past. Known as
Oregon's Antiques Capital, this lush, rural town is home to dozens of antiques shops, as
well as many examples of distinctive original architecture and one of the state's premiere
National Historic Districts. It's antiquated here, but in the very best possible way.

Founded as a religious commune in 1856 by Dr. William Keil, who named the settle-
ment after his daughter, Aurora has become a destination for those seeking everything from
a turn-of-the-century chiffarobe to a piece of hazelnut candy to simply a taste of the 19th
century.

getting there

Aurora is 8 miles north of Woodburn on US 99 E/OR 99 E.

where to go

Old Aurora Colony Museum and Historical Society. 15018 2nd St. NE; (503) 678-5754; www.auroracolony.org. The Aurora Colony was a Christian commune that existed from 1856 to 1883. Nearly 600 people, almost all German and Swiss immigrants, lived together here, subsisting on farming and manufacturing, making most of their own products including furniture, textiles, and baskets. The houses and buildings from the Aurora Colony represent one of the largest concentrations of structures built by German craftsmen in the Pacific Northwest. Today visitors can see inside the Ox Barn, Steinbach Cabin, Kraus House, Will Family Summer Kitchen, and Tie Shed, and several other buildings can be viewed as part of a walking tour. Self-guided and guided tours are available and throughout the year several special events occur, featuring quilts, craft demonstrations, and hands-on activities for adults and children. Open Tues through Sat 11 a.m. to 4 p.m. (closed for the month of Jan and on all major holidays).

where to shop

Antiques. There are nearly 20 antiques shops in the Aurora area. Here we mention a few, but as any good antiques hunter knows, your best bet is to make a day of it, wander around, hit every shop you can, and leave no stone unturned.

Antique Village. 21581 Main St. NE, #A; (503) 678-1007; www.antiquesoregon.com. Furniture, fine and costume jewelry, glass, decor, pottery, and collectibles. Open Tues through Sun 11 a.m. to 5 p.m.

Aurora Mills Architectural. 14971 1st St. NE; (503) 678-6083; www.auroramills .com. This store is a must-see for anyone interested in architectural salvage. A big warehouse is filled with unique, historic, and vintage architectural materials, such as stained and beveled glass, lighting, fireplace mantels, ornamental cast iron, clawfoot tubs, Victorian hardware, terra cotta, rustic timbers, and old growth flooring. Open Tues through Sun 10 a.m. to 5 p.m.

Home Again Antiques. 21631 Main St. NE; (503) 678-0227. Very nice store, featuring primitives.

Main Street Mercantile. 21610 Main St. NE; (503) 678-1044. One of the largest antique stores in town with possibly the best selection from multiple dealers including furniture and books. Open Tues through Sun.

Pacific Hazelnut Candy Factory. 14673 Ottaway Ave.; (800) 634-7344; www.pacific hazelnut.com. A whopping 98 percent of all hazelnuts grown in the United States are from the Willamette Valley, and the folks at the Pacific Hazelnut Candy Factory know how to turn them into delectable sweets. In addition to roasting and seasoning nuts, the Pacific Hazelnut Candy Factory also chocolate coats hazelnuts, almonds, walnuts, prunes, and pretzels. The hazelnut toffee they developed was featured in *Bon Appetit* magazine. Open Mon through Fri 9 a.m. to 4:30 p.m. and Sat 10 a.m. to 4 p.m.

where to eat

The Colony Pub. 21568 US 99 E; (503) 678-9994. Cold and hot sandwiches, seafood specials, fresh soups, salads, and burgers in this classic pub with pool table, jukebox, and lottery games. The food is much better than the average pub usually manages to produce. $–$$.

White Rabbit Bakery. 21368 US 99 E; (503) 267-9044; www.whiterabbitbakery.com. A gem of a place in a little old town, the White Rabbit Bakery offers pastries, cookies, bread, sandwiches, and cakes with names like the Tulgey Wood, the Mad Hatter, and the Fat Elvis. Owner Emily Arreola aims to bring a little comfort to folks who are missing it in the form of sweet, warm, buttery, sugary, fresh, and decadent delectables. Why White Rabbit? Arreola says it's all about following your dreams and the way life gets indisputably curiouser and curiouser. Famous for their wide variety of gluten-free offerings. Open Tues through Fri 6:30 a.m. to 4 p.m., Sat and Sun 8 a.m. to 4 p.m. $.

where to stay

Feller House Bed and Breakfast. 21625 Butteville Rd. NE; (503) 678-0268; www.the fellerhouse.com. This historic farmhouse was built in the 1880s on what is known as French Prairie. Now this old homestead is a bed and breakfast, offering 2 rooms. Breakfast is a wholesome meal with a gourmet touch featuring homegrown and local produce in season, served at the table near the woodstove in the kitchen, graced with cut flowers from the property. $$.

day trip 03

south

farm & garden:
mt. angel, silverton

mt. angel

In 1881, a contingent of Benedictine monks from Engelberg, Switzerland, came to Oregon with hopes of establishing a new American branch of their church. After visiting several locations, the Mt. Angel area was selected as the ideal location for a new abbey. Immigrants from Bavaria and Germany soon followed, and eventually the area became known as Mt. Angel (an English translation of Engelberg).

Mt. Angel Abbey was twice destroyed by fire; the current building, set high above the town on a 300-foot bluff with views of Mt. St. Helens, Mt. Hood, Mt. Adams, and the lush Willamette Valley farmland, was constructed in 1928 and remains a peaceful retreat and destination for many people annually.

The town itself retains a Bavarian old-world flavor—an aura that is encouraged by local businesses who have done up their storefronts to emphasize the city's cultural roots. Mt. Angel's German heritage especially comes to life in September, during Mt. Angel's elaborate Oktoberfest. But all year, visitors enjoy the Mt. Angel Glockenspiel—a life size, authentic work of art and piece of entertainment.

getting there

Take I-5 south out of Portland. Travel for 30 miles to the Woodburn exit, #271. Merge onto OR 214 and travel to the south and east for 10 miles to Mt. Angel.

N

Columbia River Gorge Nat'l Scenic Area

502
Battle Ground

5

503

47

Scappoose

26

Columbia River

500

205

5

30

Vancouver

Camas

Washougal

6

47

26

Fairview

84

8

Hillsboro

8

Portland

Gresham

Beaverton

99E

205

Damascus

212

Tigard

219

5

47

224

Sherwood

205

Gladstone

99W

240

Newberg

Oregon City

Estacada

Dundee

99E

Canby

Lafayette

551

Aurora

Dayton

St. Paul

211

18

153

221

Hubbard

99E

Molalla

Woodburn

153

Amity

99E

214

213

Mt. Angel

Keizer

99W

213

Silverton

0   5   10 miles

22

Salem

22

51

22

214

Aumsville

Stayton

Silver Falls State Park

99W

Lyons

22

where to go

Mt. Angel Abbey. 1 Abbey Dr., St. Benedict (just south and east of Mt. Angel); (503) 845-3066; www.mountangelabbey.org. In 1883, a group of Swiss Benedictine monks established the Mt. Angel Abbey. Today, a community of monks continues to reside here at this peaceful and exceptionally lovely spot. The abbey itself is a classic beauty of a building in red brick; the grounds are lush with many old hardwood trees, flowers, and huge stretches of lawn. The library, designed by Alvar Aalto, is world-famous and stores a priceless collection of illuminated manuscripts as well as a display of rare, hand-printed books. A seminary school of philosophy and theology operates on the grounds, as does a guest and retreat house. The abbey's gift and bookshop sells books and music, rosaries and medals, greeting cards and art. Bookstore open Mon through Thurs 10 a.m. to 4:30 p.m. Guided tours of other facilities can be arranged by appointment; the library is open to public visitors upon request.

Oktoberfest. Downtown; www.oktoberfest.org; (503) 845-6882. It only happens once a year, but boy is it a doozy. Oregon's oldest and best-loved Oktoberfest began in 1966 as a traditional harvest festival to celebrate the bounty of the earth and the goodness of creation. Today the 4-day event is Oregon's largest folk festival and features continuous live music on 4 stages, free kindergarten with rides and shows, night street dancing, more than 50 alpine food chalets, a large arts and crafts show, traditional biergarten, weingarten, and alpinegarten, and RV and tent camping.

Saint Mary's Church. 575 E College St.; (503) 845-2296; www.stmarymtangel.org. This gorgeous church has been anchoring downtown Mt. Angel and serving the community since 1912. It is Roman Catholic in faith, but with a Benedictine tradition, reflecting Mt. Angel's roots. Designed and built in the Revival Gothic style, the church is laid out in the form of a Latin cross and boasts 22 stained glass windows. The church is open for viewing upon request, and depending on private events. Of course, you can see the outside just by walking by.

where to eat

The Glockenspiel Restaurant Pub. 190 East Charles St.; (503) 845-6222; www.glocken spielrestaurant.net. The atmosphere here is comfortable and the food a fresh mixture of seasonal Northwest cuisine with a hint of Bavaria, including spätzle soup, wiener schnitzel, fondue, and the traditional Friday fish fry (long a Catholic tradition, in accordance with scriptural advisement to avoid meat on Fridays). But the real attraction at this restaurant is outdoors. Mt. Angel's Glockenspiel rises 49 feet above the restaurant. This marvel in the center of town celebrates the Native-German-Swiss-Bavarian heritage of the village and Mt. Angel's world-famous Oktoberfest held each fall. Its figures represent Mt. Angel history and dance, sing, and ring bells in celebration. Glockenspiel performances occur daily at 11 a.m. and 1, 4, and 7 p.m., and are free. Restaurant open daily 11 a.m. to 9 p.m. $$.

silverton

Silverton exudes small town charm. A historic downtown district and many old mansions perched on the surrounding hills attract visitors looking for a picturesque slice of America's past every year.

But Silverton does modern, too—the city is home to a thriving arts community with many galleries and unique shops to be discovered downtown. The Silverton Fine Arts Festival draws artists and art lovers to town each August, and transforms this little town into a small artist's enclave.

There's plenty of artistic inspiration to be found here, to be sure, especially from nature. Silverton is nicknamed "Oregon's Garden City," and the Willamette Valley is lush and beautiful here. Silverton has just enough of a hilly aspect to it to offer fabulous views of the countryside. Nearby, Silver Falls State Park boasts 10 waterfalls and is the oldest and biggest state park in Oregon. The Oregon Garden is a newer establishment with just as much beauty—20 specialty gardens bloom on site, and the only structure in Oregon designed by famous architect Frank Lloyd Wright is here, too.

Right in town, Silver Creek runs through the city, making those historic buildings all the more picturesque.

getting there

Take OR 214 south out of Mt. Angel. Silverton is 5 miles south of Mt. Angel on OR 214.

where to go

Cooley's Gardens. 11553 Silverton Rd. NE; (503) 873-5463; www.cooleysgardens.com. Founded in 1928 by Rholin and Pauline Cooley, Cooley's Gardens started as a backyard iris hobby. An amazing 83 years later, Cooley's grows and ships "The World's Finest Iris" to customers the world over. Cooley's breeds new irises as well as planting classics, and a 4-acre display garden is open to the public. Hundreds of varieties of bearded iris bloom from about May 15 through mid-June.

The Gordon House. 879 W Main St. (next to the Oregon Garden); (503) 874-6006; www .thegordonhouse.org. Frank Lloyd Wright designed a series of homes in the 1930s and later that he referred to as Usonian—a philosophy of living in harmony with the land of the United States of Northern America (USONA). Designed for Evelyn and Conrad Gordon in 1957 and finished in 1963, this house was one of Lloyd Wright's many creations that ultimately made great impact on the design and architecture of small homes for the middle class consumer. Originally located in Wilsonville, the Gordon House was moved to this site near the Oregon Garden in 2000 to save it from planned destruction by its owner. It is now registered on the National Register of Historic Places. It is the only building in Oregon designed by Frank Lloyd Wright. Tours of the interior are offered and cover the theories and practices of Frank Lloyd

Wright's architecture, the story of how an Oregon farm family commissioned Mr. Wright to design their new home, and the home's rescue, dismantling, moving, and reconstruction. Tours are offered May through Oct from 11 a.m. to 5 p.m. and Nov through Apr noon to 4 p.m., on the hour. Please call for reservations.

The Oregon Garden. 879 W Main St.; (503) 874-8100; www.oregongarden.org. A whopping 80 acres of specialty gardens is the theme at work here, and isn't it pretty. A Lewis and Clark Garden, Market Garden, Rose Garden, Oak Grove, Northwest Garden, Tropical Garden, and much more are here waiting to be explored. The Children's Garden is complete with an in-ground hobbit house, a tree fort, and furniture filled with colorful annuals. There are also waterfalls, quiet ponds, fountains, beautiful vistas, and art. A motorized tram provides visitors with an excellent overview of the garden's many features. Passengers have unlimited on-off privileges at 6 stopping points. The tram is designed for passengers with limited mobility and operates from Apr to Oct. Garden hours: May to Sept 9 a.m. to 6 p.m.; Oct to Apr 10 a.m. to 4 p.m. Admission is $5 to $10 and varies by season.

Silver Falls State Park. 20024 Silver Falls Hwy. (OR 214, 26 miles east of Salem); (503) 873-8681; www.oregonstateparks.org/park_211. As one of the most scenic places in a scenic state, Silver Falls State Park is not to be missed. The temperate rain forest here in the lower elevation of Oregon's Cascade Mountains is lush and gorgeous, and in this park 10 waterfalls can be found. Ranging from the grand South Falls (177 feet) to the delicate Drake Falls (27 feet), the Trail of Ten Falls/Canyon Trail takes them all in with a moderate hike of 6.9 miles. If you aren't feeling up to it or are traveling with folks who aren't, there are several shortcut options, so don't be afraid to venture out on the trail if just for a short distance. Keep in mind, though, that because the Canyon Trail is narrow and bordered by sharp drop-offs in spots, bicycles, skateboards, in-line skates, and pets are not allowed. It's all about the waterfalls, some of which are more than 100 feet high. The trail in several places leads through mossy caverns behind the water's shimmering descent, where you can feel the mist and the damp spray. The Canyon Trail and the falls lead to a forest floor covered with ferns, mosses, and wildflowers, as well as stands of Douglas fir, hemlock, and cedar. While thousands visit the park every year, it is large enough for solitude, too. Open all year; the park is usually snow-free even in mid-winter, but the falls and wildflowers peak from late March to May. Oregon State Parks charges a fee per car to park anywhere in the state park. Silver Falls State Park also offers RV, cabin, and tent camping in the overnight campground.

Silverton Murals. Downtown Silverton (pick up a map of mural locations at the site of the Four Freedoms mural at S 2nd and E Main Streets or download one at www.silvertonor .com/murals). In the early 1990s, local artist David McDonald painted Norman Rockwell's famous "Four Freedoms" on a wall in downtown Silverton. The idea caught on. Today there are nearly a dozen murals to be discovered in downtown Silverton, each with a historic story to tell. Make it a point to see them all or stumble upon them—they are hard to miss.

mt. angel moonshine

There was a time that Silverton was dry and Mt. Angel was wet. No, they weren't subjected to strangely alternating weather patterns. Before Prohibition, Mt. Angel could legally sell alcohol and Silverton couldn't. Commerce working the way it does, those with managed to make an industry out of providing to those without. One point of transfer was the Gallon House Bridge, the last of Marion County's original covered bridges. Located over Abiqua Creek on Gallon House Road a little more than a mile northwest of Silverton, the bridge was constructed in 1917. Soon after, the north end of the bridge became a pigeon drop, or place to exchange "white lightning" whiskey for cash. The illegal trade is long gone, but the bridge remains. It's worth seeing, and you can still make a toast while you are here—even if it's just with a swig from your water bottle.

where to eat

Lisa's on Water Street. 310 N Water St.; (503) 873-7051; www.lisasonwaterstreet.com. Here you'll find a fine dining experience that includes breakfast, homemade soups, sandwiches, soups, daily lunch and dinner specials, beer, wine, and cocktails. Open for breakfast, lunch, and dinner Mon through Sat; breakfast only on Sun. $$–$$$.

O'Brien's Café. 105 N Water St.; (503) 873-7554. Traditional small-town diner offering breakfast and lunch items like omelettes, buttermilk pancakes, chicken strips, burgers, and Philly sandwiches. A back deck overlooks Silver Creek, and O'Brien's is known for the antiques and collectibles that can be found throughout the building, including Santa's mailbox by the front door. This cafe is also a popular destination for the bus tours that come to Silverton to see the murals. $.

Silver Grille. 206 E Main; (503) 873-8000; www.silvergrille.com. This restaurant has been described as not only the best in Silverton but one of the best in the Willamette Valley. Handmade pastas, a salad called the Naughty Librarian, dishes like shrimp scampi and rockfish piccata, and tasty desserts are prepared by a high end chef in a small town in a lovely, elegant space. Open for dinner Wed through Sun 4 to 9:30 p.m. $$.

where to stay

Birdwood Inn. 511 S Water St.; (503) 873-3247; www.birdwoodbandb.com. A charming vintage home near downtown Silverton. All rooms have queen-size beds and are beautifully decorated in a classic style. Each room has a private bath with a clawfoot tub; splurge and stay in the private suite with a fireplace. Morning coffee is served to your room and a full breakfast is served in the dining room. $–$$.

Oregon Garden Resort. 879 W Main St.; (503) 874-2500; www.oregongardenresort.com. This lovely new hotel, restaurant, and resort not only has great views of the Oregon Garden, it has a full spa, lounge with nightly entertainment, fireplaces, private landscaped patios and balconies, a heated outdoor swimming pool, and a hot tub. Rooms come with a buffet breakfast. The restaurant offers fine Northwest cuisine and is open for breakfast, lunch, and dinner 7 days a week. $$–$$$.

Water Street Inn. 421 N Water St.; (503) 873-3344; www.thewaterstreetinn.com. Five well-appointed rooms in a classic Victorian home near downtown. Relax by the fire in the cozy living room, enjoy breakfast in the comfortable dining room, hold hands and swing on the front porch, or simply appreciate a good book in the backyard garden. Some rooms have whirlpool tubs or a double shower. $$.

White Oaks Bed and Breakfast. 629 Kloshe Rd.; (503) 873-1474; www.whiteoaksbed andbreakfast.com. This bed and breakfast blends French farm-style with Northwest living near the Oregon Garden. White Oaks is within walking distance of Silverton's Victorian-inspired downtown, shops, and restaurants—or you might choose to just relax in this absolutely gorgeous home and garden setting. $$.

worth more time

Willamette Valley Fruit Company. After your Silverton visit, you may decide to return to I-5 via Silverton Road SE, which heads west into Salem. If so, don't miss the chance to stop at the Willamette Valley Fruit Company. The creator and purveyor of freezer jam, raw honey, natural syrup, fruit snack bars, packaged vegetables and fruits, and divine premade cobblers and pies uses homegrown Willamette Valley fruits to make your life a little sweeter. The facility is located at 2994 82nd Ave. NE in Salem and tours are available upon request. Just call (503) 362-8678 or see www.wvfco.com.

day trip 04

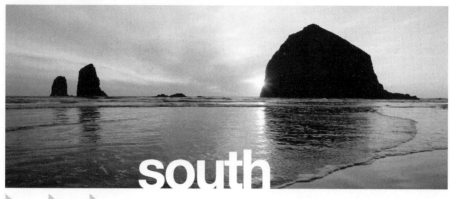

south

>>> **rivers & trees:**
mill city, detroit

mill city

The North Santiam Canyon encompasses several small towns that sit along the North Santiam River, one of Oregon's loveliest rivers. Paralleling the river is OR 22, a primary east-west highway through the Cascade Range, which summits at the Santiam Pass at 4,817 feet. Travelers are treated to many views of the North Santiam River as it falls through the canyon, its waters crisp and vibrant, the forest around it lush and beautiful.

At the time of Lewis and Clark, there were Douglas fir trees in Oregon that were more massive than the giant sequoias of California. Logging and lumbering supported entire generations of North Santiam Canyon residents. Mill City was named in 1886, when four entrepreneurs set up a mill that they named the Santiam Lumbering Company. Tucked away in the forests off of this highway are pockets of remaining old growth.

By Mill City, 30 miles east of Salem, travelers east are just beginning to leave behind the rich flats of the Willamette Valley and to get a sense of the mountainous terrain ahead. There isn't a whole lot going on in this quiet Oregon town, except for lovely scenery and plenty of recreational activities. Stop here to grab a bite to eat before you head into the mountains.

getting there

From Portland, take I-5 south to Salem, 46 miles. Pass through several Salem exits to exit 253, which indicates Detroit Lake/Bend. Take a left to turn east onto OR 22/US 22. Mill City is another 29 miles east.

where to go

Kimmel Park. 330 Santiam Pointe Loop NE. This lovely park sits on the North Santiam River and is a great spot for a picnic or family gathering. But Kimmel's primary attraction is its boat launch, and many people flock here during the warmer months to find water access for their kayaks, canoes, and whitewater rafts. It's also a great place to fish and observe nature and wildlife.

Into the Wild Equine Adventures. Headquartered in Mill City; (503) 586-8072; www .itwtrailrides.com. What better way to explore the gorgeous Monument Peak area outside of Gates than by horseback? Intimate, guided group trail rides on well-trained, well-behaved horses with an experienced guide in a small group equate to a very positive trail riding experience. During the journey, clients will encounter thick native forests, ridge tops, meadows, waterfalls, and sparkling streams with breathtaking views of the Cascade Mountains and Santiam Valley. The trail system includes nearly 20 miles of single-track trail in the foothills of the Cascade Mountains. Trips are 3-hour, half-day, and full-day; prices range from $150 to $300.

The Oregon Experience. Headquartered in Mill City; (503) 897-3291; http://oregon-experience.com. If you are itching to get out onto the waters of the North Santiam River but don't have the gear or the know-how, the Oregon Experience is the outfitter to call. Licensed Guide Arden Corey shares the extensive knowledge of forestry, wildlife, and fisheries that he has acquired during 30 years with the US Forest Service and 27 years spent on the North Santiam River on guided fishing and rafting trips. Drift boat fishing for spring Chinook salmon and summer and winter steelhead is a challenge in a beautiful place; rafting can be leisurely or thrilling—sometimes both in one trip. Rafting $40 to $55; fishing $100 to $125.

Opal Creek Ancient Forest Center. Twenty miles north of Gates on North Fork Road; (503) 892-2782; www.opalcreek.org. The Opal Creek Wilderness and neighboring Bull of the Woods Wilderness is the largest contiguous area of low-elevation old growth Douglas fir left in Oregon. The Opal Creek Ancient Forest Center exists to interpret, protect, and share this forest with the public. Many school programs and family workshops are offered during the programming season, which runs from mid-April to mid-November. You can even take a class on lichens or fungi. Or head out on an exploration of your own on the many available hiking trails—you'll likely see a great menagerie of wildlife, birds, fish, and insects (as well as those big majestic trees). Opal Creek also offers some lodging in rustic cabins. All visitors to Opal Creek need a Trail Park permit to park at the trailhead. The permits cost $5 per car for a one-day pass or $30 for a full-year pass. Full-year passes are available at most Forest Service offices and at the Santiam Sports Center in Mill City, (503) 897-2881, or you can pay per day from a self-serve pay station (cash or check only) at the trailhead.

Stayton Jordan Covered Bridge. On Marion Street off the Stayton/Sublimity turnoff from OR 22. This covered bridge has been rebuilt twice—first in 1988 after years of disrepair, and again in 1998 after a devastating fire destroyed the first rebuild. Now connecting two parks, the bridge is a lovely destination just off the highway. Stop here for a lunchtime picnic.

where to shop

Gene's Meat Market. 21991 Fern Ridge Rd., Mehama; (503) 859-2252; www.genesmeat market.com. Day tripping and meat shopping may not immediately come to mind as companionable activities, but you might think twice once you know that every smoked meat category that Gene's carries has won at least one Grand Champion Award in the past 10 years, and that many popular varieties of sausage are made on-site. Bring a cooler and stock up.

Hardwood Components, Inc. 20573 OR 22, Mehama; (503) 859-2144; www.hardwood components.com. Reminding us all that the North Santiam Canyon once made an honest living on the timber industry is this little sawmill and shop. For more than 40 years, the owners of Hardwood Components have milled native trees like big leaf maple, Oregon white oak, and wild cherry into lumber. You'll also find black walnut, alder, and ash, available in small or large amounts. Much of Hardwood Component's lumber is air dried for up to two years before kiln drying. Pick up some of Oregon's best woods for your next remodel project or woodcraft work.

where to eat

Giovanni Mountain Pizza. 146 NW Santiam Blvd.; (503) 897-2614. Hand-tossed dough and fresh ingredients make this a local's favorite for pizza. Try the spinners—made from pizza dough and stuffed with Italian sausage and ricotta cheese, served with a side of warm marinara sauce. This is a great, casual place to take the whole family, including the kids. Open 7 days a week for lunch and dinner. $.

Rosie's Mountain Coffee House. 647 Santiam Blvd.; (503) 897-2378; www.rosiesgourmet sconesandpastries.com. When traveling through the more remote areas of the beautiful Pacific Northwest, sojourners are often left disappointed after a search for a good meal (not to mention a clean restroom). Rosie's Mountain Coffee House aims to change that. Here real food is served in fresh, delightful abundance. Savory quiche, veggie and meat wraps, fruit smoothies, and fresh scones are just some of the treats you'll find at Rosie's. If you're yearning for soy milk in your Allan Brothers latte while communing with the natural world of the North Santiam Canyon, Rosie's is the place for you. $.

Sierra Mexican Restaurant and Market. 302 W North Santiam Hwy., Gates; (503) 897-2210. The skinny on this place is that the exterior is deceiving. Don't be fooled—inside you'll find fabulous authentic Mexican food. The tortillas and salsa are great and the rice has bits of carrots and peas, giving it an almost Asian twist. $.

Trexler Farm Café. 20146 Ferry Rd. SE, Stayton; (503) 859-4488; www.trexlerfarm.com. The North Santiam's newest hot spot is this little-known farm store/cafe, which serves high-quality, farm-fresh, nutritious lunches 6 days a week on a farm that was home to the old Mehama Fish Hatchery. Try the BBQ tri-tip beef sandwich, artichoke wrap, or the Greek Isle wrap. Wine tasting, organic foods, and great coffee are all here waiting to be discovered. The facility is also available for private and group events by appointment. Open for lunch Mon through Sat, 11 a.m. to 2 p.m. $–$$.

detroit

The original town of Detroit is under water. Born on the pursuits of logging and fishing, Detroit's fate changed when The Army Corps of Engineers selected the site for the Detroit Dam in the 1930s. Three thousand workers descended on the area to build the dam at the peak of construction in 1950. That was the good news. The bad news was that the proposed dam would put the town under 100 feet of water. Many businesses closed and relocated to the new town site—along with the residents, of course. Life reconvened on higher ground 1 mile north of the old town, just west of the confluence of the North Santiam River and Breitenbush River.

Today that dam makes Detroit a recreationalist's heaven. Detroit Lake is now the number one recreational lake in the State of Oregon. This is the spot for all types of water sports: fishing, boating, swimming, waterskiing, and personal watercraft. Camping, swimming, hiking, and the like are very popular, too.

getting there

Detroit is 20 miles east of Mill City directly on OR 22.

where to go

Boating. Whatever your craft of choice, Detroit Lake will float it. Folks come here to motor boat, sail, paddle, canoe, kayak and water ski. For great water skiing or wakeboarding, get out on the lake early, as skiing is best when the water is calm. Sail boaters should direct their vessel towards the dam, where the wind is the windiest and most constant. For respite, tie up in the calm waters and sheltered coves of the Breitenbush Arm (near Detroit Lake

Marina) or Blowout, located at the far southwest end of the lake, for a picnic or swim. Bon voyage!

Fishing. Detroit Lake is over 9 miles long with more than 32 miles of shoreline, and provides many accessible locations for fishermen. For good fishing from the shore, try areas where a creek enters the lake, like Tumble Creek, French Creek, and the Breitenbush River. Fishing from the Detroit Dam provides easy access with very good fishing action. There are also several high lakes around Detroit, many of which are stocked with fish. These lakes are open year round, but may be inaccessible in winter. To fish from a boat, find lake access at Detroit proper or Detroit Lake State Park, which has two boat moorage docks. Detroit Lake fishing is best April through October.

Hiking. There are many options for the hiker near Detroit, whether you'd enjoy scaling the steep hills of the Cascade Range or strolling around the flatter flanks of the lake. Try the Rocky Top Trail for the former or the Beachie Trail for the latter. To find more information on each, visit the Detroit Ranger Station, near Detroit Lake State Park on Highway 22.

where to eat

The Cedars Restaurant & Lounge. 200 Detroit Ave.; (503) 854-3636; www.thecedars restaurant.com. Marked by a tall, lit, blinking green and red tree on its roof, this family oriented restaurant has been serving food to hungry Detroit Lake visitors for more than 50 years. Breakfast is available all day long, and a large full-service liquor lounge with lottery, adjacent to the restaurant, keeps tourists happy. Cedar's, and Detroit in general, likes to advertise itself as "the friendliest place by a dam site." $–$$.

Sammy's Pizza. 195 Detroit Ave.; (503) 854-3100. Rumored to make the best pizza in Oregon, Sammy's has a loyal following from folks from all over the state who make Detroit their favorite summer vacation spot and Sammy's their favorite place to eat. The red and white exterior is modest but inviting. Open for lunch and dinner Thursday through Monday. $.

where to stay

Brietenbush Hot Springs. Ten miles north of Detroit on the Brietenbush River; (503) 854-3320; www.breitenbush.com. This lovely hot springs and retreat is tucked away in an amazing ecosystem. The landscape is 154 acres of wildlife sanctuary surrounded by national forest. The 3 Meadow hot springs pools are lined with smooth rocks and overlook the river. The 4 tiled Spiral Tubs, with increasing temperatures, are aligned in the cardinal directions and adjoined by the cedar tub cold plunge. The Sauna is a cedar cabin resting atop bubbling hot waters. Guests stay in simple, rustic cabins kept warm year-round with heat from Earth-heated waters. Some have a sink and toilet, and bathhouses are nearby. In summer and early fall, personal campsites are available. Bountiful vegetarian meals, mostly organic, are served buffet style 3 times daily. Day-use access available. Often closed for private gatherings—check website for availability and driving directions.

Detroit Lake State Park. 44000 North Santiam Hwy. SE; (503) 854-3346; www.oregon stateparks.org. What's a summer without camping? This large state park and campground offers many amenities including an amphitheater, boat launch ramp, playground, showers, evening interpretive programs, firewood, and more than 200 camping sites for RVs and tents. Day use $5; Camping $19 to $24. $.

The Lodge at Detroit Lake. 175 N Detroit Ave.; (503) 854-3344; www.lodgeatdetroit lake.com. For those who'd rather not camp, try this brand new lodge with gorgeous, wooden lodge-like exterior. Inside you'll find spacious rooms with full kitchenettes, log beds, Western decor, 42-inch flat screen TVs, jetted tubs, fireplaces, built-in air conditioning, on-demand hot water, and Wi-Fi. It's a great place to rest your head and still be near outdoor splendor. $$.

worth more time

The stunning **Estacada Detroit Scenic Byway,** only open seasonally, runs 70 miles between Estacada and Detroit past a sparkling river, thick forests, lovely bridges, and high rock formations. In the fall, beautiful foliage lines the route. A favorite for motorcycle tours. The mountain pass, which offers great views of Mt. Jefferson, snows over in the winter and this road closes.

day trip 05

south

be a duck:
eugene

eugene

The City of Eugene anchors the southern tip of the Willamette Valley. As the second largest city in Oregon and home to the University of Oregon, Eugene draws thousands of visitors each year. In addition to sports fans and students' families, the city also attracts recreationalists to its natural beauty and outdoor opportunities.

Sometimes called "Track Town USA," Eugene may be best known nationally for its famous running tradition. It's said that the tradition of jogging was born here, and the university has turned out many Olympic track stars, including Steve Prefontaine and Alberto Salazar. In 1964, the international sports company Nike was founded in Eugene by Phil Knight and Bill Bowerman, the University of Oregon track coach.

Eugene is also known as the hippie capitol of Oregon. This is said with the utmost kindness and respect. In the 1960s and 1970s, Eugene and the university were central to left-wing political activities like war protests, and folks with "alternative" lifestyles were likewise attracted to the area. In the 1970s, Eugene became an innovator in grass-roots community projects and more earth-focused ways of living. Small natural food stores, student cooperatives, and alternative schools cropped up here long before they did other places in the state or nation.

Though the city has migrated toward the mainstream since those tumultuous times, Eugene is still a great place to buy tie-dye and homemade candles, stage a political activism

N

Battle
Ground

WASHINGTON

503

500

North Bonneville

Camas   Washougal

Bridal
Veil

84

30

99E   205

Gresham

6

6

8

26

Hillsboro

Portland

Beaverton

Tigard

Damascus

Sandy

47

219

99W

205

Gladstone

Oregon
City

212

224

26

Sherwood

240

Newberg

5

Canby

Estacada

Dundee

Lafayette

Dayton

St. Paul

Aurora

211

18

221

Hubbard

Molalla

213

Mt. Hood
National
Forest

Siuslaw
National
Forest

Amity

99W

99E

214

OREGON

22

Keizer

Mt. Angel

18

22

213

Silverton

Salem

214

Dallas

22

22

22

Aumsville

Silver Falls
State Park

51

Stayton

99W

Jefferson

Lyons

22

226

223

Albany

20

Lebanon

20

Corvallis

99W

5

34

Alsea

Halsey

Sweet
Home

Monroe   Harrisburg

Siuslaw
National
Forest

Junction City

Coburg

126

Fern
Ridge
Lake

126

Veneta

Eugene   Springfield

Deschutes
National
Forest

0   5   10 miles

5

Cottage Grove

58

Curtin

campaign, and participate in cutting edge "green" projects. Eugene's residents trend towards the laid-back and happy—traits with which it can be refreshing to surround oneself for a day trip or longer.

getting there

Eugene is 110 miles due south of Portland on I-5. Take exit 194B off I-5 to merge onto OR 126 W. Travel west and follow signs for downtown.

where to go

Cottage Grove Covered Bridge Route. www.travellanecounty.org/covered-bridges. Known as the "Covered Bridge Capital of Oregon," Cottage Grove is home to this state's scenic byway. Drawing visitors from across the nation every year, this seven-bridge route also takes you on a journey past Dorena Lake, several swimming holes, the historical Bohemia mining district, and filming locations made famous by the movie *Stand By Me.*

Dorris Ranch Living History Farm. Two miles east of I-5 at the intersection of S 2nd and Dorris Streets, Springfield; www.willamalane.org/pages/parks/dorris. Established in 1892, this 250-acre farm is Oregon's oldest working filbert (hazelnut) farm and the nation's oldest commercial filbert farm still in continuous operation. George Dorris and his wife Lulu set up a farm here in 1892, ultimately creating a hazelnut legacy. More than half of all the commercial filbert trees now growing in the US originated from Dorris Ranch nursery stock. Walk through this 250-acre historic site and natural area, admiring a variety of plants, flowers, and birds. At the Masterson homestead, step back in time to the year 1852 and discover what life was like for a newly arrived pioneer immigrant family. Brochures with a map of area paths are available at the entrance kiosk. Open weekdays and weekends from 6 a.m. until dusk for self-guided tours.

Eugene Saturday Market. 8th and Oak Streets (Apr to Nov); Lane Events Center, 796 W 13th Ave. (Nov to Dec); (541) 686-8885; www.eugenesaturdaymarket.org. Saturday markets are a dime a dozen these days, but that wasn't the case 40 years ago when the Eugene Saturday Market began operations. Now it's known as the oldest weekly, open-air crafts festival in the US. Come and enjoy more than 200 craft booths, delicious food, and live entertainment every Sat, rain or shine, Apr through Oct. For the months of Nov and Dec, the market moves indoors to the Lane Events Center.

King Estate Winery. 80854 Territorial Rd.; (541) 942-9874; www.kingestate.com. One of the gems of Oregon wine, King Estate has been pleasing wine aficionados for nearly 20 years. Come here to taste the pinot noir, pinot gris, and limited amounts of chardonnay they produce each year. Also home to an award-winning restaurant dedicated to pairing Northwest wines with regional food products.

Mount Pisgah Arboretum. 34901 Frank Parrish Rd.; (541) 747-3817; www.mountpisgah arboretum.org. Don't miss this 209-acre living museum. Riverside trails, evergreen forests, a water garden, bright wildflower meadows, and open views across oak savannas delight all ages. Seven miles of all-weather trails and 23 bridges make for great exploring and hiking. Open daily from dawn to dusk, $2 parking fee per vehicle.

Olive Grand. 1041 Willamette St.; (541) 685-1000; www.olivegrand.com. Eugene's first and only olive oil tasting bar offers unique blends of fine olive oils, vinegars, herbs, and much more. Savor rich and aromatic flavors and learn to appreciate the distinctions that result from olive varieties, regional climates, and unique harvesting methods. What flavors do you most enjoy? You might be surprised to learn it's something radically different, like chocolate scones dipped in blood orange-flavored olive oil. Delicious! Open daily Mon through Sat from 10 a.m. to 6 p.m. or by special arrangement for groups and organizations.

Pacific Tree Climbing Institute. (866) OLD-TREE; www.pacifictreeclimbing.com. Everyone who ever climbed a tree as a kid and loved it will thrill at this opportunity. Pacific Tree Climbing Institute guides tree climbing expeditions in the legendary trees found in the Pacific Northwest. Their purpose is to demonstrate that remaining old growth groves have greater value as intact forests than as lumber. This message hits home as a guide takes you safely and expertly into the marvelous ecosystem that is a tree canopy. Day trips and overnighters available—yes, you get to sleep in the tree.

University of Oregon. Agate and E 13th Streets; (541) 346-1000; www.uoregon.edu. The university has been Eugene's centerpiece since its inception in 1876. The campus is a beautiful spot to take a walk, see interesting architecture, and enjoy flora and fauna, as well as witness the youth and exuberance of the student body. Keep an eye out for buildings that appeared in the 1978 film *Animal House,* which was filmed on campus. Here are a few other highlights:

> **Deady Hall.** UO's first building was completed in 1876, when university enrollment was 177 students, and faculty numbered 5. It was designated a national historic landmark in 1977.

> **Hayward Field.** Historic Hayward Field is one of the most famous track and field facilities in the world. The field was home to Bill Bowerman's famous "Men of Oregon" from 1948 to 1973—track teams that finished in the top 10 at the NCAA championships 16 times, including taking four team titles (1962, '64, '65, '70) and two second-place trophies. Hayward Field hosts many track and field events per year, including the Oregon State High School Championships, the annual Prefontaine Classic, and the Eugene Marathon. The 2008 Olympic Team Trials for Track and Field were also held here, an honor that will be repeated in 2012.

Jordan Schnitzer Museum of Art. 1430 Johnson Lane.; (541) 346-3027; www
.jsma.uoregon.edu. This premier Pacific Northwest visual arts center features Chinese,
Japanese, Korean, and American art from its historic and contemporary collections
in engaging exhibitions. Open Tues, Thurs, Fri, Sat, and Sun 11 a.m. to 5 p.m.; Wed
11 a.m. to 8 p.m. Free admission for children and University of Oregon students. The
museum also includes a cafe, Marche Museum Café, open 7 days a week.

Living Arboretum. Wander through more than 500 different species of trees on
campus. Especially in the fall, when the colors change, the campus is gorgeous.

Museum of Natural and Cultural History. 1680 E 15th Ave.; (541) 346-3024; www
.natural-history.uoregon.edu. As Oregon's primary repository for anthropological and
paleontological collections, the Museum of Natural and Cultural History houses nearly
one million ethnographic and archaeological objects and almost 100,000 fossils and
biological specimens from Oregon, the Pacific Northwest, and around the world.
Open Wed through Sun, 11 a.m. to 5 p.m.

Sporting Events. (541) 346-4481; www.goducks.com. The mascot is the duck
and the supporters willing to quack at the top of their lungs! Football and basketball
are the primary fan-pleasers, but the University of Oregon offers the chance to see
lacrosse, golf, cross-country, soccer, and even ultimate Frisbee matches. Get your
tailgate on and be a duck!

Ruth Bascom Bike Path. See www.eugene-or.gov for a downloadable map. This popular
12-mile bike path follows the Willamette River through many of Eugene and Springfield's
favorite parks and attractions. Let your kids play at the new Skinner Butte River Play playground, or search for wildlife at the Delta Ponds. Here's where you'll see all of those Eugene
joggers, too—though it's mostly called running now. Easy access to and from downtown
Eugene, and connects with a larger trail system, is the Ridgeline Trail, should you desire a
longer or more challenging hike, ride, or run.

Spencer Butte Trail. 85385 Willamette St.; (541) 682-4800. This moderate to difficult 1.7-
mile loop trail climbs 784 feet before reaching the summit of Spencer Butte. The 360-degree
view from the summit gives a great overview of the Eugene area and beyond, including
views of the Three Sisters and Fern Ridge Reservoir.

Studio West Glassblowing Studio. 245 W 8th Ave.; (541) 683-WEST; www.visitstudio
west.com. Studio West is a full production glass studio and gallery. Resident artists put on
a show in the viewable studio for visitors every Fri and Sat night from 6 to 9 p.m. This studio
also offers "blow your own" mini-workshops, allowing you to create your own keepsake
to take home. Open Tues through Thurs 11 a.m. to 5 p.m.; Fri and Sat 11 a.m. to 9 p.m.

Sweet Cheeks Winery. 27007 Briggs Hill Rd.; (541) 349-9463; www.sweetcheekswinery
.com. The 65-acre Sweet Cheeks Estate Vineyard sits on 140 acres of prime sloping hillside

the oregon county fair

*Some events just have to be experienced at least once in a lifetime, and the **Oregon Country Fair** is one of them. For 40 years, organizers have been putting on this groovy gathering in the woods outside of Veneta, 13 miles west of Eugene. In some ways, the Oregon Country Fair is just another summer celebration, with loads of entertainment, handmade crafts, and delectable foods. In other ways, the fair is a mind-blowing adventure with magical surprises at every turn. Creativity, costumes (or—ahem—lack thereof), and the nourishment of the spirit in every way imaginable are enthusiastically encouraged. The last time I visited, I saw a woman with a typewriter in her lap selling made-to-order poems, a man painted from head to toe as a butterfly (and wearing nothing but the paint), a pirate on stilts, and a gigantic bicycle-powered, paper mache vehicle called a "hippypotamus." The Oregon Country Fair epitomizes Oregon's free spirit and, if nothing else, is an entirely welcome alternative to your average summer festival. Held the second weekend in July every year. Visit www.oregoncountryfair.org.*

located in the heart of the Willamette Valley. Come for the view and the wine—pinot gris and Riesling. Open daily.

where to shop

Fifth Street Market and International Cafes. 296 E Fifth Ave.; (541) 484-0383; www.5stmarket.com. A Eugene icon, the Fifth Street Market opened in 1976 in an old poultry warehouse. Originally, local craftspeople and farmers rented booth space for two dollars a day, selling their wares and foodstuffs to a local crowd in this unique reclaimed space. Several remodels and decades later, the historic downtown Eugene marketplace is comprised of some of the Northwest's finest cafes, shops, and restaurants. Locally owned stores offer everything from shoes to suitcases to candy to cards, and local craftspeople are still able to lease a small sales space for their hand-crafted wares. Many stand-alone restaurants, as well as a bustling upscale food court area with 5 or 6 small cafes to choose from and well-lit comfortable seating, feed hungry visitors. The international cafes are a great destination if you are with a group with diverse tastes. Live music is often on hand, and the sprawling multi-level marketplace with balconies and water fountains is almost always a feast for the senses, with the smell of fresh food, fresh flowers, and fresh baked goods wafting in the air. (Exciting note: The Inn at the 5th, a 69-room boutique hotel attached to the Fifth Street Market, is set to open sometime in summer 2011. It will be the first hotel built downtown in 28 years! For more info see www.innat5th.com.) Retail shops open Mon through Sat 10 a.m. to 7 p.m., Sun 11 a.m. to 5 p.m. International cafes open Mon through Sat 8:30 a.m. to 7 p.m., Sun 9 a.m to 6 p.m.

where to eat

Ambrosia. 174 E Broadway; (541) 342-4141; www.ambrosiarestaurant.com. Italian fare is served up in this upscale environment anchored by a lovely, antique bar. A second floor balcony gives a birds-eye view of the bar and main restaurant. Open Mon through Fri 11:30 a.m. to close, Sat and Sun 5 p.m. to close. $$–$$$.

Beppe and Gianni's Trattoria. 1646 E 19th Ave.; (541) 683-6661; www.beppeandgiannis .net. Just off campus, this Italian restaurant has been voted "best" by weekly newspaper *Eugene Weekly* 8 years in a row. It is a must! Try the spaghetti, homemade fettuccine, or penne pasta with choice of sauces—puttanesca, pomodoro, pesto, and carbonara. Open for dinner nightly. $$–$$$.

Café Lucky Noodle. 207 E 5th Ave.; (541) 484-4777; www.luckynoodle.com. Serving a dynamic menu of Italian and Southeast Asian cuisine, Lucky Noodle offers everything from organic yam tempura to glass noodle stir fry to chicken Marsala. Open Mon through Fri 11 a.m. to midnight, Sat and Sun 9 a.m. to midnight. $$–$$$.

Café Zenon. 898 Pearl St.; (541) 684-4000; www.zenoncafe.com. When I was a college student in Eugene, Café Zenon was where we all wanted to eat but couldn't quite afford to eat dinner. So instead we went for dessert. An assortment of cakes, tarts, galettes, pies, éclairs, fresh fruit cobblers, macaroons, meringues, pot de crème, and cookies, served in the fancy modern space, gave us the tiny taste of decadence we craved. Zenon is still a great restaurant, and for those not on the starving-student budget, a full dinner might include Indian spiced rack of lamb with toasted curry, Southern fried pork chop with Kentucky chow-chow, or fresh fettuccine with locally foraged mushrooms. Save room—the desserts are still amazing, too. Open Mon through Sat 11 a.m. to 10 p.m., Sun 9:30 a.m. to 2 p.m. and 5 to 10 p.m. $$–$$$.

The Glenwood. Two locations: 1340 Alder St.; (541) 687-0355; and 2588 Willamette St.; (541) 687-8201; www.glenwoodrestaurants.com. The Glenwood is a Eugene tradition. I think I had my first meal at the Glenwood at about the age of 5, and every time I get back to Eugene, it's one of the places I must visit. A huge menu covers fabulous, hearty, home-cooked meals extensively, from eggs Benedict to tempeh stir fry. Big portions, reasonable prices, and a casual, comfortable atmosphere make these restaurants a favorite for everyone from college students to retirees. Alder Street location is open 7 a.m. to 9 p.m. daily. Willamette Street location open weekdays 6:30 a.m. to 9 p.m., Sat and Sun 7 a.m. to 9 p.m. $–$$.

Heidi Tunnell Catering Company. 182 South 2nd St., Creswell; (541) 895-5885; www .heiditunnellcatering.com. Heidi provides much more than just catering—she takes the farm-fresh approach to the next level. Her Barn Dinners, served Saturdays seasonally, bring foodies, farmers, guest winemakers, brewers, and food artisans such as cheesemakers or beekeepers around the table to enjoy a completely seasonal menu while discussing what went into it. Dinners are 3 courses, served family style, and each course is paired with a wine from the featured winemaker. Wednesday night dinners follow a similar format and occur once a month. Every Tuesday, a changing lunch special is served along with fresh baked bread. Call for more information and reservations. $$–$$$.

Keystone Café. 395 W 5th Ave.; (541) 342-2075; www.keystonecafe.net. Another classic Eugene restaurant that's been around since the 1970s, Keystone provides nourishing food in generous portions at reasonable prices in a warm and friendly atmosphere. The menu pleases carnivores, vegetarians, and vegans alike. Newly opened patio is the best choice for breakfast. Open 7 a.m. to 3 p.m. every day. $.

Osteria Sfizio. 105 Oakway Center; (541) 302-3000; www.sfizioeugene.com. Newly opened in 2010, Sfizio is the realization of a long-time dream of head chef Rocky Maselli of blending Northwestern sustainability, classic Italian cuisine, and contemporary design. Roasted pork loin with tomato chutney and fregola sarda, and fried eggplant, pesto, roasted garlic, mozzarella, and tomato panini are but two of many delicious menu options. Open Mon through Fri for lunch and dinner, Sat and Sun for brunch. $$–$$$.

Sweet Basil Thai. 941 Pearl St.; (541) 284-2944; www.sweetbasileug.com. Serving elegant Thai food in the heart of downtown Eugene, Sweet Basil won the prestigious Chef's Night Out Overall Best Bite Award for 2010. Open for lunch Mon through Sat 11:30 a.m. to 3 p.m., dinner Sun through Thurs 5 to 9 p.m., dinner Fri and Sat 5 p.m. to 10 p.m. $$–$$$.

The Sweet Life. 755 Monroe St.; (541) 683-5676; www.sweetlifedesserts.com. Desserts, desserts, and only desserts. Cakes, cheesecakes, tortes, pies, tarts, cupcakes, pastries, and gelato all come out of this popular patisserie. All day hours soothe the needy sweet tooth almost any time of day. Open Mon through Fri 7 a.m. to 11 p.m., Sat and Sun 8 a.m. to 11 p.m. $.

where to stay

Augusta House. 2585 Bowmont Dr.; (541) 342-8615; www.augustahouse.net. The Augusta House only has 2 rooms, but each is 700 square feet of well-appointed glory. A king-size bed plus queen sofa sleeper, each with luxurious soft bed linens and pillow menu, give you lots of room to spread out. Contemporary, luxurious accommodations with beautiful views of the city. $$–$$$.

The Campbell House. 252 Pearl St.; (541) 343-1119; www.campbellhouse.com. Built in 1892 and fully restored as a grand historic inn, the Campbell House is within walking distance of Fifth Street Market, the Hult Center, and downtown, and offers personalized service, comfortable surroundings, and all the amenities one would expect from a fine hotel. Voted one of the top 25 inns in America. $$–$$$.

Valley River Inn. 1000 Valley River Way; (800) 543-8266; www.valleyriverinn.com. Beautiful views of the Willamette River and nice rooms with Northwest charm, modern convenience, and luxurious comfort make this a Eugene mainstay. Valley River Shopping Center is right next door and offers lots of shopping, dining, and entertainment opportunities. $$–$$$.

worth more time

The McKenzie River, which runs from Clear Lake in the Cascade Range west into Springfield and Eugene, is one of the loveliest rivers in the state. Many small communities can be found along US 26 and the river, including Walterville, Vida, and McKenzie Bridge. Fly-fishing, rafting, and relaxing at one of many lovely lodgings are all wonderful outings within an hour out of Eugene. In fact, this river was the birthplace of the famed McKenzie River driftboat, and you'll see many if you don't actually choose to catch a float in one. Hike or mountain bike the spectacular **McKenzie River Trail,** or take a dip at **Belknap Hotsprings,** a developed hot springs, campground, and resort. Whatever you do, you'll be surrounded by incredible beauty and a fabulous example of the lush ecosystem of the western Cascade Range.

southwest

day trip 01

southwest

pioneer country:
newberg, dundee

newberg

Like many of its surrounding communities, the great allure of Newberg lies in its bucolic small-town charm and scenic beauty, all so near the big city. Newberg is a lovely town surrounded by forests and farmlands less than 30 miles from the Portland Metro Area. The Chehalem Mountains and the Willamette River buffer Newberg, providing a peaceful sense of place. Tourists flock here to taste the region's world-famous wine, but the rural countryside offers up opportunities beyond wine tasting—boating, fishing, hunting, and golf are popular activities. The beach is an hour west, the snowy Cascades an hour east. These advantages haven't gone unnoticed, and Newberg has grown in population in recent years. Still, it remains a relaxed and rewarding place to spend a day or a lifetime.

The Newberg area is also steeped in Oregon history. Hudson Bay Company trappers created the first European settlement in the area in a place called Champoeg, which is located approximately 7 miles southeast of Newberg. Pioneers followed, clearing the rich land for farming. Ultimately, Champoeg earned the distinction of serving as the site where Oregon's provisional government was established in 1843. Newberg has presidential roots, too. Herbert Hoover and his family lived in a home here, which you can visit.

southwest day trip 01

getting there

Take I-5 south out of Portland to the OR 99 W exit, exit 294, to Tigard/Newberg. OR 99 W will merge with Pacific Highway W; continue to follow OR 99 W/Pacific Highway W to the southwest for a total of 24 miles from the Portland City Center.

Be aware that because OR 99W travels through many suburbs of Portland, it's slow going. The 24-mile trip could easily take you an hour to drive.

where to go

Champoeg State Heritage Area. Champoeg is located south and east of Newberg. Take a left onto Champoeg Road off the St. Paul Highway.

You could spend an entire day at the Champoeg State Heritage Area, and come away with a real sense of Oregon's history as well as that of this beautiful countryside. The Champoeg prairie has been settled longer than just about anywhere in this state. Originally home to the Kalapuya Indians, this rich landscape's abundant game lured British and French Canadian fur trappers; later, its fertile farmland attracted American settlers. On May 2, 1843, Oregon's first provisional government was established here.

Champoeg may have gone on to become the state capital if not for a huge flood of the Willamette River in December 1861, which essentially destroyed the town. Settlers eventually rebuilt, but by that time the headquarters for the fledgling state of Oregon had moved to Oregon City.

There is much to do here on the banks of the Willamette at this location today. Here are a few ideas:

The Butteville Store. 10767 Butte St. NE; (503) 678-1605; www.buttevillestore.com. The oldest continuously operating retail store in Oregon sits here on the banks of the Willamette River at the end of the Champoeg walking path. This little store serves delicious homemade soups, sandwiches, salads, and desserts, including Tillamook ice cream and fresh fruit pie, with a big dose of local history. Open daily May through Oct: Sun through Fri 9 a.m. to 6 p.m. and Sat 9 a.m. to 9 p.m. Live music plays on Saturday nights.

The Champoeg Interpretive Center. 8239 Champoeg Rd. NE; (503) 678-1251; www.champoeg.org. This big red barn-like structure includes a museum that was updated for Oregon's 150th anniversary in 2009. The exhibits bring alive the ways of the Kalapuya Indians, fur trappers, explorers, and settlers. Living history events take place all summer long, and there is a really nice gift shop and book store on site, too. Open year-round, 7 days a week.

Champoeg State Park. The park features two main day-use areas, the Oak Grove and Riverside. Riverside features the old town site, an outdoor amphitheater, river access, and the Pioneer Mother's Cabin. Oak Grove has room for large groups, plus space for disc golf. Both are connected by a paved trail perfect for running, strolling, and biking. The trail snakes through dense woodland, offering peek-a-boo views of the Willamette River. More than 130 bird species have been identified in the park; ask for a Champoeg bird checklist at the visitor center. There's a campground on the east side of the park.

Hoover-Minthorn House. 115 S River St.; (503) 538-6629. The boyhood home of Herbert Hoover, 31st President of the United States, was built in 1881 by Jesse Edwards and is the first residence built and still standing in Newberg. The furniture in President Hoover's bedroom, which he inhabited from 1885 to 1889, is the actual set he used as a boy. Other furnishings in the house were gathered from homes in the countryside around Newberg. Open Mar through Nov, Wed through Sun 1 to 4 p.m.

The 99 W. Drive-in Theatre. 3110 Portland Rd.; (503) 538-2738; www.99W.com. Thank goodness for the family that has kept this old-fashioned drive-in theater in Newberg open since August 1953, when it opened with *Sea Devils* and *Under the Sahara* as its first features. Twice the screen has been destroyed by Oregon storms, but the owners rebuilt. Today the 99 W. is one of only four drive-ins left in operation in Oregon. Open late Apr or early May until late Oct.

Vista Balloon Adventures, Inc. (800) 622-2309; www.vistaballoon.com. Here's one fabulous and scenic way to see the countryside. Hot-air balloon flights are offered by this company from Newberg at dawn in Oregon's beautiful wine country. Flights take about an hour, and a lovely catered brunch is included after the flight. Flights are offered Mon, Wed, Fri, weekends, and holidays. Flight season is Apr 1 through the first weekend in Oct. All flights are weather permitting.

Wineries. So many wineries, so little time. You, day tripper, will need more than one day trip as well as a designated driver to hit all of the wineries in this area (which is why we've included tour company listings). We've only listed a handful of the wineries that exist around here. There are over 200 in the entire Willamette Valley region. See www.yamhillvalley.org for a longer list. Choose wisely and call ahead to make sure your selections are indeed open. Most wineries are up in the hills out of town—bring a good map or electronic mapping system and pay close attention to addresses.

> **Adelshiem.** 16800 NE Calkins Lane; (503) 538-3652; www.adelsheim.com. Adelshiem was established in 1971 and is one of the oldest vineyards in the valley. Today the winery uses sustainable farming practices to bring out the best in each of their unique vineyard sites. In the winery, traditional and modern techniques are combined to craft wines in a style that centers on elegance, complexity, and richness in flavor and texture. The winery is located at the base of the scenic Chehalem Mountains, and the tasting room is open 7 days a week from 11 a.m. to 4 p.m.

Bergstrom Wines. 18215 NE Calkins Lane; (503) 554-0468; www.bergstromwines .com. The Bergstrom philosophy is that winemaking is an agricultural pursuit—that the wine that you enjoy in your glass depends on a vineyard's and a farmer's performance in any given year, matched with the challenges put forth by Mother Nature. The very best Oregon pinot noir can only be achieved through non-industrial, artisan winemaking. The tasting room and patio here offer a beautiful view and are open from 10 a.m. to 4 p.m. daily.

Chehalem Wines. 106 S Center St.; www.chehalemwines.com. Well known for quality red and white wines, Chehalem focuses on cool-climate wine varieties that reflect both site and climate in complex, structured, and intensely fruited wines. Chehalem is a local Calapooia Indian word best translated as "gentle land" or "valley of flowers," phrases that capture a long-standing, almost religious reverence for the land—a philosophy Chehalem Wines tries to emulate. Varietals include pinot noir, pinot gris, chardonnay, Riesling, pinot blanc, Grüner Veltliner, and Gamay noir. Tasting fees are refundable with purchase of two bottles. Open daily from 11 a.m. to 5 p.m.

Fox Farm. 602 E 1st St.; (503) 538-8466; www.foxfarmvineyards.com. This very small production winery makes finely crafted food-friendly sensibly priced wines. In addition to their own delicious vintages, Fox Farm offers the wines of eight other local boutique wineries at their tasting room, which is open daily from noon to 8 p.m.

Hip Chicks Do Wine. 602B E 1st St.; (503) 234-3790; www.hipchicksdowine.com. These Hip Chicks make wine fun and make fun wine. The winery itself is in Portland, but pop into their Newberg tasting room to try their many varietals and soak up some good energy. Hip Chicks focuses on the grape, which means these wines are ready to drink now. It's your job to oblige that readiness. Open daily noon to 7 p.m.

Penner Ash. 15771 NE Ribbon Ridge Rd.; (503) 554-5545; www.pennerash.com. This is a truly lovely winery in a very scenic spot. On 80 acres, the winery sits on a hillside overlooking breathtaking and expansive views of the Chehalem Valley. Fifteen acres of pinot noir grapes produce great wine annually, which you can taste right here, with a view. The tasting room is open Wed through Sun from 11 a.m. to 5 p.m. Winery tours are available Sat and Sun at 10 a.m.—call for reservations.

Rex Hill Vineyards and Winery. 30835 N OR 99 W; (503) 538-0666; www.rexhill .com. Located in an old fruit and nut drying facility, this winery sits on a hill and boasts a spectacular view. Visitors can see the original tunnels into which the carts of drying racks were rolled. The winery produces chardonnay, pinot gris, and pinot noir. Rex Hill also offers harvest tours and a variety of "exploring wine essentials" seminars—call for reservations. Tasting room open daily 10 a.m. to 5 p.m.

My Chauffeur Wine Tours. (503) 969-4370; www.winetouroregon.com. This company offers 4-hour, 6-hour, and 8-hour tours of Yamhill County wineries. They will pick you up in Portland or in wine country, wherever you prefer. Travel in groups of 2 or 52. Prices begin at $50 per person and go up depending on length of tour and services (a pre-packed picnic lunch is an option).

where to eat

The Painted Lady. 201 S College St.; (503) 538-3850; www.thepaintedladyrestaurant .com. The painted lady movement restores Victorian homes using contrasting colors that bring out a building's decorative flourishes. This restaurant is located within a beautiful example of a painted lady Victorian home, and serves fabulous Pacific Northwest cuisine sourced locally. The menu is prix fixe, 4 courses for $60; with wine pairing it will cost you $100. Open Wed through Sun for dinner from 5 to 10 p.m. $$$.

Subterra. 1505 Portland Rd. Suite 120; (503) 437-4984; www.subterrarestaurant.com. Subterra serves white tablecloth dining without prices quite as high as they can go around here. The menu includes baked brie with bourbon maple figs, duck confit, and grilled lamb kebabs. Open for lunch Wed through Sat from 11:30 a.m. to 2 p.m., for dinner Wed through Sat 5 p.m. to close, and for Sunday brunch from 10 a.m. to 2 p.m. The wine bar offers small plates and affordable wines by the glass. $$–$$$.

where to stay

The Allison Inn and Spa. 2525 Allison Lane; (503) 554-2525; www.theallison.com. Getting here, you'll pass through an average suburb and maybe wonder if your intended destination is going to be all it is rumored to be. Then suddenly you'll arrive at this fabulous estate and resort and all doubt will be laid to rest. The Allison Inn, opened just a few years ago, is a truly outstanding destination. Rooms are spare but luxurious with fireplaces and soaking tubs—there is also a huge spa and fitness center on site. The restaurant, Jory, pays tribute to Oregon's acclaimed wines, microbrews, hand-crafted distilled spirits, and agricultural bounty—some of which are grown right outside in the restaurant's half-acre garden. Indulge by trying several of the offered one-ounce tasting pours. The grounds are beautiful and boast a mile-long trail around the property. Both room and board are very expensive here, but the Allison's service, attention to detail, and ambiance are world-class. $$$.

The Inn at Champoeg. 8899 Champoeg Road NE; (503) 678-6088; www.innatchampoeg .com. A splendid rural bed and breakfast at which guests can rest, rejuvenate, and explore the Champoeg Heritage Area. There are only 2 rooms here, but each is beautifully decorated and has its own private bath. The inn itself is spacious and welcoming, and there's even more wide open space outside. $$.

dundee

At a distance of only 30 miles from Portland, Dundee wears multiple hats: bedroom community, close-in day trip, dinner destination, road bike route. Despite the encroaching city (development along OR 99 from Portland to Dundee has become essentially seamless), Dundee remains relatively rural and small, with a population of just over 3,000 and a restful atmosphere. And yet, little Dundee offers a level of culture and style associated with a big city. Many highly rated restaurants are here, not to mention award-winning wineries.

Dundee's proximity to Portland also makes it a popular destination via bicycle. OR 99 W provides a protected bike lane, but cyclists often find the scenery and experience is better on side streets and country roads. Grab a map and choose to cruise the side of the city with the meandering Willamette River and Dundee's Ash Island, or the other side, where acres of vineyards are found.

getting there

Continue on OR 99 W out of Newberg, heading southwest. Dundee is 2.5 miles southwest from Newberg on OR 99 W.

where to go

Oregon Olive Mill at Red Ridge Farms. 5510 NE Breyman Orchards Rd., Dayton; (503) 864-2200; www.oregonolivemill.com. In 2005 the Durant family planted a small olive

could it be any prettier around here?

Wine grapes have only really been grown in the Willamette Valley since the 1970s. Before that, people didn't think the feat could be done. And anyway they were busy growing lots of other things in the valley's renowned rich and productive soils, like prunes, pears, apples, walnuts, and hazelnuts. Today, pinot noir grapes grow exceptionally well around here, and Oregon pinot noirs are widely favored. Some say they are the best in the world. Yamhill County is home today to dozens of wineries of all sizes and production levels. But if it's fruits and nuts you're after, you can still find those trees 'round these parts, as well as signs of the old homesteads that surrounded themselves with such pretty trees. In fact, these hardwoods interspersed with Oregon's famous evergreens dotted with the occasional grand old barn are part of what makes the hillsides and views around here so very beautiful.

orchard at Red Ridge Farms. They've been adding trees to it every year since. Today there are more than 17 acres and 13,000 trees on this site, as well as a new structure housing a state-of-the-art Italian olive press and a boutique bottling line. Taste and buy their unique olive oils at the Red Ridge Farms store, open Wed through Sun 9 a.m. to 5 p.m.

Wineries. The Dundee area, specifically the Dundee Hills AVA (American Viticultural Area), encompasses 6,490 acres of pristine wine growing country. It is home to Oregon's earliest pinot noir plantings, and considered by most to be the heart of Oregon wine country. The Dundee Hills AVA extends to the west, southwest, and northwest of Dundee, and most of the wineries are actually in these hills, not in Dundee proper. Bring a good map or electronic mapping system and pay close attention to addresses.

Archery Summit Winery. 18599 NE Archery Summit Rd., Dayton; (503) 864-4300; www.archerysummit.com. Archery Summit only makes pinot noir, and makes it very well. Visit their tasting room to sample their excellent wine, sit on the terrace, take in views of the Willamette Valley and breathtaking Mt. Jefferson, and learn more about Oregon pinot noir. A $15 fee includes tastes of four highly rated pinot noirs. Guided tours are given at 10:30 a.m. and 2 p.m. daily, by appointment only. Tours begin in the vineyard and continue through the winery, from the sorting tables to the aging caves and bottling room. Archery Summit guides will teach you more than you ever imagined there was to know about pinot noir, whether you are a fan or a novice. The tasting room is open every day from 10 a.m. to 4 p.m.

Argyle Winery. 691 OR 99 W; (888) 427-4953; www.argylewinery.com. Housed in a former hazelnut processing plant are the modern winery operations for Argyle Winery, a popular and accessible winery. Argyle produces pinot noir, dry Riesling, chardonnay, and pinot gris, as well as 3 types of vintage Oregon sparkling wines made in the méthode Champenoise: brut, blanc de Blaney, and rose. The newly rebuilt tasting room is a wonderful place to taste Argyle wines, hear live music, see local art displays, and experience some of the Oregon winemaking culture. Open daily 11 a.m. to 5 p.m. except major holidays.

Domaine Drouhin. 6750 Breyman Orchards Rd., Dayton; (503) 864-2700; www.domainedrouhin.com. Domaine Drouhin was established in the 1980s and was one of the forerunners in the Oregon pinot noir phenomenon. Their pinot noir bottlings are frequently awarded "Outstanding" scores from *Wine Spectator* and *Wine Advocate* critics, and the Domaine Drouhin chardonnay was recently named "Best New World White Wine." The winery itself has been described as "palatial," occupying the top of a hill with panoramic and amazing views. The tasting room is open Wed through Sun from 11 a.m. to 4 p.m.; there is a tasting fee of $10 for a flight of 3 wines. No appointment is necessary for groups of 7 or fewer. Domaine Drouhin does not allow picnics on their property, but the view of 90 acres of hillside vineyards on a 225-acre estate might just be enough to satisfy you.

Stoller Vineyards. 16161 NE McDougall Rd., Dayton; (503) 864-3404; www .stollervineyards.com. Stoller Vineyards offers excellent wines and friendly hospitality in a stunning setting, but their true claim to fame is their eco-friendly practices. Bill and Cathy Stoller's vision of blending vineyard stewardship with environmental sustainability was recognized in 2006 when Stoller became the first LEED certified winemaking facility in the United States. Today, the winery continues to operate sustainably as well as provide delicious pinot noir, chardonnay, and pinot noir rose as well as panoramic views including Mt. Hood. The tasting room is open daily from 11 a.m. to 5 p.m.

White Rose Wines. 6250 Northeast Hilltop Lane; Dayton; (503) 864-2328; www .whiterosewines.com. Planted in 1980 at the top of a hill near Dayton, the White Rose pinot noir vines consistently produce fruit of great character and complexity. This small winery makes some very delicious pinot noir and offers it in its adorable tasting room, open 11 a.m. to 5 p.m. daily, except in December, when it is only open by appointment. There is a $15 tasting fee.

where to eat

Dundee Bistro. 100-A SW 7th St.; (503) 554-1650; www.dundeebistro.com. This bistro with full bar and fireside, courtyard, and private party seating is as comfortable as it is satisfying. Created by the Ponzi family, who have owned and operated world-acclaimed vineyards in the Yamhill Valley for 35 years, the Dundee Bistro prepares and presents dishes that reflect culinary sophistication while also catering to the winemaker who wants to have lunch in his overalls and field boots. The menu changes daily and features locally grown organic, sustainable products—visitors might choose baby arugula with Italian plums and chevre or halibut fish and chips. Open daily 11:30 a.m. to close. $$–$$$.

Joel Palmer House. 600 Ferry St.; (503) 864-2995; www.joelpalmerhouse.com. Joel Palmer founded the town of Dayton and built this spectacular home in 1857. Today the Joel Palmer House is a renowned restaurant that features wild mushrooms and other local ingredients in excellent dishes that match the glorious wines of the local region. World-renowned chef Jack Czarnecki has been featured extensively in the media, and the Joel Palmer House has become a destination. The prices are very high, but some still believe this is the best place to eat in wine country. Open Tues through Sat for dinner. $$$.

Tina's Restaurant. 760 OR 99 W; (503) 538-8880; www.tinasdundee.com. Opened in 1991, this restaurant is a bit of a flagship for the Dundee area wining and dining scene. An understated exterior shrouds a cozy and intimate interior, with a comfortable bar and 2 dining rooms divided by a fireplace. The owners know everyone and even if they don't know you, they'll treat you like they do. The menu offers some fabulous unique items like soufflé, braised rabbit, and steamed salmon. The wine list, as you'd expect, is amazing. Desserts include fruit cobblers in season and crème brûlée. Open for dinner nightly from 5 p.m. to close, and for lunch Tues through Fri from 11:30 a.m. to 2 p.m. $$$.

where to stay

Black Walnut Inn and Vineyard. 9600 NE Worden Hill Rd.; (503) 429-4114; www.black walnut-inn.com. If you are feeling extravagant, book an overnight stay at the Black Walnut Inn. Newly constructed and reminiscent of an old Tuscan villa, this inn sits in the hills outside Dundee and is filled with modern art and amenities blended expertly with beautiful antiques, old world details, and the works of local artisans. The European elegance extends from the incredible architecture to luxurious linens, soaking tubs, king and queen size beds, and breathtaking views. The rooms run as much as $495 per night, but you'll be comforted to know that they come with a full gourmet breakfast and afternoon refreshments. $$$.

The Inn at Red Hills, Farm to Fork Restaurant, and Press, A Wine Bar. 1410 N OR 99 W; (503) 538-7666; www.innatredhills.com. If your desire is to leave the city, plop down somewhere, and not have to move an inch to experience all that wine country has to offer, this is your place. The Inn at Red Hills is Oregon Wine Country's first full-service boutique hotel and offers world-class, luxury lodging, dining, and wine tasting right in one place in lovely downtown Dundee. The inn is composed of two free-standing buildings with a charming stone courtyard in between. There are 20 luxurious and unique rooms boasting large windows with views of the countryside and small relaxation areas with either a sofa or oversized chairs. Kick back, read a book, and gaze at those vineyards. The restaurant, Farm to Fork, adjacent to the lobby, has garnered national acclaim. Focusing on farm fresh, locally sourced ingredients, the menu changes frequently with seasonal availability. Farm to Fork has a "Wall of Wine"—simply choose a bottle and carry it to your table. Press, the wine bar, showcases hard to find, small lot Oregon wines. Winemakers are very likely to turn up on site, and special flights of Oregon's best wines are always available. Finally, the Inn at Red Hills has a deli, offering a wide selection of Oregon and international cheeses, charcuterie, and fresh salads. Custom picnic baskets for a day of wine tasting, bike riding, hiking, or trail riding are available. Farm to Fork: Open for breakfast, lunch, and dinner daily. Press: Open nightly. Lodging: $$$. Dining: $–$$$.

day trip 02

southwest

wine country:
mcminnville, carlton

mcminnville

McMinnville is the county seat and the largest of Yamhill County's cities. Located at the confluence of the North and South Forks of the Yamhill River, McMinnville has a charming and thriving downtown and is surrounded by rolling and lovely pastoral hills. Also lovely is the campus of Linfield College, a four-year undergraduate liberal arts college. Pioneer Hall, built in 1882, and Melrose Hall, built in 1929, are both exquisite examples of architecture, and the campus also boasts many old and lovely trees.

McMinnville had its 15 minutes of national fame back in 1950, when photographs of a reported unidentified flying object were taken from a local farm and published in the city's newspaper. Within a month, the photos had made it into *LIFE* magazine. A debate has raged ever since about the validity of the photos, and more than once photographic experts were hired to prove or disprove the case, to no avail. McMinnville residents took the whole affair lightly, however, and to this day hold a UFO Festival each year in May, the biggest such gathering in the Pacific Northwest.

If you don't make your day trip around UFO season, definitely shoot for wine tasting and shopping season (which, luckily, is all year). McMinnville is full of both opportunities, as well as some truly fabulous restaurants.

southwest day trip 02

getting there

Take OR 99 W out of Portland, heading southwest. Travel through Tigard, Sherwood, Newberg, and Dundee. Turn left onto OR 18 W/SE Dayton Bypass. After 6 miles, take the Salmon River Spur ramp to make a slight right onto NE Three Mile Lane/OR 18 Spur, which will immediately turn into McMinnville's 3rd Street.

Be aware that because OR 99 W travels through many suburbs of Portland, it's slow going. It will likely take you more than an hour to drive 35 miles.

where to go

Evergreen Aviation and Space Museum. 500 NE Captain Michael King Smith Way; (503) 434-4180; www.sprucegoose.org. This massive facility has an aviation museum, a space museum, an IMAX theater, and an estimated 5-hour tour time! Even if you don't have that much time, consider popping in to see the famous *Spruce Goose.* The single hull flying boat capable of carrying 750 troops was designed by Howard Hughes and flown only once before being stored for years. Finally, it was donated to this museum, where it is treated as the crown jewel. This living museum celebrates aviation's rich history, honors the patriotic service of our veterans, and offers enlightening educational programs in aviation. Set to open in summer 2011 is a new water park—with a real 747 airplane parked on the roof. Open every day, including weekends, from 9 a.m. to 5 p.m. Tickets vary in price from $9 to $27 depending on age and whether or not the visitor chooses to include an IMAX movie.

Farms: You-Pick, Produce, and Christmas Tree. It's not all about wine around here. Some farms do what they've always done in the rich, organic Willamette Valley soil and grow vegetables, raise sheep and cows, and even grow Christmas trees.

> **Draper Farms.** 11105 SW Baker Creek Rd.; (503) 472-2358. You-pick raspberries and tomatoes when posted or advertised. Farm stand season is May 1 through Oct 31 from 9 a.m. to dusk daily. Call for availability.

> **Farmer John's Produce and Nursery.** 15000 SW Oldsville Rd.; (503) 474-3514; www.farmerjohnsproduce.com. This family farm has been growing wonderful things since 1882. Today, the farm follows organic practices but without the organic certification. Farmer John's is open to the public mid-May through Oct 31 and offers a wide array of products depending on the season including bedding plants, hanging baskets, strawberries, pumpkins, kiwi, Indian corn, artichokes, tomatoes, and potatoes.

> **Foxridge Tree Farm.** 2960 NW Hill Rd. N; (503) 835-9606. This you-cut Christmas tree farm offers noble, Douglas fir, and grand trees to take home. Open weekends only between Nov 26 and Dec 19.

Ramsby's Tree Farm. 16460 SW Oldsville Rd.; (503) 843-3149; www.nwtrees.com. Between Thanksgiving and Christmas, cut a Christmas tree at this lovely farm south of McMinnville. Choose from noble, Douglas fir, grand, Turkish, and Nordmann fir, all grown here in the rich soil of Yamhill County. Open daily 9 a.m. to 5 p.m. Nov 26 through Dec 20.

Wheatland Ferry. Wheatland Ferry Road; (503) 588-5304; www.wheatlandferry.com. Located 1 mile north of the Yamhill–Polk county border in Oregon, the Wheatland Ferry shuttles passengers across the Willamette River, linking Marion with Yamhill and Polk counties. It's a little old fashioned blast from the past and a fun ride. Hours of operation: daily 5:30 a.m. to 9:45 p.m. year-round. Closed Thanksgiving and Christmas. Cost is $2 for passenger cars.

Wineries. The Oregon wine country bounty continues in McMinnville. If you aren't in the mood to drive to surrounding wineries, visit 3rd Street, downtown, and simply begin wandering. There are several wine bars on this street, and more seem to appear all the time. If you prefer to go to the source, here's a partial list, some in town, some out. See www.yamhillvalley.org for a longer list.

Panther Creek. 455 NE Irvine St.; (503) 472-8080; www.panthercreekcellars.com. Panther Creek is located in McMinnville's former power plant, just off the main street in downtown. This enormous brick building built in 1923 makes the location just as unique and interesting as the wines. Panther Creek's tasting room is located right inside the main winery production area, allowing guests to feel right at home amongst tanks and barrels. All of the winery's currently released wines, which include pinot noir, pinot gris, and chardonnay, are offered daily in the tasting room, open noon to 5 p.m. There is a $5 tasting fee, which is refundable with wine purchase.

R. Stuart and Co. Wine Bar. 528 NE 3rd St.; (503) 472-4477; www.rstuartandco .com. This little downtown tasting room is done up in warm colors, big street-front windows, and chandeliers. Their wines—primarily a pinot noir and pinot gris—are delicious. The wine bar is the perfect setting to linger over a glass of something and a snack with friends, or purchase wine to take home. For a little variety, R. Stuart also offers a couple of local microbrews and Portland Roasting Company organic espresso. Open Sun through Wed noon to 6 p.m. and Thurs through Sat noon to 8 p.m.

Willamette Valley Vineyards. 8800 Enchanted Way SE, Turner; (800) 344-9463; www.willamettevalleyvineyards.com. Willamette Valley Vineyards is a popular spot with tourists for many reasons besides just their excellent wine. Not only does their world-class winery have sweeping views of the vineyard and Yamhill Valley, the folks that work here really want you to learn something. Tours are offered daily at noon on a first-come, first-served basis for a fee of $10 per person. Wine tastings come with the amazing story of Willamette Valley Vineyards beginnings. Try their pinot noir, pinot gris, chardonnay, and Riesling. The tasting room is open from 11 a.m. to 6 p.m. daily.

where to shop

Brigittine Monks' Gourmet Confections. 23300 Walker Lane, Amity; (503) 835-8080; www.brigittine.org. This Roman Catholic monastery manufactures quality gourmet fudge and truffles as its means of self-support. It's great candy that receives accolades from candy experts and customers alike. The store, at the monastery, is open Mon through Sat from 9 a.m. to 5 p.m. and Sun from 1 to 5 p.m.

La Bella Casa. 406 NE 3rd St.; (503) 435-2313; www.shoplabellacasa.com. This gorgeous shop is filled from floor to ceiling with uniquely chosen gifts for your beloved home, kids, pets, and everyone else you may know and love. Shop for Vietri Italian pottery, glass tableware, fragrant candles and soaps, pajamas and bathrobes, jewelry, stationery, dog collars, and more. This is the ideal location to find that perfect gift for baby showers, weddings, and birthdays. Free gift-wrapping available. Open Mon through Fri 10 a.m. to 6 p.m., Sat 10 a.m. to 5 p.m., and Sun 11 a.m. to 4 p.m.

Red Berry Boutique. 303 NE 3rd St.; (503) 472-6993; www.redberryboutique.com. Red Berry brings a taste of city fashion to McMinnville. Their hand-picked selection of women's and men's apparel, accessories, and shoes trends toward the trendy, and inventory changes frequently. Jewelry, shoes, accessories, and some home decor items are here, too.

Retro Rama. 448 NE 3rd St.; (503) 434-5303. This store occupies the former JC Penney building—an appropriate location, as their trade is nostalgia. Glassware and other items from the 1950s and 1960s are offered up alongside treats such as Big Hunks, Abba Zabbas, Chic-O-Sticks, jawbreakers, and root beer fizzies. You'll also find mid-century furniture, old tins, and nearly antique pottery. Open Tues through Sun.

Third Street Books. 334 NE 3rd St.; (503) 472-7786; www.thirdstreetbooks.com. Every small-town downtown needs a really great book store, and this is McMinnville's resident book lover's dream. Third Street Books is a general interest bookstore with mostly new books, but some used books are on the shelves as well. There is also a great selection of magazines, cards, and other unique gift items here to discover. Open Mon through Sun 10 a.m. to 6 p.m.

where to eat

Bistro Maison. 729 NE 3rd St.; (503) 474-1888; www.bistromaison.com. Authentic French food including coq au vin, steak au poivre, cassoulet, mussels, and fondue is offered at this lovely little bistro in an old house in historical downtown McMinnville. Bistro Maison makes an incredible brunch, and in the summer, the gardens and patio are delightful places to spend a mealtime. Open for lunch and dinner Wed through Sun. $$$.

Crescent Café. 526 NE 3rd St.; (503) 435-2655. More refined than your average breakfast cafe, Crescent Café puts out phenomenal, well-put-together local foods, including daily homemade breads that are to die for. Daily specials are truly special—try the Carlton Farms pork biscuits and gravy or the blood orange juice. Open until about 1:30 p.m. Wed through Sun—expect a wait on weekends. $.

Golden Valley Brewery and Pub. 980 NE 4th St.; (503) 472-2739; www.goldenvalley brewery.com. This downtown building was a working warehouse in the 1920s and now houses a brewery, brewpub, and restaurant. This small craft brewery, founded to revive a traditional style of brewing, is dedicated to producing ales and lagers of rare complexity and great balance. But their menu is pretty great, too. Golden Valley has always had a kitchen garden and sources produce and meats locally. And guess what? They even serve Oregon wines. Open every day for lunch and dinner. $$–$$$.

La Rambla Restaurant and Bar. 238 NE 3rd. St.; (503) 435 2126; www.laramblaonthird .com. You can't miss this beautiful bright red and orange stucco building in McMinnville's downtown. The interior is vibrant and richly detailed, too, but the main attraction is the food. La Rambla creates Northwest inspired cuisine from Spain by blending classics with Spanish influences and the best food the Pacific Northwest has to offer. Hot and cold tapas plus larger plates are available to pair with a selection from the incredible wine list, which includes more than 400 local and Spanish wines. Open for lunch and dinner 7 days a week. $$–$$$.

Nick's Italian Café. 521 NE 3rd St.; (503) 434-4471; www.nicksitaliancafe.com. Since 1977, Nick's has served multi-course fixed meals and à la carte dishes that helped to put McMinnville on the gastronomic map. The menu features local foods made with true Italian style, including Dungeness crab and pine nut lasagna, Cornish game hen, and lamb. Open for lunch and dinner Tues through Sat (closed from 2:30 to 5 p.m.). $$–$$$.

Red Fox Bakery and Café. 328 NE Evans St.; (503) 434-5098; www.redfoxbakery.com. McMinnville's first independent artisan bakery in the heart of downtown features true hand-crafted breads and pastries. A light lunch of sandwiches and soups is served daily, as well. Your sweet tooth will not be neglected—Red Fox makes some delightful brownies and rather addictive macaroons. Try the sbrisolona (almond butter cookie). Open Mon through Sat 7 a.m. to 4 p.m., Sun 8 a.m. to 2 p.m. $.

Thistle Restaurant. 228 NE Evans St.; (503) 472-9623; www.thistlerestaurant.com. The dining room, menu, and portions might be small at this McMinnville restaurant, but the flavors are interesting and intense. The menu changes daily, is written up on a chalkboard, and usually lists about 12 items of "playful American cuisine." The chef works hand in hand with farmers, ranchers, and fishermen to bring the very best meals to your table—most ingredients are sourced within 45 miles. Open for dinner Tues through Sat. $$$.

Wildwood. 319 NE Baker St.; (503) 435-1454. This is a classic breakfast joint offering up big fat traditional breakfasts, good prices, and big portions. Egg beaters and old memorabilia cover the walls, giving the place a retro chic. A word of warning—Wildwood is popular and the wait can be lengthy, especially on weekends. Open for breakfast and lunch. $.

where to stay

Hotel Oregon. 310 NE Evans St.; (503) 472-8427; www.mcmenamins.com. Hotel Oregon anchors the heart of downtown McMinnville, just as it has since 1905. Once home to a restaurant and lounge, banquet hall, Greyhound bus depot, Western Union, soda fountain, and beauty parlor, this handsome 4-story building, renovated by the McMenamin brothers, is a delightful destination in the heart of Oregon's wine country. Take a trip to the subterranean bistro-style Cellar Bar or magnificent Rooftop Bar, which boasts a breathtaking 360-degree view of city lights, vineyard-laden hills, and the Coast Range. If you haven't had enough, stay overnight in one of 42 European-style guest rooms, or hit the restaurant for omelets, burgers, pastas, salads, or one of McMenamins 200 signature ales. $$.

carlton

Carlton puts the "I" in idyllic. This little town brims over with charm, from the quaint and appealing downtown to the sweeping vistas and rolling hills that surround it. Rich soil covers those hills, and settlers began farming this land 150 years ago. Eventually a railroad went in and Carlton grew a little—but not much. Today it's still a tiny hamlet, albeit a tiny hamlet sprinkled with riches, both metaphorical and actual. Investors and retirees have scooped up ranches and vineyards around this small town, and the growth of the wine industry has beckoned a smattering of top-notch restaurants and shops. Park and walk the entire downtown—there are several wine bars and tasting rooms as well as a few attractive shops.

At the same time, there are still plenty of people living simple lives around here, and doing so with a lot of hometown spirit. Residents take seriously the city's motto—"A great little town."

getting there

Head north out of McMinnville on OR 99 W. After just a couple of miles, turn left onto OR 47 N/Tualatin Valley Highway. Continue 4 miles into Carlton.

where to go

Wineries and Tasting Rooms. "Where to Go" translates to "where to go to taste some wine" here in Carlton. You can park your car and walk to all of these destinations.

Barking Frog. 128 W Main St.; (503) 702-5029; www.barkingfrogwinery.com. According to Native American lore, the barking frog is a symbol of prosperity, considered friendly as it is said he signals to mankind that all is well with the environment. At Barking Frog winery, the winemaking style is to utilize fully ripe fruit and to maximize and build complexity with structure in all wines. The winemakers want to allow the uniqueness of each wine's terroir to be expressed. Open Fri through Sun 1 to 5 p.m. or by appointment.

Cana's Feast Winery. 750 W Lincoln St.; (503) 852-0002; www.canasfeastwinery .com. Located in a Tuscan-inspired building just north of historic downtown Carlton, Cana's Feast Winery has a rich history of combining the tradition of bold, Northwest red wines with good food, hospitality, and celebration. They produce Burgundy, Bordeaux, and Rhone-style red wines, and host lunch and dinner for guests on occasion, usually in the summer on the weekends, pairing great foods with great wines. The west terrace offers spectacular views of the Coast Range and is the perfect place to relax. Two Bocce ball courts host lively games on the lawn. The tasting room is open daily, 11 a.m. to 5 p.m.

Carlton Winemakers Studio. 801 N Scott St; (503) 852-6100; www.winemakers studio.com. This place is as revolutionary as it is a fabulous destination. The idea behind the studio was to create a space where artisanal wine producers could come together under one roof in a state-of-the-art facility to produce and promote their ultra-premium wines. In that way, the Carlton Winemakers Studio has become an incubator for small boutique winemakers. As many as 10 vintners can operate within the studio walls at one time, and each showcases his or her current releases in the shared Tasting Room, itself a totally cool modern room with a concrete bar and large windows. This place is not to be missed. Open daily from 11 a.m. to 5 p.m.

Scott Paul Wines. 128 S Pine St.; (503) 852-7300; www.scottpaul.com. Scott Paul Wines is a bit of an anomaly in that not only do they produce their own Oregon pinot noir, they also import champagnes and burgundies from over 20 small family artisanal producers in Burgundy and Champagne, France. At this tasting room, you can try all of these wines. There is a $10 tasting fee, which is waived with a 3-bottle purchase. Tasting room open Dec through Mar on Sat only from 1 to 5 p.m. From Apr to Nov, Scott Paul is open Fri through Sun from 1 to 5 p.m.

The Tasting Room. 105 W Main St.; (503) 852-6733; www.pinot-noir.com. This tasting room, one of Carlton's original wine tasting establishments, offers dozens and dozens of yummy wines in a lovely space downtown. Specializing in showcasing the fruits of the labors of smaller wineries that don't have their own tasting rooms, the Tasting Room is a great opportunity to try a wide variety of the valley's wines. Open noon to 5 p.m. Thurs through Mon (but call ahead, as hours vary seasonally).

Tyrus Evan. 120 N Pine St.; (503) 852-7010; www.tyrusevan.com. Ken Wright, known for his highly rated, single-vineyard pinot noir, introduced a new label in 2003.

Tyrus Evan, producing claret, syrah, malbec, and cabernet franc, isn't available for tasting at the winery, so Wright created this new shop in a beautifully restored train station in historic downtown Carlton. Tyrus Evan crafts expressive warm-climate varietals from southern Oregon and Washington State. Production always includes a claret and syrah from each region, along with individual bottlings of cab franc and malbec as the fruit warrants. Tasting fee refundable with full case purchase. Call for hours.

where to eat

Cuvee. 214 W Main St.; (503) 852-6555; www.cuveedining.com. French country cuisine is elevated at this local's favorite restaurant to elegant comfort food. Fresh seafood, select meats, seasonal vegetables, and house-made breads are served with the very best Oregon wines. Cuvee is as comfortable for quiet romantic dinners for two as it is for energetic celebrations. Hours vary seasonally—call ahead. $$$.

Filling Station Deli. 305 W Main St; (503) 852-6687; www.fillingstationdeli.com. Enjoy breakfast, lunch, ice cream, and a full espresso bar on the deck at this old gas station in downtown Carlton. The building isn't as appealing as the food, which is delicious. Try the breakfast and lunch sandwiches (on a fresh baguette) or the soup of the day. Open 7 a.m. to 3:30 p.m. daily except Wed; closed Jan 1 through Feb 15. $.

where to stay

Abbey Road Farms Bed and Breakfast. 10501 NE Abbey Rd.; (503) 852-6278; www.abbeyroadfarm.com. Ever slept in a silo? Most folks surely have not. This unique lodging consists of 3 renovated silos, converted into lovely modern suites. They sit on an 82-acre working farm that cultivates 3 unique crops—maraschino cherries, grass seed, and dairy goats. The farm and gardens are beautiful, the silo suites comfortable. Get used to farm living—coffee is available at 7:30 a.m. and the breakfast bell rings at 8:15 a.m. $$$.

The Winery Lofts. (503) 852-7010. This is a bit of a best-kept secret. These 1-bedroom studio fully furnished lofts sit right in downtown Carlton over the tops of the storefronts and are available to rent for a weekend or week away. Each unit is beautifully appointed has a kitchenette with complimentary breakfast items and light snacks. Wireless Internet access, cable TV, and DVD are provided. Staying right downtown in Carlton means you can hit all of the wine tasting spots and restaurants without having to step into your car. $$.

day trip 03

southwest

be a beaver:
corvallis

corvallis

Corvallis is the kind of place that sneaks up on you. At first glance, the small city located at the confluence of the Willamette and Mary's Rivers can come off as sleepy, old-fashioned, and dripping wet. Catch Corvallis on a bad day and all you'll see are shuttered storefronts and the arc of your umbrella.

On a good day, however, the sun lights up the lovely old neighborhoods, hundreds of leafy hardwood trees in over a dozen parks, and classy college campus that define this town. Add to that Corvallis's educated, cultured population—by some accounts this city has a higher education rate per capita than any other city in the State of Oregon, surely something to do with the presence of Oregon State University. It may be subdued here, but things are definitely smart and interesting.

Joseph C. Avery first laid claim to the land here in 1845. He's the one credited with coining the word "Corvallis"—an amalgam of the Latin words for "heart of the valley." The plateau upon which the city is built extends into the foothills of the Coast Range, which offer great opportunities for hiking and wildlife spotting. The forest and fields here can be soaking wet, it's true. But all of that rain only makes things greener and more beautiful come summer, when Corvallis has its chance to shine.

getting there

Take I-5 south out of Portland. Drive 72 miles to the OR 34 W exit, exit 228. Take this exit and turn right (west). Continue to follow OR 34 W for 10 miles to Corvallis.

where to go

Alley Art. www.visitcorvallis.com. Tour more than 25 sculptures and enamel-on-metal reproductions of poems, photographs, silkscreen prints, and more on this self-guided tour of public art along Madison Avenue from the riverfront to Central Park. The tour begins on the north side of Madison Avenue at 8th Street (adjacent to Central Park); art pieces are numbered consecutively to the riverfront and back. See website for more information and a downloadable tour brochure.

The Corvallis Arts Center. 700 SW Madison Ave.; (541) 754-1551; www.theartscenter .net. Located in the heart of downtown Corvallis on the edge of a rose-filled park, The Arts Center showcases local art by well-known and emerging artists from all around Oregon. Housed in an historic church, the Arts Center also hosts classes and workshops year-round, and is home to a fun gift shop filled with local goods. The Main Gallery features solo, small group, and juried exhibitions that change monthly. See the website for current show information. Open noon to 5 p.m. Tues through Fri.

Oregon State University. (541) 737-1000; http://oregonstate.edu. Founded in 1868 and originally an agricultural college, Oregon State University is one of Oregon's oldest public institutions. The campus was designed by the Olmsted Brothers in 1909, emphasizing trees and an architectural harmony anchored by basic classical forms in brick. Though the campus has grown considerably since then, the current design is laid on a grid of wide, tree-lined streets, has a classic old-American feel, and is lovely to stroll through, particularly in the fall when the trees change color.

Athletic Events. www.osubeavers.com. Oh yes, you can bet your bottom dollar that Oregon State University fans come out in droves regularly to root for their mascot, the Beavers, and their athletes. Men's crew on the Willamette River, football in Reser's Stadium, women's basketball, swimming, soccer, track—you name it, you can see it at Oregon State University.

Irish Bend Covered Bridge. The west side of campus is dedicated primarily to agricultural research. This covered bridge and historic landmark is on a path through the research farm. Moved from its original location here in 1988, the bridge is between 35th and 53rd Streets on the west side of the OSU campus, spanning Oak Creek.

Oregon State University Tour of Trees. Oregon State University has won many awards for its tree diversity and forestry program. Take a self-guided tour of the historic OSU campus with the help of a brochure available at the Corvallis Tourism Visitor's Center at 553 NW Harrison (541-757-1544).

Tyee Century Farm and Wine Cellars. 26335 Greenberry Rd.; (541) 753-8754; www .tyeewine.com. Located on a Century Farm just south of downtown Corvallis, Tyee Wine Cellars is a family owned and operated vineyard and winery. The vintage milking barn still stands today on this former dairy farm. Visit the on-site art gallery adjoining the tasting room, which offers pinot noirs, chardonnays, pinot gris, and more. Open Apr through Dec, Sat and Sun, noon to 5 p.m.

where to shop

Beekman Place. 601 SW Western Blvd.; (541) 753-8250. Feel like poking around in the past? This is a great little antiques mall full of vintage clothing, furniture, and oddities. The fun thing about an antiques shop is that you just never know what will turn up. Come and see if you'll find a treasure or two to carry back home as a day trip souvenir.

Camellia Vintage and Antique Jewelry. 221 NW 2nd St.; (541) 758-1100; www .camelliacollection.blogspot.com. This charming little shop specializes in antique diamond and platinum engagement rings as well as antique jewelry from the 1880s to the 1950s. The store also offers stunning vintage-inspired bridal gowns. Other finds include vintage pottery, linens, and art pieces from the 1920s to the 1960s. Hours vary—call ahead.

Corvallis Brewing Supply. 119 SW 4th St.; (541) 758-1674; www.lickspigot.com. It may not occur to you to shop for home brewing equipment on a day trip—or maybe it will, as there is nothing like a relaxing day out of town to make one ponder picking up a leisure activity. In any case, this place is worth a stop for its wide range of rather exciting and exceptionally brilliant commercial beer, wines, hard ciders, sake, mead, and craft sodas. Open Tues through Fri 11 a.m. to 6 p.m., Sat 10 a.m. to 5 p.m.

Oregon Coffee and Tea. 215 NW Monroe Ave.; (541) 752-2421; www.oregoncoffee andtea.com. We here in the Pacific Northwest do worship our coffees. Teas, too, have recently earned a rather hyper level of fanaticism. Here's the place to come and indulge your beverage fancies. This beautiful and newly expanded shop stocks more than 400 teas and dozens of coffee varieties to choose from. If that just sounds overwhelming, rely on the very helpful staff. Open Tues through Fri, 10 a.m. to 6 p.m., Sat 9 a.m. to 5 p.m.

Sibling Revelry. 145 NW 2nd St.; (541) 754-1424; www.siblingrevelry.com. Find pottery, garden art, jewelry, socks, hats, and more at this clothing and gift shop that operates with just a touch of whimsy. This is a great place to pick up a gift or something for you. Open every day: Mon through Sat 10 a.m. to 6 p.m. and Sun noon to 5 p.m.

Soft Star Shoes. 521 SW 2nd St., #201; (866) 763-2525; www.softstarshoes.com. These soft and flexible shoes are crafted on the premise that barefoot is best. If one must wear

> ## one enchanted afternoon

The Enchanted Forest is part Oregon legend, part every kid's fantasy day trip. This attraction built into a forested hillside just off I-5 near Turner has been a part of the local scenery and culture since the 1970s. It's much more than a theme park. Within its magical boundaries are a log ride, dragons, monsters, a storybook lane, a Western town, a kiddie train, bumper cars, a haunted house, an English village, gnomes, cowboys, princesses, and Humpty Dumpty. It's all a little bit quirky—no flashy over-produced style here. That vibe is what makes the place so special. Kids love it, and adults are charmed, too. The whole project remains in the hands of its creator, Roger Tofte, and his family. That love and undivided attention shows. Prices vary by attraction but are generally very reasonable. The Enchanted Forest is located at 8462 Enchanted Way Southeast in Turner. Use exit 248. Because of its convenient location on I-5 between Salem and Albany, a visit to this fun park would be easy to include in a couple of other day trips in this book, including Eugene and Mill City. See www.enchantedforest.com or call (503) 363-3060 for more information.

a shoe, than choose a Soft Star, which mimics barefoot conditions. Customers have the option of customizing shoes down to the very last detail, or choosing from a variety of pre-made shoes. Visitors can also take a tour at this unique shoe factory located in downtown Corvallis.

where to eat

Aqua. 151 NW Monroe Ave.; (541) 752-0262; www.aquacorvallis.com. Aqua's beautiful riverfront location is not to be missed, but the proof of the place is in the food. Showcasing Hawaiian regional cuisine and delicious Pacific Rim fare exquisitely, Aqua offers dishes like Lokelani prawns and Shichimi Togarashi diver scallops. The menu can be fairly expensive, but the food is prepared impeccably. Don't miss the hibiscus-infused butter. Open for dinner Tues through Sat. $$$.

Big River. 101 NW Jackson; (541) 757-0694; www.bigriverrest.com. A Corvallis classic, this restaurant offers fine dining in a cool old building on the riverfront. Big River never disappoints with a consistently marvelous Pacific Northwest menu offering local organic produce, natural meats, sustainable seafood, and mouthwatering desserts. A wide range of pizzas, seafood and meat dishes, salads, and yummy starters pleases a diverse crowd, and the bread bakery, located on-site, crafts artisan loaves daily. Big River's bar features local and regional wines, single malts, seasonal martinis, and jazz on weekends. Open for lunch Mon through Fri and dinner Mon through Sat. Call for reservations. $$–$$$.

Block 15 Brewery and Restaurant. 300 SW Jefferson; (541) 758-2077; www.block15 .com. While Block 15 is a relatively new brewery on the Pacific Northwest beer scene, it has already made quite a name for itself. These folks are willing to push the envelope continually to put forth fabulous beers. Be sure to try one of their stone-fruit ales. The kitchen produces honest casual food, much sourced from Oregon, including Painted Hills Natural beef burgers, slow smoked Carlton Farms pork, pastas, crisp salads, beer battered fries, and vegetarian options. Stop in for a quick snack, an extended meal, or "hoppy hour" from 3 to 6 p.m. Open Sun through Wed 11 a.m. to 11 p.m. and Thurs through Sat 11 a.m. to 1 a.m. $–$$.

Cloud 9 Atmospheric Eatery. 126 SW 1st St.; www.dinecloud9.com. This intimate space on Corvallis' historic riverfront serves slow-cooked, handmade American fare. The space's red tables and dangling globe lights will make you feel like you are on Cloud 9 (and isn't that just the perfect name for a restaurant?). The menu focuses on local and largely organic comfort food, including world famous, award-winning, pan-made, fresh-to-order mac-and-cheese. Live music plays on weekends at this fun, family-friendly place that also showcases both local and student art. Open for dinner Mon through Sat. $–$$.

Gathering Together Farms. 25159 Grange Hall Rd., Philomath; (541) 929-4270; www .gatheringtogetherfarm.com. Gathering Together Farm is both a restaurant and a farm that specializes in certified organic vegetable and fruit production. Shop their farm stand for the best seasonal organic vegetables in the valley or visit the restaurant for a truly unbelievable meal. The store is open 9 a.m. to 5 p.m. Tues through Sat, seasonally. Lunch is served at the restaurant Tues through Fri, breakfast is served on Sat, and dinner is served Thur and Fri nights, though hours vary seasonally and you should definitely check ahead of time and make a reservation. The menu might include leg of lamb with fingerling potatoes, carrot ginger soup, and cherry crème brûlée to finish. $$.

LUC. 134 SW 4th; (541) 753-4171; www.i-love-luc.com. An intimate setting with an ever-changing menu that showcases the best of what Corvallis and Benton County have to offer in wines and food. Any given evenings' offerings are limited and subject to change, but are also guaranteed to be delicious. Duck leg confit, parsnip mash, mustard crème fraîche, braised pork shoulder, sunchokes, black kale, gastrique and Kumamoto oysters (served raw), or rice wine mignonette might just hit the spot. $$–$$$.

Nearly Normals. 109 NW 15th St.; (541) 753-0791; www.nearlynormals.com. For a casual meal, Nearly Normals is my favorite Corvallis restaurant. There is nothing you can't get here, and all of it is fabulous. The menu focuses on vegan and vegetarian foods, but proteins of all varieties are happily added to the food. The huge selection offers everything from curry to burritos to pasta to pad Thai. Nearly Normals emphasizes fresh ingredients (organic when available), original recipes (born from creative chaos), and thoughtfulness in preparation—a combination of ethics they call "gonzo cuisine." The building and design are as eclectic and wild as the food, and the outdoor patio is a marvelous garden with shading trellises. If you are craving a tofu stir fry or Tijuana tempeh enchiladas, this is the place for you. Open Mon through Sat for breakfast, lunch, and dinner. $$.

New Morning Bakery. 219 SW 2nd St.; (541) 754-0181; www.members.peak.org. This downtown bakery is roomy, cheery, accessible for all, and is the perfect stop for breakfast or brunch. Muffins, scones, bagels, croissants, Danishes, coffee cakes, cinnamon rolls, pecan sticky buns, pies, cookies, brownies and bars, pastries, soups, stews, calzone, wraps, lasagna, polenta, spanikopita, ravioli, panini, and chowders . . . are you hungry yet? Open Sun 8 a.m. to 8 p.m., Mon through Thurs 7 a.m. to 9 p.m., and Fri and Sat 7 a.m. to 10 p.m. $.

where to stay

Alder Creek Guest House. 7920 NW Skillings Dr.; (541) 719-8525; www.aldercreekcottage .com. This cute converted barn has easy access to biking and walking trails and is the perfect location for a little relaxation. Kick back in this newly renovated, stand-alone vacation lodging with a luxurious bed, fireplace, kitchenette, deck, and bath. Prices are reduced the longer you stay. $–$$.

Hanson Country Inn. 795 SW Hanson St.; (541) 752-2919; www.hcinn.com. This charming country home holds a treasure trove of antiques, museum quality art, and splendid architectural details. As an inn, it embodies an atmosphere brimming with beautiful gardens, balconies, cozy warmth, unique charm, and elegant ambiance. Rooms are spacious, beautifully decorated with antiques, and feature original built-in cabinetry and sitting rooms. Come morning, enjoy a full gourmet breakfast in the sun-filled dining room. Close to downtown. $$.

Harrison House Bed and Breakfast. 2310 NW Harrison Blvd.; (541) 752-6248; www .corvallis-lodging.com. Several elegant, tasteful, large, and comfortable rooms are available in this beautiful Dutch Colonial home just steps from the Oregon State University Campus. Guest rooms have private baths, 2 comfortable chairs, reading lights, and an interesting selection of books and magazines. The owners are former restaurant owners and the breakfasts here are truly gourmet. $$.

Leaping Lamb Farm. 20368 Honey Grove Rd., Alsea; (541) 487-4966; www.leapinglamb farm.com. This is a pretty cool option for those of us who wanted to live on a farm when we were kids. A self-contained cabin on this property, which was homesteaded in 1896 and has been farmed ever since, is rented to guests. Formerly known as Honey Grove Farm, it has been a working farm since the fields were first cleared, growing hay, raspberries and blueberries, garlic, apples, pears, plums, and grapes, and raising turkeys, cattle, and sheep.

The lodging includes 2 bedrooms with queen-size beds, a full bath, a complete kitchen and eating area, a large, airy living room with a double-futon couch, and a multi-level deck with views overlooking orchards and pastures. The kitchen comes with a do-it-yourself breakfast, with cereals, fruits, bread, juice, coffee, teas, waffles, and anything else you can think to whip up from the provisions in the cupboard and fridge. Guests can buy eggs and other produce from the farm. It's a great family-friendly farm stay where you can learn as much as you want about farming or just sit back and just relax. Two-night minimum on weekends. $$.

day trip 04

southwest

all the fish in the sea:
newport

newport

Newport lies on the Central Oregon Coast, about halfway between California and Washington. The city strikes a balance between the artsy coastal towns of the northern Oregon coast and the working coastal towns of the southern Oregon coast. Many Newport folks work hard at traditional hands-on jobs in the forest or sea—fishing, logging, or tending to oyster beds—but there's also a big contingent of artistic types residing in Newport, from painters to writers. These diverse communities come together and blend their lives just fine, which is part of why Newport is known as "the friendliest town on the Oregon Coast."

Newport got its start on oysters. A whole batch of them was discovered in Yaquina Bay in 1862, and the delicious sea delicacies began to be exported to San Francisco and beyond. Soon after that the area opened for settlement, and a thriving tourism industry popped up immediately—an especially amazing fact given that there wasn't even a road to Newport until 1927.

From the get-go, development in Newport centered around two distinct areas: the Bayfront and Nye Beach. These remain the city's primary gathering places, each with its own character. Recently rejuvenated Nye Beach is an artsy village, home to many fine dining establishments—it's also the primary access to a world class sandy beach. The Bayfront is a traditional coastal vacationer's dream—galleries, saltwater taffy and ice cream vendors, beer, fish and chips, and carnival-type attractions abound. Don't overlook the Highway

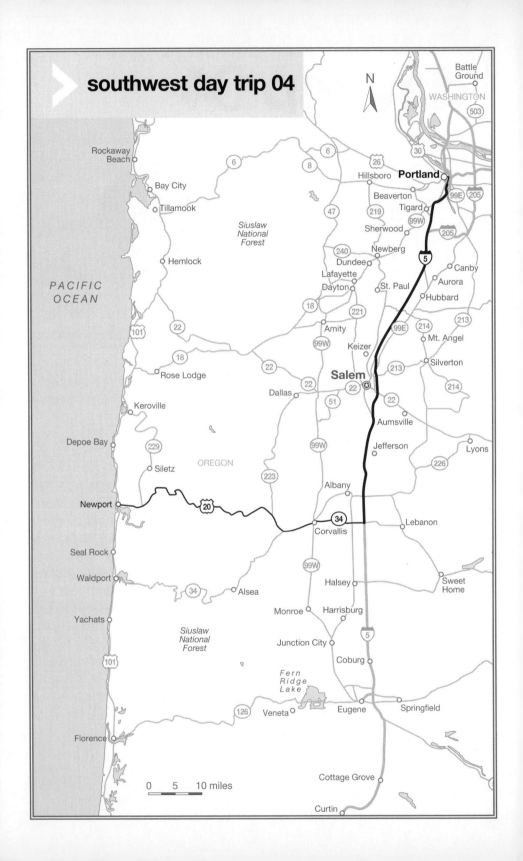

southwest day trip 04

101 Corridor and South Beach, the location of the Oregon Coast Aquarium and Rogue Breweries.

No matter where you go, take a jacket—like all of the Oregon Coast, it can be windy here. And don't forget your appetite! Newport is home to more than 80 restaurants, ranging from four-star dining to small, cozy cafes.

getting there

Take I-5 south out of Portland for 72 miles to exit 228. Turn right onto OR 34/Corvallis-Lebanon Highway. When you reach the outskirts of Corvallis, turn left to stay on OR 34 (it will become the Corvallis-Newport Highway). Continue west for 21 miles, at which point OR 24 will turn into US 20. Continue west for another 30 miles until you reach Newport.

where to go

Hatfield Marine Science Center. 2030 S Marine Science Dr.; (541) 867-0126; www .hmsc.oregonstate.edu. The public wing of Oregon State University's Mark O. Hatfield Marine Science Center showcases live marine animals, interactive marine science puzzles and games, and other aspects of our amazing ocean planet. Trained volunteers and a fabulous bookstore are major perks. Last time I was there, the lobby was home to a gigantic, touchable octopus. Open year-round: 7 days a week in summer, Thurs through Mon fall through spring. Free admission, but a suggested donation of $5 per person or $20 per family is gratefully accepted.

Mariner Square. 250 SW Bay Blvd.; (541) 265-2206; www.marinersquare.com. Three attractions in one in this Bayfront establishment, priced at a bargain if you catch them all. Hours vary seasonally.

Oregon Underseas Gardens. Catch an underwater view of all manner of fish, an octopus, and a wolf eel in a kelp forest. Continuous dive shows are filled with action, special effects, and surprises, all expertly narrated by knowledgeable tour guides and scuba divers equipped with underwater communications.

Ripley's Believe it or Not. Robert Ripley captured the bizarre, which is definitely what can be found here, from shrunken heads to the magic harp. Don't get lost for all eternity in the deep-space hall of mirrors.

The Wax Works. Hundreds of sculptures, each elaborately molded and detailed from wax, in the form of Hollywood legends to sci-fi creatures. Creepy, but cool.

The Newport Aquarium. 2820 SE Ferry Slip Rd.; (541) 867-3474; www.aquarium.org. A truly worthy destination, the Oregon Coast Aquarium is home to more than 15,000 marine animals in a beautiful setting. Resident species include sea otters, sea lions, octopuses, sharks, tufted puffins, and an array of tropical fish, and the grounds are gorgeously, natively landscaped with salal, boxwood, shore pine, and wildflowers. The ocean crashes nearby, and exhibits offer a close-up view of what lies in its depths. Don't miss the jellyfish—they are magical. Open every day except Dec 25. Open in winter 10 a.m. to 5 p.m. daily, summer 9 a.m. to 6 p.m. daily.

Newport Visual Arts Center. 777 NW Beach Dr.; (541) 265-6540; www.coastarts.org. The Newport Visual Arts Center, located at the historic Nye Beach Turnaround, is a municipal public art exhibition and programmatic space and for art education programs. Two shows every month feature Northwest artists. Open Tues through Sun, 11 a.m. to 6 p.m. Free admission.

The Rogue Brewery Brewers on the Bay. 2320 OSU Dr.; (541) 867-3664; www.rogue .com. This big red warehouse is where Rogue makes its famous, award-winning microbrews. Visit for brewery tours, lunch or dinner at the upstairs pub, and a taste from—count 'em—50 taps. There is also plenty of logo wear for sale and a panoramic view of Yaquina Bay and the marina. Open Sun through Thurs 11 a.m. to 8 p.m., Fri and Sat 11 a.m. to 9 p.m. Brewery tour at 3 p.m. daily.

Yaquina Head. 750 NW Lighthouse Dr.; (541) 574-3100. This 100-acre Outstanding Natural Area is an absolute don't-miss. There's no better view of the ocean, wildlife, and the Yaquina Head Lighthouse than from this natural peninsula just north of Newport. Harbor seals, brown pelicans, auklets, and up to 300,000 common murres inhabit the rocks off the point. Whale-watching is a winter and spring seasonal delight. Several trails allow for small

nye beach

One of my favorite walks anywhere is on Nye Beach. Park in the Nye Beach turn-around off of Coast Street and hit the sand. One can walk either direction, but I like to head north first, toward Yaquina Head. As the waves roll in to your left, admire shore pine-and-salal cliffs to your right. It's about 2 miles all the way north to the beach's terminus to the base of Yaquina Head, and to get there you may have to traverse a stream running across the sand to the ocean. If you do make it to the north end of Nye Beach, you'll likely see some surfers braving the waves. Then check out the tide pools at the base of the rocky cliff. Starfish, anemones, tiny fish, barnacles, and urchins are visible at low tide. Birds nest above. Waves crash against the rocks. The best part—you still have the long walk back, but this time, the wind is at your back, your legs are wearing out, the smile is lodged on your face, and all of this activity has earned you your evening's allotment of fish and chips.

hikes with killer views. There is a great Interpretive Center on site that sheds light on the natural and human history of Yaquina Head. The wind blows powerfully here and storm-watching can be excellent. But the pièce de résistance is Cobble Beach. Over millennia, chunks of basalt have fallen from the hillside, tossed and bashed in the surf, and morphed into hundreds of gorgeous black round rocks known as cobbles. These comprise the small beach nestled out of the north wind at the base of the head. As soon as you hear the satis-fying crunch of your feet working their way through thousands of lovely spherical stones, as soon as you see the way the black stones illuminate the ocean water in an entirely unique way, you'll know you are someplace special. But the real thrill is to come. Waves arrive on the beach as they do on any beach anywhere—large or small, high or low—but as the waves recede through the basalt cobbles, the most wonderful and unusual sound results—a watery tinkling, a musical waterfall. You've never heard anything like it. Yaquina Head is open daily; hours vary per season. $7 per vehicle.

where to shop

The Kite Company. 407 SW Coast Hwy.; (541) 265-2004; www.thekitecompany.com. This enormous retail space houses the largest kite store on the Pacific Coast. Every kind of kite you could dream of can be found here, including delta kites, dragon kites, box kites, diamond kites, stunt kites, and parafoil kites. Catch the wind!

Latitude 44. 255 NW Coast St.; (541) 574-7696; www.latitude44newport.com. High-quality apparel for men, women, and children made from organic materials, including cotton, bam-boo, hemp, and silks from free trade countries. You won't find anything from China, but you will find some great clothing.

Peerless Puffin. 742 NW Beach Dr.; (541) 265-3153. Find fun gifts, cards, and bath and body care items in this cute little shop with all the windows, right by the beach.

Toujours Boutique. 704 NW Beach Dr.; (541) 574-6404; www.toujoursboutique.com. Lovely clothes for women. Separates in beautiful color combinations, bags, hats and shoes, scarves, and jewelry all coordinate to create a look that is comfortable and natural, yet sharp and sophisticated. Some great jewelry, too.

where to eat

April's at Nye Beach. 749 NW 3rd St.; (541) 265-6855. Fine Northwest cuisine served with a view of the ocean. The interior is cheery with watercolor paintings and white linens. The food is delicious seafood and pastas. Don't pass up anything with saffron as an ingre-dient, or the decadent house-made desserts. Open Wed through Sun, 5 p.m. to close. Reservations recommended. $$–$$$.

Café Mundo. 711 NW 2nd Court; (541) 574-8134; www.cafemundo.us. This place is a groovy, hidden treasure. On what was not so long ago a vacant lot with a small kitchen/

trailer on it now sits one of the coolest restaurants around. Behind a row of hedges is a 2-story structure, the inside of which is painted plywood and Sitka spruce, hung with eclectic local art and a massive kite, and interspersed with skylights. Redwood driftwood salvaged from the beach was used to create the barn-style doors that open the ground floor to the outdoor garden seating area. Mundo hosts an open mic night weekly and frequent live music. The menu boasts sushi to omelettes to bento. Tourist or not, you'll feel like a local here. Open Tues through Sat 11 a.m. to 10 p.m., Fri and Sat 11 a.m. to midnight. $–$$.

The Chowder Bowl. 728 NW Beach Dr.; (541) 265-7477. A Nye Beach tradition. Simple traditional beach cafe with award-winning clam chowder, seafood, burgers, beer, wine, and lots of other goodies, like bread pudding with hard sauce. You'll often find a line outside. $–$$.

Kam Meng. 4424 N Coast Hwy.; (541) 574-9450. Genuine Hong Kong–style cooking in a big green and yellow building on US 101. The exterior is deceiving, but the food speaks for itself. The black bean sauce, seafood hot pot, and green bean chicken are all excellent. $–$$.

Local Ocean. 213 SE Bay Blvd.; (541) 574-7959; www.localocean.net. A casually sophisticated fish market and grill unlike any other, and quite possibly the source of the very best seafood on the Oregon Coast. Market-style dining is accented with a central open kitchen where chefs prepare fresh grilled seafood dishes. Diners sit near floor-to-ceiling windows

arr place

There's a great little restaurant in Nye Beach that you'd never know about if you didn't stumble upon it or get sent there by a loyal convert. It's called **ARR Place**—the A, R, and R being the first initials of the first names of the family of three who run the place and live above it. This trio doesn't take kindly to the norms of restaurant management, including a set menu and regular hours, but also eschews serving less than unquestionably superb food. In fact, their motto is "actual food touched by human hands." You might find teriyaki albacore, mushroom and leek quiche, or bread pudding on that day's menu—always, there's some sort of scramble/hash option that's a mix of whatever is fresh, available, and yummy. Whatever you choose, it will be cooked and served by the owners, and will taste delicious. Call (541) 265-4240 or see www.arrplace.com for more information—though like the building, the website won't tell you much. Best just to wander by 143 SW Cliff St. and check the chalkboard in the window for this week's hours.

with roll-up glass doors, which overlook fishing boats in the harbor and the Yaquina Bay Bridge in the distance. The fish and chips are heavenly and the crab po' boy sandwich is completely refreshing. I never visit Newport without eating at Local Ocean at least once, even if I'm not hungry. Open 7 days a week for lunch and dinner. $$–$$$.

Mo's. 657 SW Bay Blvd.; (541) 265-7512; www.moschowder.com. Mo's has been an Oregon Coast mainstay for nearly 60 years. With a unique, informal, and friendly style, traditional beach fare is served at long wooden tables. You can't go wrong with the chowder. $–$$.

Nana's Irish Pub. 613 NW 3rd St.; (541) 574-8787; www.nanasirishpub.com. Outdoors it's light and airy, indoors dark and moody. Nana's is a quintessential Irish pub with surprisingly excellent food. Homemade and hearty pot pies, fish and chips made with house beer batter, savory Reuben sandwiches, and homemade soups and salad dressings are all freshly prepared and wonderful. Naturally, there's plenty of beer on tap. Open Sun through Thurs 11 a.m. to 12 a.m., Fri and Sat 11 a.m. to 1 a.m. $–$$.

Panini Bakery. 232 NW Coast St.; (541) 265-5033. Great pizza, excellent scones, and pastries that aren't overly sweet. The lunchtime sandwiches change daily, are excellent and sell out quickly. Very limited seating, cash only. $.

The Rogue Ales Public House. 748 SW Bay Blvd.; (541) 265-3188; www.rogue.com. If you don't make it to the brewing facility (above in Where to Go), at least hit the brewpub on the Bayfront. Rogue Ales are made with the finest hops and barley malt, free range coastal water, and proprietary yeast. What the food lacks in imagination, it makes up for in volume. And anyway, with all of those beers on tap, who needs food? Open Sun through Thurs 11 a.m. to 1 a.m., Fri and Sat 11 a.m. to 2 a.m. $–$$.

where to stay

Elizabeth Street Inn. 232 SW Elizabeth St.; (541) 265-9400; www.elizabethstreetinn.com. The rooms here are fairly standard, but the view and location can't be beat. Located on a bluff overlooking the magnificent Oregon Coast in the heart of Nye Beach, it's the perfect place to stay to take in all of Newport. $$–$$$.

Fairhaven Vacation Rentals. Coast Avenue; (888) 523-4179; www.fairhavenvacation rentals.com. If you are traveling with a group or extended family, rent one of these gorgeous Victorian and Cottage-style homes in Nye Beach. Just a few blocks from the beach, shopping, and great restaurants; several have views, hot tubs, and more. $$$.

Greenstone Inn. 729 NW Coast St.; (800) 480-2477; www.greenstone-inn.com. Located in Nye Beach, the newly constructed Earth-friendly Greenstone Inn consists of 20 beautiful new units, all with ocean views, balconies, and fireplaces. The inn benefits from solar-generated electricity and waste-water heat recycling. Choose from studios or 1- and 2-bedroom units, some with kitchenettes. Stairs out front lead directly to the beach. $$–$$$.

Sylvia Beach Hotel. 267 NW Cliff St.; (541) 265-5428; www.sylviabeachhotel.com. Not for everyone, but those who love this place love it with both arms open and a ravishingly loyal happiness. The funky old 4-story hotel could be described as ramshackle, or full of awesome character, depending on your point of view. It's a hotel with a theme, and the theme is books. Each room is decorated to reflect a single author. Sleep with Mark Twain, Agatha Christie, Dr. Seuss, and many more. There is no TV, no Wi-Fi, no telephones, no radio. Relax, read, visit quietly in front of the fireplace in the common library with a spectacular ocean view. Come for romance, come for solitude, come to make new friends. A fabulous breakfast is served each morning with a view of the ocean. Tip—while some rooms are quite expensive, there is a dormitory-style lodging option on the hotel's top floor that's a steal, especially considering it includes breakfast. $–$$$.

west

day trip 01

farm country:
forest grove

forest grove

Forest Grove was born a small farming town, and once produced a significant amount of Oregon's strawberries. Over the years, the city has evolved to a bedroom community for Portland, and the bucolic countryside and small-town quiet has changed significantly. This small city is still a farming town of sorts, but these days the land that surrounds it is more likely to produce Oregon's famous pinot noir than strawberries, corn, and beans.

But especially since the small-farm renaissance of the last five years, a freshly picked, homegrown strawberry can still be found around here, as well as a fresh zucchini, carrot, and apple. The city has encroached on this section of Washington County, but there is still open farmland to be discovered. Wildlife, especially birds, continue to frequent the area, probably hoping for a bite of the same vittles we crave. Visit the surrounding countryside for fresh produce, good old-fashioned pumpkin patches, and a taste of the way things used to be.

Settled in the 1840s, the town was the first established in Washington County and is home to the oldest chartered university in the West, Pacific University. Ten of Forest Grove's buildings are on the National Register of Historic Places and an entire 18-block district represents history with homes dating as far back as 1854. Wandering downtown, visitors can still get a sense of what life was like 100 years ago, when Portland—only 25 miles away—was a true destination. Now Forest Grove is the best of both worlds—rural charm with a few big city accoutrements thrown in.

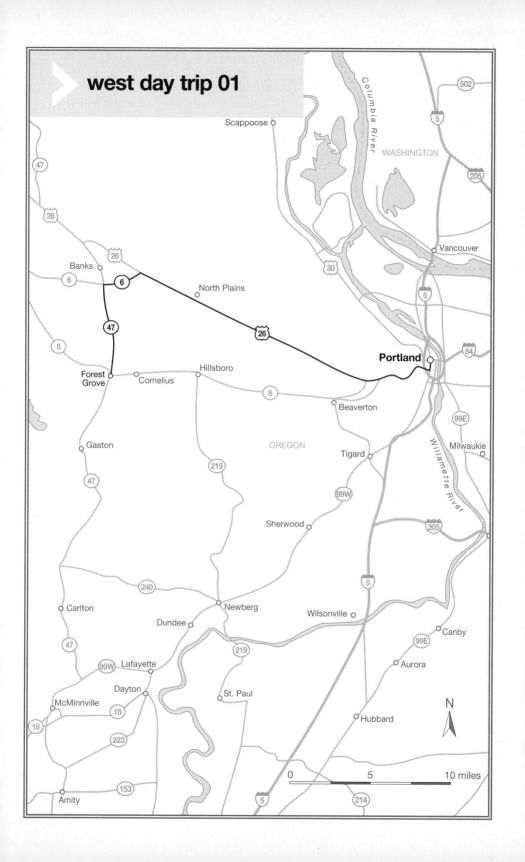

> ## strawberry fields forever
>
> *My mother grew up in Forest Grove. For 40 years, my grandparents ran a hardware store downtown. Some of my mother's fondest childhood memories are of walking directly from school to the store each day, where she would do her homework and help her parents until it was closing time. She also recalls being released from school early, in May instead of June, to go pick Oregon's famous strawberries. The rich soil of the northern Willamette Valley produced oodles of the delicious fruit beginning around mid-May, and the region's schoolchildren temporarily became day-laborers. They were paid by the flat, and went home with sticky fingers. During the 1950s and 1960s, Oregon farmers grew 90 to 100 million pounds of strawberries. Today, that number is closer to 20 million, and Oregon ranks third in the nation in strawberry production—a distant third to Florida and California. Still, many Oregonians—including my mother—would argue that ours are the best.*

getting there

Forest Grove is 25 miles west of Portland. Take US 26 W west out of Portland to merge with OR 6 W. Travel southwest another 2.6 miles and take the OR 47 (Banks, Forest Grove) ramp. Head south on OR 47 and follow signs into Forest Grove.

where to go

Killin Wetland. NW Killin and NW Cedar Canyon Roads, outside of Banks. Killin Wetlands is one of the largest remaining peat soil wetlands in the Willamette Valley and is a haven to wildlife. Its 373 acres harbor an uncommon willow species, Geyer's willow, as well as a breeding population of the state-sensitive red-legged frog. Birding enthusiasts are given the opportunity to see a nice population of breeding American bittern, sora, and Virginia rail. Many species of waterfowl are frequently spotted, too. Breeding plumage and courtship behavior are on stage as early as mid-February through mid-May. The area also attracts many species of migrating shorebirds looking for a rest.

Old Town. www.historicforestgrove.org. The 18-block Clark District is peppered with homes dating as far back as 1854, and several dozen pre-1900. Wander from downtown and soak up the atmosphere—it's pretty hard to get truly lost in a sweet little town like this.

Pacific University. 2043 College Way; (503) 352-6151; www.pacificu.edu. Forest Grove's Pacific University is the oldest chartered university in the West. Originally Tualatin Academy, the school was granted its original charter on September 26, 1849—predating statehood by 10 years, and serving as the first formal act of the territorial government. Pacific's Old College Hall, built in 1850, housed the original academy and is the oldest educational building in the West. Today, Pacific is a comprehensive liberal arts and health-care university with 3,200 students. The campus is beautiful and a great opportunity to see some lovely old architecture and trees. Forest Grove itself was named for a grove of oak trees that still stands on campus. See the website for a guide to trees and more information.

Pumpkin Ridge Golf Course. 12930 NW Old Pumpkin Ridge Rd., North Plains; (503) 647-9977; www.pumpkinridge.com. En route to Banks on US 26 is North Plains, home to Pumpkin Ridge Golf Course, which has repeatedly been named one of the top courses in the state of Oregon. The course opened in the spring of 1992 to rave reviews and quickly became host facility to some of the game's best championships. There are 2 courses: the public course, Witch Hollow, and the private club, Ghost Creek. The course is known for stillness and quiet; just you, your clubs, and 36 holes of championship golf in a truly great setting.

Tree to Tree. 2975 SW Nelson Rd., Gaston; (503) 357-0109; www.treetotreeadventure park.com. This one isn't for everyone, and it kind of doesn't fit with the classy wineries, bucolic farms, and quaint small-town offerings in the rest of this day trip. But if you've been yearning to fly through the tippy tops of trees, here's your chance. Southwest of Forest Grove on Hagg Lake in Scoggins Valley Park is a "playground in the trees" that features aerial ropes courses, zip lines, and tree-top obstacles. Visitors move from platform to platform (tree to tree) via wobbly bridges, tightropes, zip lines, and more. Warning: not for the acrophobic (those fearful of heights).

You-Pick Farms. Grocery stores are great, but sometimes you want to do the work of gathering food from the ground it grew in yourself. Washington County is a great place to find farms of many varieties, several of which allow visitors to pick the fruits and vegetables of their labors. Teach the kids where their food comes from and what it takes to harvest it while enjoying some family time in the great outdoors at these farms.

> **Bays Farms.** 14550 NW Bays Dr., Banks; (503) 324-0261. Bays Farms offers many varieties of produce to hungry Portlanders every summer season, including peaches, plums, nectarines, apples, pears, and kiwis. This is a destination in the winter, too, when you can come and choose a Christmas tree here. Open mid-July to Dec 23.

> **Gordon's Acres.** 48360 NW Narup Rd., 3 miles west of Banks (Take OR 6 to milepost 46, turn north on Cedar Canyon Road, and follow signs 0.7 mile); (503) 901-7971. You-pick, ready-picked, or picked to order blueberries, raspberries, and kotatas. Open 7 a.m. to 6 p.m. daily July through Aug.

> **Jim Dandy Farm Market.** 45770 NW Sunset Hwy.; (503) 324-3954. Jim Dandy's greenhouse opens in early May and features hanging baskets and vegetable plants.

The fruit stand opens around June 1 when local strawberries ripen; other crops include blueberries, blackberries, raspberries, cherries, peaches, apples, pears, and assorted vegetables, including pumpkins, in season.

Wineries (and one Sakery). Some of the Pacific Northwest's best wineries are in the lush hills of Washington County. Try to include at least one in your day trip—not only do these vineyards offer great wine for the taste buds, they are a feast for the other senses, as well. Smell the rich soil, gaze upon the lovely vineyards, enjoy an afternoon at a winery.

Apolloni Vineyards. 14135 NW Timmerman Rd.; (503) 330-5946; www.apolloni .com. Apolloni Vineyards specializes in the production of traditional pinot noir and Italian-style wines. The tasting room is open Fri through Sun, noon to 5 p.m.

David Hill Winery and Vineyards. 46350 NW David Hill Rd.; (877) 992-8545; www.davidhillwinery.com. David Hill Vineyards offers sweeping views of Oregon's Coast Range and tastes of excellent pinot noir, pinot gris, Riesling, chardonnay, and Gewürztraminer from some of the oldest vines in the state. The tasting room is located in a farmhouse that was built in 1883, and the grounds are open for impromptu picnics.

Montinore Estate. 3663 SW Dilley Rd.; (888) 359-5012; www.montinore.com. A family-run winery, Montinore Estate holds high standards in sustainable agriculture and careful craftsmanship. Here you'll find estate-grown and -bottled, balanced pinot noir, pinot gris, Riesling, Gewürztraminer, and Muller-Thurgau wines. The tasting room and gift shop are open daily.

Purple Cow Vineyards. 52720 NW Wilson School Rd.; (503) 330-0991; www .purplecowvineyards.com. At Purple Cow Vineyard, the owner, winemaker, and vineyard manager are all the same person, and only 500 cases of wine are produced per year. This is a unique Oregon winery that specializes in a seamless process from vineyard to bottle. Open Saturday from Valentine's Day through Thanksgiving weekend.

SakéOne. 820 Elm St.; (800) 550-SAKE; www.sakeone.com. How did the the only American-owned and operated saké (or sake) brewery in the world end up in a little farming town in Oregon? It's all about the water. Pure water is crucial to saké, and the Pacific Northwest has it. SakéOne's founders set up shop in Forest Grove, Oregon, at the edge of a rain forest, in 1997. SakéOne brews premium Junmai Ginjo styles in a range of distinct saké profiles for their Momokawa and Moonstone lines. Tours and tastings daily.

Shafer Vineyard Cellars. 6200 NW Gales Creek Rd.; (503) 357-6604; www.shafer vineyardcellars.com. Shafer Vineyard Cellars has been producing estate-grown and bottled wines since 1978. Pinot noir, pinot gris, chardonnay, Riesling, Muller-Thurgau,

Gewürztraminer, sparkling wine, and dessert wines come out of this lovely winery, which boasts a picnic area with a spectacular view. The tasting room is open 11 a.m. to 5 p.m. Thurs through Sun, except in Jan and Feb, when it's open weekends only.

Tualatin Estate Vineyard. 10850 NW Seavey Rd.; (503) 357-5005; www.tualatin estate.com. Wine grapes from Tualatin Estate's 145-acre vineyard have produced world-renowned wines for 28 years, and the winery is now a part of Willamette Valley Vineyards. The tasting room is open Sat and Sun from noon to 5 p.m., Mar through Dec.

where to eat

Izgara Middle Eastern Cuisine. 2036 Main St.; (503) 352-9306. Izgara is in an old building downtown, serves excellent authentic Middle Eastern cuisine, and features belly dancing on Saturday nights. A free salad sampler is served before each meal, and the kebabs, hummus, and mint tea are awesome. Try the shawarma pita or laffah, too. $$.

Maggie's Buns. 2007 21st Ave.; (503) 992-2231; www.maggiesbuns.com. Maggie's Buns has been serving breakfast and lunch to happy people for a long time. From omelets or Maggie's McBagel at breakfast to fresh soups, chicken piccata, Greek orzo salad, and a handful of wraps, you can be sure that something at Maggie's will make your belly happy. Open Mon through Fri 6:30 a.m. to 5:30 p.m. and Sat 7 a.m. to 2 p.m. $–$$.

Pac Thai. 1923 Pacific Ave.; (503) 992-1800. Whether you like your Thai food spicy or sweet, you'll like Pac Thai. Vegetarian and vegan meals are available, and the portions are really good. The Thai ice tea is just right—not too sweet with a great tea flavor. Open for lunch and dinner—take out, too. $$.

Stecchino. 2014 Main St.; (503) 352-9921. This bistro, just opened last year, serves a combination of French and Italian bistro–style cuisine, made from fresh local foods at good prices. Open for lunch Tues through Fri, dinner Tues through Sat. Don't miss the flourless chocolate cake. $$.

where to stay

McMenamins Grand Lodge. 3505 Pacific Ave., (503) 992-9533; www.thegrandlodge .com. Built in 1922 as a Masonic and Eastern Star home, the Grand Lodge is an incredible building that was neglected until the amazing McMenamin brothers came along and renovated it. Reopened in 2000, the Grand Lodge now offers 77 European-style guest rooms, restaurants, small bars, an outdoor soaking pool, wine tasting, a 10-hole disc golf course, Ruby's Spa, and loads of the fantastic, eclectic artwork that McMenamins is known for. The stately columns, winding drive, and epic green lawn (it's truly enormous) beckon, drawing in visitors for what might turn out to be more than they bargained for (Hotel California, anyone?). Dine in the Ironwork Grill or enjoy a casual meal at the Yardhouse Pub. The Doctor's

Office Bar offers pool and a gorgeous antique back bar. Take in a movie in the Compass Room Theater. Get a room—you might be here a while. Restaurants and lodging: $–$$.

Old Recreation Inns. 1721 22nd Ave.; (971) 242-9904; www.oldrecreation.com. This old home built in 1925 is now a bed and breakfast with modern amenities. History remains with original fir floors and moldings, leaded mirrors, and a large furnished porch. Old Recreation is decorated, furnished, and painted with warmth and comfort in mind. $.

day trip 02

west

catch a wave:
tillamook, pacific city

tillamook

Tillamook is known for two things—cheese and fire.

In 1909, a farmer-owned dairy cooperative was established that would lay the ground-work for what would become a nationally recognized dairy products producer. Tillamook Cheese is distributed widely and dairy farming continues to be a staple of the Tillamook County economy.

Between 1933 and 1951, a series of forest fires swept through the Northern Oregon Coast Range near Tillamook, ultimately destroying 355,000 acres of old-growth timber. The fires not only caused huge setbacks to the logging industry (during the Great Depression, no less), but also laid waste to large swathes of forest along the highway from Portland, making the devastation apparent to travelers and tourists who made trips to the county. The Tillamook Burn, as the series of fires are known, are still the stuff of legend to Oregonians.

Today, the forest has recovered and Tillamook Cheese continues to flourish. Drivers pass through lovely trees to descend into the Tillamook Valley, where dairy farms dot the landscape. The city itself isn't considered one of the Oregon Coast's hotter destinations, but continues to thrive as a pleasant small town, bordered by the ocean on one side and hundreds of cows on the other.

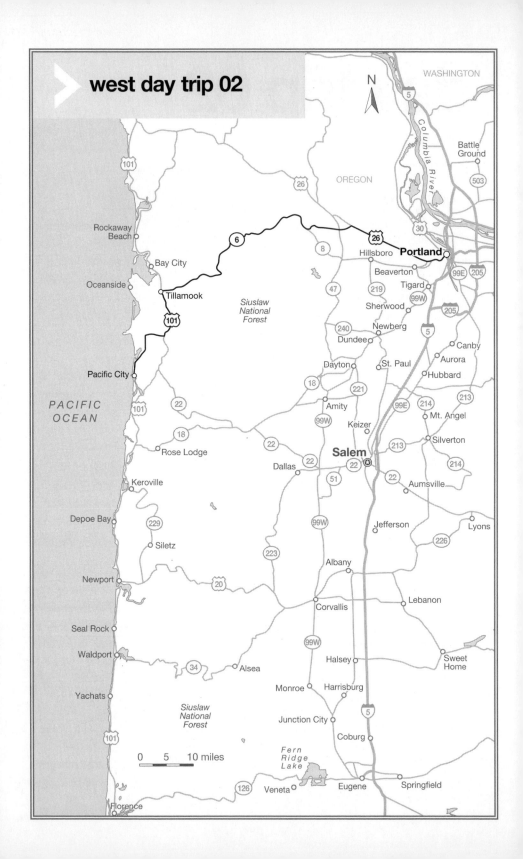

west day trip 02

getting there

Take US 26 W/OR 26 W out of Portland and continue 20 miles to the junction with OR 6 W. Follow OR 6 W toward Banks/Forest Grove/Tillamook. Continue for 51 miles, at which point OR 6 W will dead-end into US 101, and the City of Tillamook.

where to go

Blue Heron French Cheese Company. 2001 Blue Heron Dr.; (503) 842-8281; www.blue heronoregon.com. Celebrating more than a quarter century on the Oregon Coast, the Blue Heron French Cheese Company is known for their famous brie. The shop includes a deli, unique gifts, and gourmet food. The kids will love the petting farm. Open 7 days a week: 8 a.m. to 8 p.m. in the summer; 9 a.m. to 5 p.m. in the winter.

Cape Meares Lighthouse and State Scenic Viewpoint. Off US 101 10 miles west of Tillamook; (800) 551-6949; www.capemeareslighthouse.org. Cape Meares is the site of the Cape Meares Lighthouse, an informational kiosk, viewpoints, the Three Arch Rocks National Wildlife Refuge, nature trails, and the Oregon Heritage Tree known as the Octopus Tree. From its headland, visitors get an excellent view of one of the largest colonies of nesting common murres on the continent. Bald eagles and a peregrine falcon have also been seen here. Cape Meares has more than 3 miles of hiking trails—one winds through old-growth spruce trees, including Oregon's largest Sitka spruce. In winter and spring, the cape can be a great place from which to spot whales. The park is open daily, throughout the year, from 7 a.m. to dusk with no day use fee. The Cape Meares Lighthouse was constructed in 1889 and is the shortest lighthouse in Oregon. It is open daily Apr through Oct from 11 a.m. to 4 p.m. Free admission.

The Tillamook Air Museum. 6030 Hangar Rd.; (503) 842-1130; www.tillamookair .com. One of the finest collections of World War II war birds, including a P-38 Lightning,

water, water everywhere

Tillamook is an Indian word meaning "land of many waters," and isn't that the truth. This place is locally famous for sogginess. The pastures just west of Tillamook become so waterlogged during particularly wet winter storms that OR 6 can sometimes be closed. If you see cows wading, keep your eyes on the road to avoid turning your car into an aquamobile. In truly wet weather, call ahead or check the Oregon Department of Transportation's www.tripcheck.com to access road condition information.

F4U-Corsair, P51-Mustang, PBY Catalina, and SBD Dauntless dive bomber, is right here in Tillamook. The war planes and an exhibit hall featuring rare historical wartime and aviation artifacts are all housed in a rare World War II blimp hangar, the largest wooden structure in the world. Open to the public daily 9 a.m. to 5 p.m. except for Thanksgiving and Christmas.

Tillamook Cheese Visitor Center. 4175 US 101 N; (503) 815-1300; www.tillamookcheese .com. Back in 1909, a farmer-owned collective of dairy farms was founded in the Tillamook Valley to ensure that locally produced cheese was the best it could be. The Tillamook County Creamery Association eventually expanded to include all of the small, independent cheese plants in the county, and today, the association is made up of approximately 110 dairy families. They collectively own Tillamook Cheese. At the visitor's center, see cheesemakers at work, learn about the cheesemaking process, and best of all, taste award-winning cheeses and 38 flavors of ice cream. Open daily 8 a.m. to 6 p.m. Labor Day through mid-June; 8 a.m. to 8 p.m. mid-June through Labor Day. Closed Thanksgiving and Christmas.

The Tillamook County Pioneer Museum. 2106 Second St.; (503) 842-4553; www.tcpm .org. From the Tillamook Indians to Captain Gray's 1788 voyage into Tillamook Bay, the Tillamook coast has a fascinating history. Open Tues through Sun from 10 a.m. to 4 p.m.

The Tillamook Forest Center. Located 20 minutes east of Tillamook on OR 6; (503) 815-6800; www.tillamookforestcenter.org. Located at the heart of the Tillamook State Forest, the region's newest interpretive and educational center showcases the legacy of the historic Tillamook Burn through a wealth of innovative exhibits, programs, and interactive displays. Free admission. Open 7 days a week from 10 a.m. to 6 p.m. during summer season; open from 10 a.m. to 4 p.m. Wed through Sun in winter.

where to eat

Alice's Country House. 17345 Wilson River Hwy.; (503) 842-7927. This little homey place is quaint, cozy, and tucked away in the beautiful rural coastal woods. Home-cooked burgers, pie, milk shakes, Philly cheese steaks, and prime rib please guests. There's nothing fancy here but the food will fill you up nicely on a rainy day. $.

The Farmhouse Café at the Tillamook Cheese Visitor Center. 4175 US 101 N; (503) 815-1300; www.tillamookcheese.com. The Visitor's Center houses a restaurant, the Farmhouse Café, that's a local's favorite lunch spot. What's on the menu? Grilled cheese sandwiches, omelets with cheese, and burgers with cheese, of course. Breakfast and lunch are served here to tourists and local regulars, both of whom leave happy. $.

Roseanna's Café. 1490 Pacific Ave., Oceanside; (503) 842-7351; www.roseannascafe .com. Roseanna's is one of the most delicious restaurants on the coast, in one of the most gorgeous small communities. On the menu you'll find chowder, sandwiches, a variety of fishes, prawns, scallops, oysters, chicken, steak, pastas, quiche, wine, domestic beers, and microbrews. Last but not least, homemade desserts—pies, cakes, puddings, cobblers, ice cream, and more. Open 7 days a week for lunch and dinner. $–$$.

where to stay

Thyme and Tide Bed & Breakfast. 5015 Grand Ave., Oceanside; (503) 842-5527; www .thyme-and-tide.com. Only 2 bedrooms at this tiny bed and breakfast, but they are beautiful, and Oceanside is a lovely, small alternative to Tillamook. A hearty breakfast will get you going for your day spent walking the beach or hiking the hills. $$.

pacific city

Imagine this as you drive to Pacific City—early visitors came by buckboard and horseback from the Willamette Valley, so excited by the prospect of the beach that they were willing to travel two days over a mountain pass to achieve a glimpse of the sea and hold sand in their own hands. Many of these early travelers had come from the Midwest on the Oregon Trail, and had never seen the ocean. Imagine their reaction when they crested that last hill.

Campgrounds and lodgings to accommodate these vacationers were some of Pacific City's first business endeavors. The other primary economical focus was fish. Salmon used to swim thick as seaweed in Nestucca Bay, at Pacific City. A commercial cannery was built on the east side of the bay in 1886, where it thrived for many years, canning and shipping 12,000 cans of salmon a year. Fishing, logging, and eventually dairy farming became the primary occupations in the Nestucca Valley.

Today, the fishing is still pretty good, at least recreationally, and plenty of travelers come to visit—but, thankfully, the journey is much easier.

getting there

From Tillamook, head south on OR 101/US 101 S/Oregon Coast Highway for 11 miles. Turn right onto Sandlake Road and follow for 10.7 miles. Take a left on Ferry Road and follow it 2.3 miles into Pacific City.

where to go

Dory Fishing. Pacific City is the only place on the Oregon Coast that is home to a large dory fleet. Visitors to Pacific City's beach can't miss the flat-bottomed boats and their trademark manner of taking off and landing—right through the waves onto the sand. Commercial dory fishermen have been fishing for salmon out of Pacific City since the early 1900s, and were the area's primary fishermen in the 1960s and 70s. Today the fleet is more modest but still impressive to watch, the salmon still taste great, and all dory fish are still caught with a hook and line. Try out salmon fishing from a dory with one of these outfitters.

Haystack Fishing. (503) 965-7555; www.haystackfishing.com. Haystack Fishing is a licensed, beach launched, dory fishing charter that offers ocean fishing for salmon, bottom fish, halibut, and crab. Captain Joe Hay leads the way! From June through Sept only due to ocean conditions.

Eagle Charters. (503) 801-3464. Captain Dave Stiles leads beach-launched dory fishing trips.

Surfing. Pacific City is one of the best places to surf on the Oregon Coast, and is especially good for beginners (I surfed for the first time there, and was pummeled by the waves in only the gentlest fashion). The break off Cape Kiwanda, on good days, provides a nice rolling surf. On bad days, well, kick back and watch the storm instead. For rentals and lessons, visit the Kiwanda Surf Co. (see below, in Where to Shop).

Oregon Hang Gliding. (541) 913-1339; www.oregonhanggliding.com. Pacific City, Oregon, and Cape Kiwanda have been central to the development of the sport of hang gliding in Oregon. Consistent and smooth winds have brought enthusiasts to this beach for nearly 40 years. If you just can't stand the thought of keeping your feet on the ground, call Oregon Hang Gliding for a lesson and take to the skies.

Basket Case Wine. 6424 Pacific Ave., Unit B; (503) 932-1744; www.basketcasewine .com. Basket Case Wines was started by Chenin and Sean Carlton in 2006, who hoped to radically change the wine business, or at least one tiny corner of it. At Basket Case, it's not about exclusivity, arrogance, elitism, or pomposity—it's about having fun. Offering a cabernet sauvignon and a syrah.

it's a secret

"You aren't going to tell anyone about Pacific City, are you?" I got this response more than once when I confided to friends that I was writing a travel guide book. Still a bit of a hidden gem, Pacific City holds a special place in the hearts of many Oregonians. Folks who've been around Pacific City for a long time say it's changed significantly, but compared to other coastal towns, it remains relatively undeveloped—an unincorporated community with no mayor or city council, awesome beaches, great restaurants, and a very sociable attitude. Enjoy this friendly, beautiful town . . . but Shhhh . . .

where to shop

Kiwanda Surf Co. 6305 Pacific Ave.; (503) 965-3627; www.kiwandasurfco.com. Kiwanda Surf Co. is the Pacific City surfer's hub. This funky little shop looks just like a North Shore surfing joint, and offers an excellent line of quality surfboards, surf apparel, and rental equipment including surfboards, body boards, skim boards, wetsuits, hoodies, booties, and fins. You can also rent a kayak here and set forth on the Nestucca River.

where to eat

Delicate Palate. 35280 Brooten Rd.; (503) 965-6464; www.delicatepalate.com. Fine dining, Pacific City style. This AAA three-diamond-rated bistro offers a tasty bar menu as well as fine dining. Feast on Dungeness crab cakes, braised baby back ribs, tomato soup in puff pastry, Fuji apple and gorgonzola salad, pan seared wild salmon, herb crusted halibut, and grilled natural New York steak. $$$.

Grateful Bread Restaurant Bakery. 34805 Brooten Rd.; (503) 965-7337. The stuff of legends. First known for their fresh bread and pastries, Grateful Bread is now famous for their great breakfasts, lunches, and pizzas. You will leave this lovely, well-lit establishment stuffed and happy. Open Thurs through Mon 8 a.m. to 4 p.m. Bakery open until 5 p.m. $–$$.

Pelican Pub and Brewery. 33180 Cape Kiwanda Dr.; (503) 965-7007; www.pelican brewery.com. Situated practically right on the beach, Pelican Pub and Brewery is a great place to hang out and watch the surf, eat great food, and drink award-winning microbrews. Awarded Large Brewpub of the Year at the Great American Beer Festival in 2006, Pelican Pub is the place to be in Pacific City. Open Sun through Thurs 8 a.m. till 10 p.m., Fri and Sat 8 a.m. to 11 p.m. $$.

where to stay

Cape Kiwanda RV Resort. 33305 Cape Kiwanda Dr.; (503) 965-6230; www.capekiwanda rvresort.com. In keeping with the casual, beachfront, surfer atmosphere, many visitors to Pacific City simply bring their RV, or even a tent. In this case, the Cape Kiwanda RV Resort is the place to be. Right across from the beach, it offers not only easy access to the surf, but also an exercise room, heated pool and spa, and a full market stocking fresh seafood, clothing, souvenirs, espresso, and fresh-scooped Tillamook ice cream. How many RV parks can say that? The park is also an excellent place to set your kid loose on a bicycle to lap the campground, make new like-minded friends, and pick up some surfing tips. $.

Inn at Cape Kiwanda. 33105 Cape Kiwanda Dr.; (503) 965-7001; www.innatcapekiwanda .com. Boasting an ocean view from every room and cozy gas fireplaces, the Inn at Cape Kiwanda is the perfect quiet, relaxing, and romantic getaway in Pacific City. Downstairs at this multi-storied hotel you'll find restaurants and shops. From the room, views of Haystack

Rock, cozy gas fireplaces, and plush pillow-top beds with feather pillows will leave you satisfied. $$–$$$.

The Inn at Pacific City. 35215 Brooten Rd.; (888) 722-2489; www.innatpacificcity.com. A self-described "mom and pop operation," this inn is a nice inexpensive alternative to the fancier resorts. The 16-unit motor lodge is conveniently located within walking distance to shopping and dining. It's comfortable, affordable, and close to the action. $.

day trip 03

west

life's a beach:
cannon beach, manzanita

cannon beach

Cannon Beach is Oregon's resident artist. Galleries abound, in each a plethora of eclectic artistic talent. Cannon Beach offers all of the other things a coastal town should, too—gorgeous beach walks, tasty fish and chips, kites for sale, and rooms with a view. But here, it all comes with a bit more class.

As for the cannons of Cannon Beach, you can catch a glimpse of them, too. In 1846, the US Naval schooner *Shark*, part of a surveying fleet under Lieutenant Neil M. Howison, arrived off the mouth of the Columbia River. The ship landed in Astoria, and after a month, disembarked again only to encounter troubled waters and run up against rocks. The captain ordered the jettison of all cannons, and ultimately several washed ashore south of Cannon Beach at Arch Cape. One is installed at the Cannon Beach History Center.

Interestingly, two more cannons were uncovered very recently. In February 2008 after an especially low tide, the sand had been washed away from the beach at Arch Cape to reveal two cannons, presumably also from the wreck of the *Shark*. History has a way of staking its claim on even the most modern and stylish city.

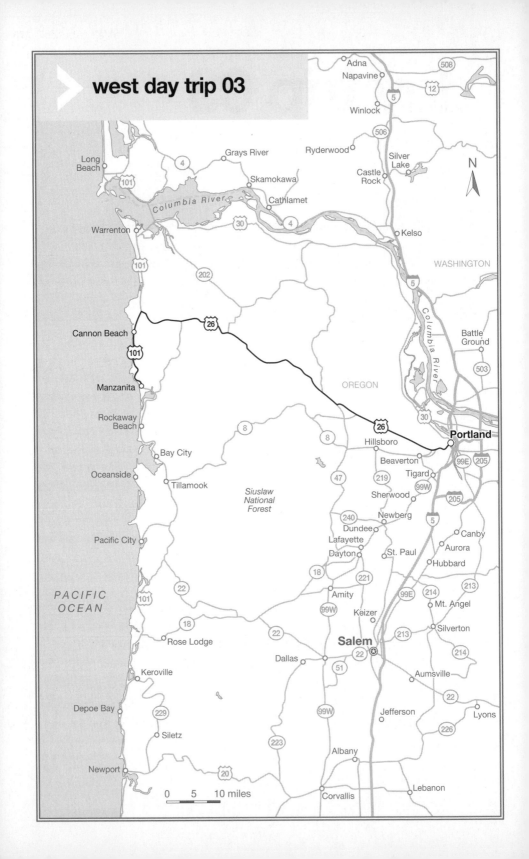

getting there

From Portland, take OR 26/US 26 W west 73 miles until you reach OR 101/US 101 S/ Oregon Coast Highway. Turn south on US 101 and proceed 4.3 miles to the Cannon Beach exits. Follow signs into town.

where to go

Cannon Beach History Center. 1387 South Spruce St.; (503) 436-9301; www.cbhistory .org. Before and after the cannons, Cannon Beach history has been pretty interesting stuff. This museum and history center features a Native American longhouse, a rotating quilt show, concerts, lectures, and more. There's also information to be found here about the History Center's fabulous, well-marked historical walking tour of Cannon Beach, which focuses on buildings in the downtown area. Open Wed through Mon, 1 to 5 p.m. Free admission.

Ecola State Park. Off US 101, 2 miles north of Cannon Beach; www.oregonstateparks .org/park_188. Here's your "dramatic coastal views" destination. A paved road leads from Cannon Beach through the thick forest of this headland. After winding through Sitka spruce, visitors emerge to a gorgeous view of the Pacific Ocean. Hiking, picnicking, and explora- tion of the new Clatsop Loop Interpretive Trail are all fun things to do at Ecola State Park. Surfers enjoy Indian Beach and tide pool aficionados do, too. Migrating whales pass by in winter and spring, and wildlife and birds are here year-round. Daily use $5; yearly use $30.

Haystack Rock. www.cannon-beach.net/haystack. Haystack Rock is a 235-foot tall monolith (or sea stack) rock formation, the third-tallest such intertidal structure in the world.

haystack rock trivia

- *Haystack Rock is a common name for geographical features of similar shape and size to the one in Cannon Beach, and there are several others even in Oregon. One is off the coast of Pacific City, next to Cape Kiwanda, and the other is in Coos County near Bandon.*

- *Cannon Beach's Haystack Rock is accompanied by two smaller rocks. Most people call them the Needles, but I've also heard a rumor that to some others, the tall, elegant one will always be known as Sven, and the shorter, clumsy one as Lori.*

- *Haystack Rock has been featured in many movies, including* The Goonies, Kin- dergarten Cop, *and* Sometimes a Great Notion.

That means it can be reached by land on foot during low tides. Get a tidal table to plan your trip to the popular tourist destination, on the beach at Cannon Beach. Its tide pools are home to many animals, including starfish, sea anemone, crabs, limpets, and sea slugs. The rock is also home to many sea birds, including terns and puffins. During the summer, volunteer interpreters are on the beach at low tide. Words of warning—the sea life that Haystack shelters is fragile. Treat it with care and do not step on sea life. Stay on sand and bare rocks only. And many people each year become temporarily trapped on Haystack Rock when high tide returns, making them unpopular with the local authorities. Pay attention to the tide.

Hug Point State Recreation Area. Four miles south of Cannon Beach on US 101. Before the highway was built, stagecoaches used to run along the beach here. North of the parking area at this site you can still walk along the original trail carved into the point. Look for the hidden waterfall around a small headland. The view north from Hug Point includes Silver Point Rock and Cannon Beach's famous offshore icon, Haystack Rock.

"Terrible Tilly" Tillamook Rock Lighthouse. Located 1 mile off shore of Tillamook Head, which is just a few miles north of Cannon Beach. You can't actually visit Terrible Tilly, but you can check her out from the shore—which might be preferable anyway. The lighthouse is nicknamed Terrible Tilly because of its location on a rock in the middle of the tumultuous Pacific Ocean. The now-decommissioned lighthouse was built in 1881 by the US Army Corps of Engineers, and lighthouse keepers actually had to be hoisted onto the rock with a derrick. The lighthouse was shut down in 1957 when it had become the most expensive US lighthouse to operate. Access today is by helicopter only. Enjoy Tilly from safe vantage points, Cannon Beach or Ecola State Park.

where to shop

Art Galleries. A visitor could make an entire day trip out of just Cannon Beach's art galleries. We couldn't list them all here, but this is a start. Bring your favorite art critic and your credit cards. Call for hours—many coastal establishments close up shop for a couple of mid-week days in the winter off-season.

Bronze Coast Gallery. 224 N Hemlock St., Suite 2; (503) 436-1055; www.bronze coastgallery.com. Specializing in limited edition bronze sculptures, the Bronze Coast Gallery has been in Cannon Beach for more than 17 years and has become one of the Oregon Coast's premiere fine art galleries. The gallery also spotlights original painting, photography, and gicleé reproductions, and features more than 30 award-winning regional, national, and international artists.

DragonFire Studio and Gallery. 123 S Hemlock St., Suite 106; (503) 436-1533; www.dragonfirestudio.com. DragonFire offers surprisingly affordable original art by local, regional, and national artists in media ranging from paint to fiber to metal.

beach art

For nearly 50 years, Cannon Beach has hosted a sandcastle building contest in June. Everyone is invited to enter, from 6-years-and-under "Sand Fleas" to more experienced "Sand Masters." But given that Cannon Beach is repeatedly voted one of the best beaches in the United States, it's worth coming on down to the sand and crafting a masterpiece out of sand any old time. See www.cannonbeach.org for more information.

Seasonal 2- and 3-day workshops in everything from portrait composition to watercolors are offered, and live music occasionally accompanies the art.

George Vetter Foto Art. 231 N Hemlock St.; (503) 739-1415; www.georgevetter fotoart.com. George Vetter specializes in color and texture-rich photography that captures the essence and beauty of Cannon Beach. Gicleé prints on canvas or paper.

IceFire Glassworks. 116 East Gower St.; (888) 423-3545; www.cbgallerygroup .com/icefire. Glass art is a particular favorite of mine. It seems to fit even better at the beach, where the sparkle of the sea complements the beauty of blown and sculpted glass works, here by artists James Kingwell, Suzanne Kindland, Michelle Kaptur, and Mark Gordon.

Modern Villa. 224 N Hemlock St.; (503) 436-2428; www.modernvillagallery.com. Paintings by David Marshall, Sarah Goodnough, Ford Smith, Anne Packard, and others brighten the walls of this contemporary gallery, and maybe your house next.

Primary Elements Gallery. 172 N Hemlock St.; (503) 436-0220; www.primary elementsgallery.com. Photography, wall art, sculpture, glass—the art at Primary Elements is inspired by nature and elemental forms.

White Bird Gallery. 251 N Hemlock St.; (503) 436-2681; www.whitebirdgallery.com. One of the first galleries to fully incorporate fine art with fine craft, White Bird has been making a mark on the Cannon Beach art scene since 1971.

Center Diamond. 1065 S Hemlock St.; (503) 436-0833; www.centerdiamond.com. A favorite with quilters and textile artists, Center Diamond offers special contemporary fabrics including a large selection of batiks, Asian, and seashore-related designs.

Dena's Shop on the Corner. 123 S Hemlock St., Suite 101; (503) 436-1275; www .denasshop.com. Higher-end contemporary women's clothing in a charming atmosphere. You'll find the brands Kut From The Kloth, Testimony, Allen Allen, 3 Dots, Johnny Was, Not

Your Daughters Jeans, and Miss Me. Open Mon through Sat 10 a.m. to 6 p.m. and Sun 10 a.m. to 5 p.m.

Found. 1287 S Hemlock St.; (503) 436-1812. A great mix of antiques, repurposed objects, cool artisan jewelry, artwork, stained glass, furniture, and table top finds. Found's finds run with a beachy theme—this is the place to find something to decorate your beach house or remind you of your beach vacation once you get back home.

La Luna Loca. 107 N Hemlock St.; (503) 436-0774; www.lalunaloca.com. The moon may or may not be crazy, but you'd be not to stop in and see La Luna Loca's handcrafts and fair trade items. Artisan-made clothing, sarongs, jewelry, and decor beat the rhythm of distant lands.

Maggie and Henry. 170 N Hemlock St.; (503) 436-1718; www.maggieandhenry.com. Henry's used to be a small imprinted sportswear store. Maggie's specialized in casual women's fashion. Then Maggie and Henry got married. Maggie and Henry is a blend of the two original stores, providing casual comfort for both women and men.

where to eat

Driftwood Inn Restaurant and Lounge. 179 N Hemlock St.; (503) 436-2439; www.drift woodcannonbeach.com. Locals' favorite for seafood and steaks for 60 years. The exterior has a Bavarian flavor, and a new outdoor patio has become prime real estate for happy diners, especially on sunny summer afternoons. Try the salmon, filet mignon, or steamed clams. $$–$$$.

EVOO Cooking School. 188 S Hemlock St.; (503) 436-8555; www.evoo.biz. Not your run-of-the-mill dinner experience, EVOO is like purchasing a ticket to a live show—one at which you learn something and are fed a delicious dinner. At EVOO (named for a frequently used ingredient, extra virgin olive oil), guests gather around the chef's kitchen-bar and watch him or her prepare three full meal courses paired with three wines, followed by a great dessert. A lively discussion about food and wine comes with the experience, too. This place is not to be missed and has become a full fledged destination! See website for class offerings and availability. $$$.

JP's. 240 N Hemlock St.; (503) 436-0908; www.jpsatcannonbeach.com. JP's website says it best: "[Chef] Bill loves to cook. He calls himself a food hacker. He takes tradition and builds on it without getting weird about it." JP's crew prides themselves on serving real food, artfully prepared, with all the color and flavor it was meant to have. Children's and gluten-free menus available. $$$.

Lush Wine Bar. 1235 S Hemlock St.; (503) 436-8500; www.lushwinebar.com. Relaxed, friendly, comforting, delicious, and fun—just like the beach. A modest-sized menu serves delicious small bites and salads, and the wine list offers just enough variety to please about everyone—even beer drinkers. Open Tues through Sat, but hours vary seasonally. $–$$.

Newman's at 988. 988 S Hemlock St.; (503) 436-1151; www.newmansat988.com. Newman's at 988 serves classic French/Italian cuisine with a focus in the Piedmont and Genoa areas of Italy. Newman's at 988 serves an à la carte menu as well as a chef's prix fixe menu that changes nightly. Chef Newman uses the finest, freshest ingredients the North Coast has to offer and serves them in an intimate dining atmosphere enhanced by the music of legendary singers such as Frank Sinatra and Tony Bennett. Open daily in summer, Tues through Sun after Oct 15, 5:30 to 9 p.m. $$$.

Sweet Basil's Café. 271 N Hemlock St.; (503) 436-1539; www.cafesweetbasils.com. Chef John Sowa conceived Sweet Basil's as a change in his own lifestyle and diet, after cooking Cajun food for years. We all get to benefit from his "fork in the road." Natural, organic, and wild ingredients go into healthy foods that still excite the palate. A nice selection of vegetarian and vegan choices as well as seafood, poultry, and pork dishes by way of salads, cold and hot sandwiches, wraps, panini, and fusion dishes all tickle the taste buds. Open for lunch; a recently added wine bar is open evenings and serves tapas. $–$$.

where to stay

Blue Gull Inn. 487 S Hemlock St.; (503) 436-2714; www.haystacklodgings.com. Cannon Beach's hacienda by the sea, the Blue Gull, brings a little Mexico to Cannon Beach. Each cottage has handcrafted wooded furniture made in the Blue Gull's own woodshop, and is located around a central courtyard with a Spanish-style fountain. $–$$.

The Lodges at Cannon Beach. 132 E Surfcrest Ave.; (503) 440-6310; www.lodgesatcb hotel.com. The Lodges are beautiful new, fully furnished Cannon Beach townhomes with state-of-the-art kitchens, great rooms, and open floor plans. Units with 2 or 3 bedrooms accommodate up to 6 adults; furnishings are warm, cozy, and comfortable. $$$.

The Ocean Lodge. 2864 S Pacific St.; (503) 436-2241; www.theoceanlodge.com. One of the loveliest and most hospitable inns on the whole coast. With hints of a 1940s beach resort, the Ocean Lodge is great place for simple family fun and nostalgic pleasure. Amenities like a library of games and books on site and a cookie jar aim to please all generations. $$–$$$.

Sea Sprite. 280 Nebesna; (866) 828-1050; www.seasprite.com. Three great locations— Sea Sprite at Haystack Rock, Sea Sprite on the Estuary, and Sea Sprite Retreat—with one great sense of beachside charm. Sea Sprite prides themselves on creating lodgings with unique personalities. Each place is special with lovely little suites and great views. $$–$$$.

The Stephanie Inn. 2740 S Pacific St.; (800) 633-3466; www.stephanie-inn.com. The Stephanie Inn is widely known in Oregon for luxury and romance. With views of majestic

Haystack Rock, the Pacific Ocean, and the lovely Oregon Coast Range, the oceanfront Stephanie Inn combines the charm and casual elegance of a New England country inn with the sophistication of a boutique resort hotel. The four-star Stephanie Inn Dining Room serves a complimentary breakfast buffet each morning, and the chef prepares a four-course dinner nightly, which features the freshest in seasonal Northwest ingredients. $$–$$$.

manzanita

Manzanita is Cannon Beach's sister—another artsy town with an impeccable beach and oodles of wood-shaked buildings selling beach-friendly items to happy coastal visitors. But Manzanita is just a little bit smaller and a little bit mellower, and as a result, you, day tripper, might just feel a little bit more relaxed and comfortable. Manzanita is the sort of place that causes visitors to sink into the atmosphere so deeply they don't want to leave.

Nearly everything shop- and service-wise in Manzanita is located on Laneda Avenue, the town's main business street. It leads directly to the sea and a wide, flat beach just begging for a stroll. You'll see examples of the town's namesake plant on Laneda, too—look for clumps of small, shiny green leaves.

getting there

Manzanita is 13.7 miles south of Cannon Beach on US 101.

where to go

Nehalem State Park. Three miles south of Cannon Beach on US 101; www.oregonstate parks.org/park_201. Known for 900 acres of forest trails and awesome vistas, Nehalem State Park offers camping, horseback riding, beachcombing, crabbing, and fishing. RV and tent campgrounds, yurts, a horse camp with corrals, airstrip with fly-in camping, and a hiker-biker camp give plenty of overnight options. Take a short walk over the dunes to the beach and watch the sun set over the ocean, in the shadow of Neah-Kah-Nie Mountain.

Oregon Beach Rides. Between Nehalem and Manzanita on US 101; (971)-237-6653; www.oregonbeachrides.com. Did you know that horse hooves squeak when they hit the sand? Come and find out with a horseback ride on the beach. One-hour, two-hour, half-day, and full-day rides are offered right on the beach. Cost ranges from $95 to $400.

Oswald West State Park. Five miles north of Manzanita; www.oregonstateparks.org/park_ 195. A favorite destination for wildlife viewing, tide pooling, and surfing. The beach is a quarter-mile walk from US 101 and is nestled in a cove that provides you with a feeling of total privacy. Several different trails lead to the beach and the Cape Falcon overlook or to the Oregon Coast Trail. Surrounded by the mountains, the beach at Oswald West offers great views and lovely picnic sites.

where to shop

Great Northern Garlic Company. 868 Laneda Ave.; (503) 368-7700. Fear garlic? Don't fear the Great Northern Garlic Company. There's much more here than the famed cloves. Good selection of wine, beer, cheese, snacks, gifts, local art, Northwest wine, locally made bread, cheese, and lots more.

Manzanita Bikes and Boards. 170 Laneda Ave.; (503) 368-3337; www.manzanitabikes andboards.com. Cycle rentals, bike rentals, surf rentals, a retail store with boogie boards, skim boards, bike-related items, beach toys, kites, footwear and headwear, sunglasses, and watches. Whew! Rental season Mar through Oct.

Manzanita Grocery and Deli. 193 Laneda Ave.; (503) 368-5362; www.manzanitadeli .com. This is one of those fun groceries where you can buy staple food items, fine wine, or a great deli sandwich and rent a movie all in one stop. A 10 percent senior discount is offered every Tues. Open 7 days a week.

Nehalem Bay Winery. 34965 OR 53, Nehalem; (503) 368-9463; www.nehalembaywinery .com. There aren't a whole lot of wineries on the Oregon Coast—most are inland in the valley. Vintner Ray Shackelford has been making wines here at the ocean for 36 years. Try his traditional pinot noir or innovative Valley Peach varietals.

Unfurl. 447 Laneda Ave., Unit 3; (503) 368-8316. Natural and eco-clothing for the hippie and the yuppie alike. Men's and women's clothing, shoes, accessories, and the like, all very fashion-forward. You'll find lots of eco-fiber clothing and planet friendly accessories for baby and child. Open 7 days a week.

where to eat

Bread and Ocean. 154 Laneda Ave.; (503) 368-5823; www.breadandocean.com. A fantastic bakery, take-out, and weekend dinner restaurant that serves fresh-baked pastries, hot-from-the-oven bread, homemade soups, and creative fresh dinners. Open Wed through Sat for breakfast and lunch, Fri through Sun for dinner. No credit cards. $–$$$.

San Dune Pub. 127 Laneda Ave.; (503) 368-5080; www.sandunepub.com. A local's favorite, this pub and restaurant offers sandwiches and seafood alongside a wide selection of domestic and imported beers. Warm your bones next to their big stone fireplace and have your favorite drink from the full-service bar. On the weekends, dance to live music. In the summer, enjoy the patio with bistro tables and market umbrellas. Closed Monday. $–$$.

Vino. 387 D Laneda Ave.; (503) 368-8466. Break away from the usual beach fare at this wonderful little place, which is great for whiling away the evening, savoring something small to eat while sipping fabulous wines. It's a bit hidden—don't let the nondescript exterior fool you. Specials like the chicken pot pie will warm your bones. $$.

where to stay

The Inn at Manzanita. 67 Laneda Ave.; (503) 368-6754; www.innatmanzanita.com. A tranquil spot for a romantic weekend, this inn is ensconced in coastal pine and spruce in an open coastal garden. Thirteen rooms each have Jacuzzi tubs, fuzzy robes, fireplaces, wet bars, down comforters, and private decks. $$.

Spindrift Inn. 114 Laneda Ave.; (503) 368-1001; www.spindrift-inn.com. Built in 1946, Spindrift Inn still retains quaint charm and cozy appeal with beachy, comfortable decor. Affordable rooms open onto a private inner flower garden, where you can relax away from the bustle outside. Quilted bedspreads and kitchenettes make this place cozy and convenient. $–$$.

northwest

day trip 01

northwest

holiday by the sea:
seaside

seaside

Seaside has been the Northwest's beach playground for 150 years. Even back when settlers had barely arrived in the Willamette Valley and hardly recovered from their journey on the Oregon Trail, some were drawn the final 100 miles over the Coast Range to experience the breathtaking beauty of the Oregon coast. Even the fact that there were no roads didn't daunt these early tourists—vacationers came by water down the Columbia to Astoria and then traveled by stagecoach to the beach. The first guest house opened in Seaside in 1850, and a tourist town was born.

Back then, not surprisingly, Seaside beach vacations were a luxury primarily available to the prosperous. Around the turn of the century, the wealthy and fashionable alone made the trip to Seaside, and when they did, they stayed in elegant comfort.

Eventually, roads went in, more people adventured to the ocean, and services began to pop up for the common family. Today, Seaside continues to be one of the most visited places on the Oregon Coast, and is also considered one of the most accessible. Everything is within walking distance and most places are wheelchair accessible, making it easy for all to explore. Visitors can still choose pricey accommodations, but there are plenty of more affordable options available, too. Seaside is the rare Oregon Coast city with amenities more common to east coast beach towns, including a promenade, carousel, and arcade. In the summer, the streets are packed with families carrying bags of saltwater taffy and ice cream cones, waiting for their turn at the go-carts.

northwest day trip 01

Of course, the amenities that brought visitors here in the first place are still there—the beach and the ocean. For those who require no more than fresh air and sand in their toes for entertainment, Seaside is still a great place to visit.

getting there

Take US 26 W west out of Portland. Travel 74 miles to merge with US 101 N/Oregon Coast Highway, traveling north towards Seaside/Astoria. Seaside is 4 miles north of this intersection on US 101 N.

where to go

Arcades. When it rains, Seaside tourists head indoors. In that case, there are a few options—eat, shop, or hit one of the arcades. These two are very popular destinations, rain or shine. Both advertise their hours the same way—"open whenever there is a crowd."

Funland Entertainment Center. 201 Broadway; (503) 738-7361. Just about every video and arcade game you can hope for is here, and then some.

Interstate Amusement Co. 110 Broadway; (503) 738-5540; www.shopseaside .com. Bumper cars, tilt-a-whirl, and miniature golf alongside classic arcade games. The snack bar serves "pronto pup" hot dogs, slushies, soft serve ice cream cones, chips, and other snacks.

Camp 18 Museum and Restaurant. 42362 US 26, Elsie; (800) 874-1810; www.camp18 restaurant.com. On the highway between Portland and the coast is this huge facility—part museum, part restaurant. This massive wood building includes an 85-foot ridgepole that's the largest such piece in the United States and weighs approximately 25 tons, cool wood carvings, 2 fireplaces built with approximately 50 tons of rock found locally, and a fireplace mantle of solid black walnut. The logging museum exists inside and out and includes a huge collection of old logging equipment, including multiple steam donkeys, a large bandsaw from a sawmill, a self-propelled Ohio steam crane, Caterpillar-style tracked vehicles that worked in the woods, a railroad skeleton log car and other heavy equipment, plus a wide variety of large and small hardware. If this doesn't do it for you, hit the restaurant, which features log-cabin-like decor including a burl table entirely carved from one hunk of wood. The menu would fill up any logger with rib-sticking dishes like ribs, pork chops, sirloin steak, and fish and chips. For breakfast, try one of Camp 18's famous cinnamon rolls. They're so big you're definitely going to need some help. $$–$$$.

Saddle Mountain. Off US 26 W, 8 miles northeast of Necanicum Junction. Saddle Mountain is the highest point in northwest Oregon and one of the most popular hikes in the state of Oregon. That's because it's easy to get to, traverses flower-filled meadows unparalleled in this part of the state, and boasts a view on top that stretches from the ocean to the mouth of the Columbia River to the Cascades. A 5.2-mile round-trip hike to the top through rough terrain and steep grades makes for challenging climbing, but you'll be so busy marveling at the natural beauty you won't mind. As you climb to the rocky summit, gaze upon mature forest and fields of wildflowers. The view from the apex is a floral show that only exists at that elevation. The temperature is very different at the summit than in the parking lot, so come prepared with a jacket.

Seaside Aquarium. 200 N Prom; (503) 738-6211; www.seasideaquarium.com. Founded in 1937, the Seaside Aquarium is one of the oldest on the West Coast. This old building on the waterfront is full of fun discoveries, including underwater areas that provide a glimpse of a fascinating world of unusual and rare life forms. An underwater viewing tank and a touch tank with sea anemones, sandpaper textured starfish and prickly sea urchins are beautiful and full of life. Don't miss the family of seals. Open daily at 9 a.m. (winter and summer hours may vary at closing time).

Seaside Museum, Historical Society and Butterfield Cottage. 570 Necanicum Dr.; (503) 738-7065; www.seasidemuseum.org. This cool old museum includes exhibits on the history of Native Americans in the Seaside area, logging, and local hotels and tourism. The Seaside Museum is the only beach cottage museum in Oregon, existing in and interpreting the Butterfield Cottage to the era circa 1912. Built in 1880 as a beach cottage for a wealthy Portlander, the Butterfield Cottage sits on beautiful grounds. The adjacent gift shop sells all sorts of fun gifts and souvenirs. Open 7 days a week year-round, but call for specific hours.

Seaside Promenade and Turnaround. Seaside's Broadway Avenue leads west directly to the Seaside Turnaround, the epicenter of Seaside with a magnificent view of the Pacific Ocean and a statue of Meriwether Lewis and William Clark that commemorates the explorers' historic expedition. Intersecting the turnaround is the popular Promenade, or Prom, a

run, play, party

The **Hood to Coast Relay,** considered to be the world's largest annual relay, begins on the slopes of Mt. Hood and finishes on the beach at Seaside. The event brings 12,000 runners, their support teams, race staff, and volunteers to this small city each year—numbers that can total 60,000. In effect, a second city is temporarily created to accommodate the masses. Dozens of tents are erected on the beach, a footbridge is installed over US 101, and local businesses stock way up on beer and hot dogs. Depending on your point of view, race weekend—the third weekend of August—might be a great time to visit Seaside or a great time to avoid Seaside. One thing is for sure, with 60,000 extra people in town, this is where the party is. See www.hoodtocoast.com.

1.5-mile paved walkway that leads walkers and runners past grand Seaside homes on one side and gorgeous dunes and beach views on the other. Everybody loves the Prom, which is lined with benches for relaxing.

Wheel Fun Rentals. 407 S Holladay Dr.; (503) 738-8447; www.wheelfunrentals.com. At Wheel Fun, you can rent just about anything. Set yourself loose on the streets of Seaside in an electric fun car, including mini-Hummers, mopeds, and a 1923 Ford Roadster. Pedal-powered options include single, double, and triple surries, kids' bikes, tandems, coupes, choppers, and cruiser bicycles. For some cash, you can even rent kayaks, boogie boards, surfboards, baby joggers, and sandcastle kits. Whatever your beach vacation can't live without, these folks have. Rental prices are $10 to $85 per hour. Summer hours: open daily 9 a.m. to sunset. Winter hours: open Mon through Fri 9 a.m. to 5 p.m. and weekends weather permitting.

where to shop

Seaside Carousel Mall. 300 Broadway; (503) 738-6728; www.seasidecarouselmall.com. Everyone loves a carousel. Twenty unique shops surround a full-size classic carousel in this cheery, colorful mall. Shops offer dining, snacks, coffee, specialty gifts, art, imports, framing, kites, games, clothing, jewelry, toys, candies, ice cream, old time photos and portraits, and much more. The carousel horses are replicas of original hand-carved vintage carousel horses from the early 1900s. Open 7 days a week, though hours change seasonally.

Shearwater Gallery. 111 Broadway; (503) 738-0328; www.shearwatergallery.com. This spacious, 2-story gallery features the work of numerous artists, many of them local, in a variety of media and styles. You'll find functional art including furniture, lighting, tabletop dishware, garden art, wall art, jewelry, pottery, and much more, including cards, candles, and soaps. Open daily from 11 a.m. to 5 p.m.; extended summer hours.

where to eat

Lil' Bayou & Magnolia Lounge. 20 N Holladay; (503) 717-0624; www.lilbayou.net. A gorgeous and colorful mural lines the wall over the bar in this joint, where the south meets seaside. Three distinct and different cuisines are offered here: Cajun, Creole, and Northwest seafood. Cajun food is a little spicy but hearty, Creole food is cooked using traditional European techniques with local ingredients, and Northwest seafood is just delicious. Try jambalaya, gumbo, and shrimp salad for a taste of Louisiana; crab cakes, rib eye steak, and coho salmon for more traditional Pacific Northwest items. Every Thursday night hosts live jazz and blues. Open for dinner every night except Tues. $$–$$$.

Maggie's on the Prom Restaurant. 581 South Prom; (503) 738-6403; www.theseaside inn.com. Located on the main floor of the Seaside Oceanfront Inn, Maggie's is a favorite for locals and tourists alike. Guests enjoy stunning views of the Pacific Ocean and Tillamook

Head. The restaurant decor is Northwest contemporary with a river rock fireplace, solid wood tables and chairs, box-beamed 10-foot ceilings, wrapped windows, and custom millwork. Outdoor dining is available. The seasonal menus offer fresh seafood, salads, sandwiches, chowder and soups, pasta dishes, specialty poultry and meat dishes, vegetarian and gluten-free dishes, and desserts. Maggie's has a large bar. Reservations are recommended. Open for breakfast, lunch, and dinner daily. $$$.

Norma's Ocean Diner. 20 N Columbia St.; (503) 738-4331; www.normasoceandiner .com. Norma's has been a Seaside standard since 1976. This restaurant's amazing food has been called "best beach fare," "unpretentious," and "best road food" by national magazines. Simply prepared and excellent seafood, steaks, and pasta dishes are served for lunch and dinner daily in a nice, comfortable, recently remodeled room. Dinners include your choice of a cup of Norma's world-famous clam chowder or dinner salad with shrimp. $$–$$$.

Taste of Tuscany. 1815 S Roosevelt Dr.; (503) 738-5377; www.tasteoftuscanyseaside .com. Fine Italian dining is served in this upscale restaurant. Catering to all, Taste of Tuscany has a family-friendly dining room and an adults-only dining room as well as a patio on the sunny south side of the restaurant, surrounded by lovely landscaping, open when the weather is warm. Taste of Tuscany serves pasta, seafood, steak, pizza, and salads, and boasts the largest collection of wines on the North Coast. Open for dinner every day but Tues. $$–$$$.

Zinger's Homemade Ice Cream. 210 Broadway; (503) 738-3939; www.zingersicecream .com. The only ice-cream place in town that makes their own homemade ice cream with ultra-premium 16 percent butterfat that is fresh, smooth, sweet, and creamy. More than 50 flavors are made, and rotated, so that visitors can try everything over the course of a season. Try butter brickle, egg nog, blue moon, black walnut . . . and many, many more. Zinger's is only open seasonally. Call for hours. No debit or credit cards.

where to stay

Beachside Inn. 300 5th Ave.; (503) 738-5363; www.beachsideinnseaside.com. Beachside Inn offers a clean and cozy beach bungalow atmosphere with 12 rooms just 4 blocks to downtown and less than a block from the beach. This lodging is clean, quaint, and a little quieter than some places. Complimentary lobby snacks and a few restaurants nearby make your stay even more convenient. $–$$.

Edgewater Inn on the Prom. 341 S Prom; (503) 738-4142; www.edgewaterinnon theprom.com. Oceanfront rooms on the promenade with views of the Pacific Ocean and Tillamook Head make this simply decorated lodging a great place to relax and enjoy your Seaside stay. Fireplaces and Jacuzzi tubs will mellow you out; fall asleep to the sound of the waves. $–$$.

Gilbert Inn. 341 Beach Dr.; (800) 410-9770; www.gilbertinn.com. The Gilbert Inn is a romantic Queen Anne Victorian home built in 1892. Rooms are fancy and floral. Only 300 feet from the Prom and 1 block south of Broadway, the location is as convenient as it is luxurious and beautiful. No children, smokers, or pets. $–$$$.

day trip 02

northwest

in the footsteps of lewis & clark:
astoria

astoria

Astoria has been basking in the past lately. The years 2005 and 2006 marked the bicentennial of the long, wet, and cold winter that Lewis and Clark spent at Astoria's Fort Clatsop. This year, 2011, marks the city's bicentennial. These milestones have been cause for much hoopla, and visitorship to the small coastal Oregon city at the mouth of the great Columbia River has climbed accordingly.

The attention is well deserved. Astoria is the oldest American settlement west of the Rockies, and has more historical markers than anywhere else in Oregon. The small city makes for a charming, atmospheric weekend getaway. The town boasts impressive old architecture including hundreds of Victorian homes perched on Astoria's steep hillsides and a revitalized 1920s-era downtown. The main part of town sits on a hilly peninsula, and the 360-degree views of the ocean, river, and temperate rain forest that surround Astoria are those of tremendous natural beauty.

Astoria was named after the American investor John Jacob Astor. His American Fur Company founded Fort Astoria, which would become the first permanent US settlement on the Pacific coast, in 1810. Eventually, Portland, Seattle, and San Francisco surpassed Astoria as the West Coast's main port cities, and Astoria was left to thrive quietly on the pursuits of fishing and logging. Today, tourism is a primary industry. In the last decade, Astoria has caught the attention of cruise ships, which can disembark 2,000 passengers at a time.

northwest day trip 02

> ## best seller
>
> *American writer Washington Irving mythologized John Jacob Astor and his 3-year reign as head of the Pacific Fur Company in Astoria (1835). Though much of what Irving wrote was romanticized and overly dramatic—he referred to fur traders as "Sinbads of the wilderness"—the book was a success, and the region was forever planted in the American psyche.*

getting there

Take US 26 W/OR 26 west out of Portland for 73 miles. Merge onto OR 101/US 101 N toward Seaside/Astoria. Continue north for 19 miles until you reach Astoria. An alternate route, and one that the locals find to be more scenic, is to take US 30 along the Columbia. This way, it's a 95-mile drive, all on US 30. The route you choose will likely depend on the time of year, weather, and where you are starting from.

where to go

Astoria Column. At the top of Coxcomb Drive off 15th Street; (503) 325-2963; www.astoria column.org. For the best view in town, drive up to the top of Astoria's Coxcomb Drive and then climb another 165 steps on foot to the top of the Astoria Column. The column is an Astoria icon, built in 1926 as the dream child of Ralph Budd, president of the Midwest-based Great Northern Railroad, with support from Vincent Astor, great grandson of businessman John Jacob Astor, whose Pacific Fur Company settled Astoria. Stunning views of the Columbia River to the north, the Cascade Range to the east, and the Pacific Ocean to the west wow those willing to test their lungs with the climb up the winding staircase. This is a great place to go when you first arrive in Astoria to begin to get the lay of the land. Parking comes with a suggested $1 per car donation; the park is open dawn to dusk.

Astoria Riverfront Trolley. 1 Basin St.; (503) 325-6311; www.homepage.mac.com/cearl /trolley. Adding to downtown Astoria's charm is this restored 1913 trolley, which makes a 2.6-mile run along the Columbia River. The conductor does his part by narrating to passengers tales of Astoria's history and attractions. You can catch a ride on the trolley from just about anywhere on the riverfront between Basin and 39th Streets. Round-trip ride is $1; an all-day pass is $2. The round trip takes about an hour. Hours change seasonally; check website.

Clatsop County Historical Society. 714 Exchange St.; (503) 325-2203; www.cumtux .org. The society has three museums. Call for hours and details.

The Flavel House. Corner of 8th and Duane Streets. Captain George Flavel was a prominent sea captain and one of the wealthier residents of early Astoria. This quaint late Queen Anne Victorian home was built for him in 1885 and features park-like grounds, original Eastlake-style woodwork interiors, and exotic hardwood fireplaces with imported tile surrounds.

The Uppertown Firefighters Museum. Corner of 30th Street and Marine Drive. Astoria's downtown was twice destroyed by fire, in 1883 and 1922, and more recently Fort Clatsop burned to the ground. With Astoria's history of fire, it's no surprise they have a museum dedicated to firefighters. This museum in an old red-brick fire station houses an extensive collection of firefighting equipment and memorabilia from Clatsop County dating back to 1877, including a horse-drawn ladder wagon and a 1912 American LaFrance fire truck.

Heritage Museum. Corner of 16th and Exchange Streets. A historical exhibit includes Chinook and Clatsop Indian baskets and a partially constructed Astoria saloon. Pick up a booklet here to help guide you on a walking tour of Astoria's famous historical homes. Opening for Astoria's bicentennial is a new exhibit, "The Astor Party and the Founding of Astoria."

Columbia River Maritime Museum. 1792 Marine Dr.; (503) 325-2323; www.crmm.org. Brave souls have been tackling the ocean by boat for hundreds of years. Here you can explore marine transportation from the age of dugout canoes to sailboats to the present. A film introduces the history of life and commerce on the Columbia River. A new exhibit titled "Crossing the Bar: Perilous Passage" takes an exciting look at the legendary Columbia River entrance, where the forces of the mighty Columbia and the Pacific Ocean meet, creating waves that can exceed 40 feet during bad winter storms. See videos captured while working with the US Coast Guard and the Columbia River Bar Pilots during fierce winter storms. Open daily 9:30 a.m. to 5 p.m.

Fort Clatsop National Memorial. 92343 Fort Clatsop Rd.; (503) 861-2471; www.nps .gov/lewi. Lewis and Clark spent a winter here, hoping that a ship would pass by to return them to their homes on the east coast. When that didn't happen, in the spring of 1906, they returned the way they'd come—but not before getting a solid taste of a Pacific Northwest winter. The facility includes the reconstructed fort, a visitor center and museum, historical exhibits, a canoe landing, picnic area, trails through the wetlands, and a rain forest of young Sitka spruce and western hemlock. During the summer months, experience living history demonstrations depicting fort activities. Open daily: summer 9 a.m. to 6 p.m.; winter 9 a.m. to 5 p.m.

Fort Stevens State Park. 100 Peter Iredale Rd., Hammond; (503) 861-3170; www .oregonstateparks.org/park_179. Fort Stevens was the primary military defense installation at the mouth of the Columbia River, serving from the Civil War through World War II. Today the site is a great place to access and walk the beach, as well as catch a glimpse of the wreck of the *Peter Iredale*, an oceangoing ship that was destroyed near the mouth of the Columbia River in the early part of the century. The wreck can still be seen at low tide. Fort Stevens State Park is great for all sorts of recreation, including boating, swimming, picnicking, hiking, and biking. Every Labor Day weekend, there's a Civil War reenactment on the site. $3 daily fee; camping also available.

Oregon Film Museum. 732 Duane St.; (503) 325-2203; www.oregonfilmmuseum.org. Astoria's beauty and architecture have attracted many to the area, including filmmakers. To celebrate the 25th anniversary of the Steven Spielberg film *The Goonies*, the Oregon Film Museum was born in 2010. Housed in the historic Clatsop County Jail, which was featured in the opening scene of *The Goonies,* the new museum is dedicated to preserving the art and legacy of Oregon films and filmmaking. Other movies filmed in Astoria include *Overboard, Short Circuit, The Black Stallion, Kindergarten Cop, Free Willy, Free Willy 2: The Adventure Home, Teenage Mutant Ninja Turtles III, Benji the Hunted, The Ring, The Ring Two, Into the Wild, The Guardian,* and *Cthulhu*. Open daily 10 a.m. to 5 p.m.

Walk the Waterfront. 1 11th St. The Astoria Waterfront provides many opportunities to stretch your legs with a walk and take in the sweep and scope of the Columbia River. Visit Maritime Memorial Park, the 6th Street Viewing Platform, the 14th Street Pier, and the 17th Street Dock. Most of the walking paths are paved.

where to shop

The Astoria Co-op. 1355 Exchange St., Suite #1; (503) 325-0027; www.astoriacoop.org. This is the place to pick up picnic supplies for an outing to Fort Stevens or the beach. Great variety of to-go salads, sandwiches, soup, cookies, and more. Pick up one of their lovely organic cotton reusable totes to take along, too.

Commercial Street Antiques and Collectibles. 969 Commercial St.; (503) 325-4388. This is the destination for great finds from the past and lovely old objects to take home and beautify your living space. There are lots of small items here, from housewares to records.

Josephson's Smokehouse. 106 Marine Dr.; (800) 772-FISH; www.josephsons.com. For nearly 90 years, Josephson's has sold the finest local smoked, canned, and jerked seafoods. At their historic smokehouse, an unequaled variety of seafood is smoked daily, sold at retail fresh from the smokers, packed for individual mail order to customers and restaurants, and shipped worldwide.

Phog Bounders Antique Mall. 892 Marine Dr.; (503) 338-0101. Here you'll find everything from low-end collectables to high-end and rare antiques in more than 3,000 square feet of small retail spaces.

> ## a fire in the night

*In October 2005, just weeks before the Lewis and Clark Bicentennial celebration was to commence, **Fort Clatsop** was ruined by fire. A stray ember from a fireplace was thought to be the cause. The fort was a replica of the original and had been built in 1955, but nevertheless, the loss was devastating to supporters of the National Memorial. The timing was particularly tough, but such a significant setback also served as a powerful motivator to the community. Fourteen months later, with the help of 700 workers and volunteers, Fort Clatsop had been rebuilt.*

Vintage Hardware. 475 14th St.; (503) 325-1313; http://astoriavintagehardware.com. The owners met at a flea market, and the rest is history. This brand-new store on the ground floor of the historic Astor Hotel is very impressive.

where to eat

Astoria Coffeehouse and Bistro. 243 11th St.; (503) 325-1787; www.astoriacoffeehouse .com. Astoria Coffeehouse makes everything from scratch—even the ketchup. This top-notch coffee house serves Stumptown Roasters coffee, fresh gourmet pastries, homemade soups, salads, and a wide variety of hot and cold beverages, plus cocktails, beer, and wine. Centrally located right downtown—look for the neon coffee cup on 11th Street. Open 7 days a week for breakfast, lunch, and dinner. $$.

Baked Alaska. 1 12th St.; (503) 325-7414; www.bakedak.com. Voted "best happy hour" by the locals, this fine dining and public house serves delicious food inspired by the region and the season. Wild, natural, and sustainable fare dominates the menu. Try the applejack halibut or thundermuck tuna. Bonus: Baked Alaska overlooks the Columbia River and offers lovely views. $$$.

Blue Scorcher Bakery Café. 1493 Duane St.; (503) 338-7473; www.bluescorcher.com. Operating as a worker collective with the motto "joyful work, delicious food, and strong community," Blue Scorcher creates artisan breads, pastries, and handcrafted seasonal foods using local and organic ingredients. A children's area features a play kitchen and makes this restaurant a natural gathering place for families. Located in the historic Fort George building with view of the Columbia River. Open Mon through Fri 8 a.m. to 5 p.m. and Sat and Sun 8 a.m. to 4 p.m. $.

Bowpicker. Located across from the Columbia River Maritime Museum, at the corner of 17th and Duane Streets, in a converted gillnet boat; www.bowpicker.com. Though you'll never leave land, just eating here will make you feel like you've had an adventure on the high seas. Bowpicker is locally famous for their beer-battered albacore tuna and steak fries—the best fish and chips in town. Open Wed through Sun in summer season, Fri through Sun in winter season, weather permitting (high winds can shut this boat/restaurant down). $.

Bridgewater Bistro. 20 Basin St., Suite A; (503) 325-6777; www.bridgewaterbistro.com. This well-lit, high-ceilinged, attractive, and modern wood and metal space in a renovated boatyard provides river and bridge views from every table. The menu is composed of creatively prepared seafoods, meats, soups, and vegetarian entrees. Choose tables in the family-friendly casual bistro setting or on the fine dining mezzanine. Open 7 days a week for lunch and dinner; brunch on Sun. $$–$$$.

Clemente's. 1198 Commercial St.; (503) 325-1067; www.clementesrestaurant.com. Healthy, local, organic, seasonal, wild, and consistently excellent foods are served here in a lovely but casual space. Specialties include poke and gluten-free fish and chips. Open for dinner Tues through Sun. $$.

Columbian Café. 1114 Marine Dr.; (503) 325-2233; www.columbianvoodoo.com. Three businesses in one: A funky renovated lunch counter that serves only the very best fresh local foods including seafood and lots of spicy vegetarian options, open for breakfast, lunch, and dinner Wed through Sun. The Voodoo Room next door opens at 5 p.m. daily for pizza and music. And finally there's the Columbian Theater, which shows one picture at a time and offers beer and pizza to go with it. $–$$.

Fort George Brewery and Public House. 1483 Duane St.; (503) 325-PINT; www.fort georgebrewery.com. Pub food and seafood are served in this popular, hip brewpub. Try the sausage sampler with spicy mustard or the albacore tuna melt. Enjoy live music on some weekends. Open 7 days a week for lunch and dinner. $$.

Gunderson's Cannery Café. 1 6th St.; (503) 325-8642; www.cannerycafe.com. Four generations of Gunderson family members fished the Columbia River for salmon, beginning at the turn of the century. In this old cannery by the river, the family created an excellent breakfast, lunch, and dinner restaurant with a killer view. Open 7 days a week for breakfast, lunch, and dinner. $$.

Pig 'N Pancake. 146 W Bond; (503) 325-3144; www.pignpancake.com. There are six Pig 'N Pancake Restaurants in Oregon, five of them on the coast. They serve 35 breakfast options including pancakes, crepes, omelettes, and the like all day, prepared fresh in a fun, family-friendly atmosphere. Open daily for breakfast, lunch, and dinner. $.

Ship Inn. 1 2nd St.; (503) 325-0033. You might just feel like one of Astoria's long-ago mariners here. Cornish pasties, great fish and chips, and calamari are served in a true English pub atmosphere. Don't miss the fabulous views of the Columbia River, and of course, there are lots of great beers on tap. $$.

Silver Salmon. 1105 Commercial; (503) 338-6640; www.silversalmongrille.com. The historic Fisher Building that houses this restaurant was built in 1924, but it's got nothing on the bar that sits inside. The Silver Salmon's ornately carved antique bar is 120 years old, is constructed of Scottish cherry wood, and was shipped around Cape Horn in the 1880s. This romantic, historic restaurant in downtown offers great food, drinks, and desserts. $$–$$$.

T. Paul's Urban Café and Supper Club. 1119 Commercial St.; (503) 338-5133. Fresh eclectic cuisine including wonderful salads, sweet potato fries, and clam chowder is served at this eclectically decorated restaurant. The prices are good, and live blues, jazz, or folk plays on Fri and Sat nights. $–$$.

Wet Dog Café and Brew Pub and Astoria Brewing Company. 144 11th St.; (503) 325-6975. Microbrews, burgers, and the like delivered to guests on Astoria's waterfront. Wet Dog offers a full menu and 20 Northwest craft beers on tap, including 9 different handcrafted ales brewed on site. Open Mon through Sat for lunch and dinner. $–$$.

where to stay

Cannery Pier Hotel. 10 Basin St.; (888) 325-4996; www.cannerypierhotel.com. Built on the site of the former Union Fish Cannery 600 feet into the Columbia River, this hotel is the ultimate in comfort and luxury, Astoria style. Guests have unparalleled views of a real working river, as well as glimpses of the Cape Disappointment Lighthouse. Each room has a private balcony and fireplace; halls are decorated with wonderful historical photographs of Astoria. A daily ship log allows guests to track ships going in and out of the Columbia River. Free wine and hors d'oeuvres in the evening; continental breakfast in the morning. A free chauffeur-driven limo service in the evenings uses classic old cars. Expensive, but worth every penny. $$$+.

Clementine's Bed and Breakfast. 847 Exchange St.; (503) 325-2005; www.clementines-bb .com. This beautiful 2-story classic 1888 Victorian house offers fresh flowers, featherbeds, down pillows, and duvet comforters in each of its 5 rooms. The grounds are done up with gorgeous English gardens, and some rooms have private decks with spectacular views. $$–$$$.

Grandview Bed and Breakfast. 1574 Grand Ave.; (503) 325-5555; www.grandviewbed andbreakfast.com. This lovely and romantic Victorian house on the Historic Homes Walking Tour features wonderful Columbia River views. Three 2-bedrooms and three 1-bedroom lodgings with private baths have lace and floral decor. $–$$.

Hotel Elliott. 357 12th St.; (503) 325-2222; www.hotelelliott.com. Built in 1924, Hotel Elliott has undergone a dramatic 3-year transformation that preserves its classic ambience. This beautifully restored old hotel has a fabulous rooftop terrace, cellar wine bar, and proximity to downtown restaurants. The rooms are designed for relaxed comfort. $$–$$$.

Rose River Inn Bed and Breakfast. 1510 Franklin Ave.; (503) 325-7175; www.roseriver inn.com. Just 3 blocks from downtown and 4 from the riverfront, this Craftsman-style home built in 1912 is on the National Register of Historic Places. Five private guest rooms have names like the Iris Garden and Cloud 9, and are filled with antiques; in the morning, enjoy a full breakfast. $–$$.

day trip 03

northwest

clams, kites & cranberries:
the long beach peninsula, wa

the long beach peninsula

The 28-mile Long Beach Peninsula juts out of Washington State's southwest corner, just across the bridge from Astoria. Long, narrow, and picturesque, the Peninsula is bounded on the west by the Pacific Ocean, the south by the Columbia River, and the east by Willapa Bay.

On the Pacific Ocean side, a sandy beach stretches continuously for 28 miles. This strip of beach is great for kite-flying, walking, sandcastle building, and more, but not so great for swimming. The water is cold and dangerous—in fact, because of the confluence of the Columbia River and the Pacific Ocean, it's some of the most dangerous water on the West Coast.

Many small communities dot the Peninsula, but only Ilwaco and Long Beach are incorporated. The residents of the Peninsula think of themselves as one community, called the Long Beach Peninsula. The principal industry of the Long Beach Peninsula has become tourism, though fishing, crabbing, oyster farming, and cranberry farming are also important components of the local economy.

From spring break through mid-October, the Peninsula is hopping with visitors, festivals, and activity. The rest of the year, it's awfully quiet around here. Winter can still be a great time to visit, especially if you want to get a glimpse of some of the epic winter storms that strike the Pacific and the Columbia River.

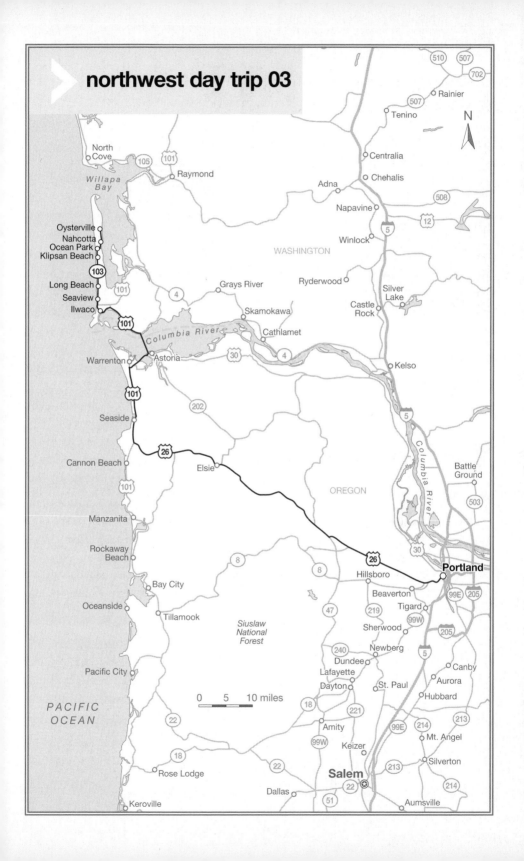

getting there

Take US 26 W/OR 26 W out of Portland and continue 74 miles to the coast. At the US 101 junction, go north for 36 miles, crossing the Astoria Bridge into Washington State. US 101 will turn into WA 103/Pacific Ave. S, which traverses the entire Long Beach Peninsula.

Note—in the winter, when US 26 can be icy, consider taking US 30 north and west out of Portland, to intersect with US 101 at Astoria.

where to go

Cape Disappointment State Park. South end of Peninsula, south of Ilwaco off WA 100. Cape Disappointment State Park is the most visited park in the Washington State Parks system. Here you can walk a flat sandy beach, explore bunkers of an old military fort, wander through coastal forests, have a picnic, camp, and take in spectacular vistas. The park has an old-growth forest, lakes, freshwater and saltwater marshes, streams, ocean tidelands, and lots of watchable wildlife. "Cape D" encompasses 1,882 acres and is fronted by both the Pacific Ocean and Baker Bay. The park is open year round for camping and day use, 6:30 a.m. to dusk.

Within its boundaries are these highlights:

Cape Disappointment Lighthouse. On the southeast tip of the Peninsula, off WA 100. There are two lighthouses on the south end of the peninsula—the Cape Disappointment and the North Head. Only the North Head is open to the public. Enjoy Cape Disappointment Lighthouse from the outside, knowing that it's the oldest operating lighthouse on the West Coast.

North Head Lighthouse. North Head Lighthouse Road, off WA 100 in Ilwaco; (360) 642-3078. The 65-foot North Head Lighthouse was completed in 1898. Tours include history and gorgeous panoramic views of the Peninsula and Pacific Ocean. Incidentally, North Head is the windiest lighthouse area on the West Coast and the second windiest in the nation. Winds of 120 miles per hour have been recorded at the

a powerful & yawning sea

The waters off the Long Beach Peninsula are considered some of the most treacherous in the world. Known as the Graveyard of the Pacific, the stretch of water where the Pacific Ocean meets the Columbia River has claimed more than 2,000 ships since the late 1700s. The US Coast Guard set up a Lifeboat School here—perfect training ground for wild and wooly ocean rescues.

site. The lighthouse grounds are open at no charge, year-round, dawn until dusk. Call for tour hours, which change seasonally.

Waikiki Beach. On the southern end of the Peninsula off WA 100. Waikiki Beach is considered the only swim-safe beach on the Peninsula. Still, whether or not you actually want to venture into the water will depend on your fortitude and/or the air temperature—the water here isn't exactly as warm as the other Waikiki, in Hawaii.

Lewis and Clark Interpretive Center. Cape Disappointment State Park, off WA 100 on the south end of the Peninsula; (360) 642-3029. Perched on a cliff 200 feet above the mouth of the Columbia River, the Lewis and Clark Interpretive Center tells the story of the journey of the Corps of Discovery, focusing particularly on their Pacific Coast stay. During winter and spring, volunteers help visitors spot migrating gray whales. Open year-round from 10 a.m. to 5 p.m. daily.

Columbia Pacific Heritage Museum. 115 SE Lake St., Ilwaco; (360) 642-3446; www .columbiapacificheritagemuseum.org. Explore the history of the region where the Columbia River meets the Pacific Ocean. Artifacts, images, and stories interpret the Chinook Indians, European explorers, 19th-century pioneers, fishermen, cranberry growers, loggers, and summer people who have made the Long Beach Peninsula what it is today. Open 10 a.m. to 4 p.m. Tues through Sat, noon to 4 p.m. Sun, closed Mon. Free admission for children ages 12 and under.

Discovery Trail. North end access is off 26th Street in Long Beach; south end access is off the corner of Elizabeth Street and Waterfront Way in Ilwaco. The Discovery Trail was created to commemorate the Lewis and Clark Expedition and parallels Capt. William Clark's hike to the Pacific Ocean in November 1805. Stretching 8.3 miles between Long Beach and Ilwaco, the trail is closed to motor vehicles and horses and offers peaceful, scenic passage to pedestrians and bicycles. Interpretive markers and several bronze statues can be found on the route. The trail is relatively easy and flat from the northern terminus to Beard's Hollow. The trail gets more challenging at that point, rising in elevation as much as 300 feet between Beard's Hollow and the southern terminus at the Port of Ilwaco.

Green Angel Gardens Farm Store. 6807 Sandridge Rd., Long Beach; (360) 244-0064; www.greenangelgardening.com. Stocked with organic greens grown on site, local fresh eggs, and a variety of certified organic produce obtained from regional growers. The Green Angel Farm promotes education and is family-friendly, encouraging kids and adults to come and learn how quality food is grown. Open daily 10 a.m. to 4 p.m.

Knappton Cove Heritage Center. Right on WA 401 just north of the Astoria Bridge; (503) 738-5206; www.knapptoncoveheritagecenter.org. Everything that happened at New York's famous Ellis Island happened at other US ports during the waves of immigration in the 1800s and early 1900s, only on a smaller scale. In Astoria, boats from overseas anchored and were boarded by an inspector. If fumigation for infestation and disease was deemed necessary, the boats were sent here, across the Columbia River to the US Columbia River Quarantine Station, the only point for federal quarantine on the West Coast north of San Francisco. Today it's a National Historic Site, set on preserving the history of this unique location and the role of the US Public Health Service. Open summer Saturdays 1 to 4 p.m. or by appointment.

Long Beach Boardwalk. Access at Bolstad Avenue and Sid Snyder Drive in Long Beach. *The Today Show* named the Long Beach Boardwalk one of the top five in the nation, calling it the "most unique." That's because, unlike many US boardwalks, the half-mile boardwalk in Long Beach isn't lined with hot dog stands and sunglasses vendors, but instead surrounded by grassy dunes. Interpretive exhibits dot the route, and spectacular views of the ocean, beach, and North Head Lighthouse make this a must-walk.

Pacific Coast Cranberry Research Foundation Museum and Gift Shop. 2907 Pioneer Rd., Long Beach; (360) 642-5553; www.cranberrymuseum.com. Cranberry farming in the southwest corner of Washington State has a more than 100-year history and remains an important part of the local economy. This 1,200-square-foot facility next to a 10-acre demonstration cranberry farm interprets the history and cultivation of this garnet-colored berry, and offers a self-guided walking tour of cranberry bogs year-round. September is the most spectacular month, when the berries are ripening. Open daily 10 a.m. to 5 p.m., Apr through Dec.

Painted Lady Lavender Farm. 1664 US 101, Ilwaco; (360) 642-3531. This charming 2-acre farm grows lavender and also includes a chicken coop, rabbits, and a guest cabin. Open daily until dusk. Call or stop in for guided tours of the plantings of lavender and other organic herbs.

the clamshell railroad

The Ilwaco Railway and Navigation Company operated a narrow-gauge railroad that ran for more than 40 years from the bar of the Columbia River up the Long Beach Peninsula. Steamers could only reach the Ilwaco wharf, where the railroad began, to unload their take after the tide was in mid-flood. Therefore the railroad's schedule was based on the tide charts. A schedule for April, 1905, shows times of departure from Astoria for the steamer Nahcotta *as varying from as early as 5 a.m. to as late as 8:30 a.m. The railroad had a number of nicknames, including the "Clamshell Railroad."*

World Kite Museum and Hall of Fame. 303 Sid Snyder Dr., Long Beach; (360) 642-4020 www.worldkitemuseum.com. The kite is 2,500 years old. This museum showcases 1,500 kites from around the world and preserves the kite's past, to record its present developments and to honor the people dedicated to kites. Open 11 a.m. to 5 p.m. daily in the summer, Fri through Tues, Oct through Apr.

where to eat

Bailey's Bakery & Café. 26910 Sandridge Rd., Nahcotta; (360) 665-4449; www.baileys bakerycafe.com. Bailey's is famous for their "Thunder Buns," an amazing cinnamon roll described as "the most outrageous on the planet" that sells out early each day. If you miss out on those, there are lots of other treats to tempt you, including bread, scones, sausage rolls, and fresh soups. Open Thurs through Mon 8 a.m. to 3 p.m., Sun 9 a.m. to 3 p.m. $.

Depot Restaurant. 1208 38th Place, Seaview; (360) 642-7880; www.depotrestaurantdining .com. Discover great food and ambiance at this restaurant in a 120-year-old depot building at the end of the old "Clamshell Railroad." Entrees include "landfood" and "seafood." The Depot's chowder is to die for, with leeks and steamer clams. They offer a regional and international wine list with 6 microbrews on tap. $$$.

Nanci and Jimella's Klipsan Market Café. 21712 Pacific Way, Klipsan Beach; (360) 665-4847. Jimella Lucas is famous on the Peninsula for her way with fish, and has been called the "sturgeon general." She and Nanci Main offer casual café dining with delicious seafood entrees, appetizers, desserts, and breads complemented by excellent wines. This location is also a seafood market and community store mecca of fine fresh fish, cheeses, local produce, fresh herbs, wines, and smoked and cured meats, plus exclusive takeout specialties beginning with Jimella's clam chowder and a tasty array of gourmet sandwiches. $$–$$$.

Pelicano Restaurant. 177 Howerton Way SE, Ilwaco; (360) 642-4034; www.pelicano restaurant.com. Contemporary fine dining with a wonderful view of the Port of Ilwaco. The menu is Mediterranean in inspiration, changes with the season, and features the bounty of the Pacific Ocean, Columbia River, Willapa Bay, and local farms. Open Tues to Sun at 5 p.m. $$–$$$.

where to stay

Boreas Bed & Breakfast Inn. 607 Ocean Beach Blvd. N, Long Beach; (360) 642-8069; www.boreasinn.com. This oceanfront boutique inn only has 5 rooms, making it peaceful and private. A 3-course award-winning brunch is served daily. Boreas is nestled in the dunes and within walking distance of the Discovery Trail and Long Beach Boardwalk. $$–$$$.

China Beach Retreat. 222 Robert Gray Dr., Ilwaco; (360) 642-5660; www.chinabeach retreat.com. China Beach is the perfect place to unwind. Decorated with an eclectic selection of European and Asian antiques and original artwork, frequently visited by deer, waterfowl, and bald eagles, China Beach Retreat has a view of the mouth of the Columbia River and Baker Bay and offers private spa tubs and gourmet breakfast. With just 3 guest rooms, you may never see another person—aside from the one you bring with you, that is. $$$.

Klipsan Beach Cottages. 22617 Pacific Way; Ocean Park; (360) 665-4888; www.klipsan beachcottages.com. Classic traditional beach cottages, kept up impeccably, the cottages at Klipsan Beach sit on a ridge facing the Pacific Ocean and are surrounded by beautifully landscaped grounds. Well-appointed kitchens, fireplaces, and the ocean nearby—what more do you need? $–$$.

Shelburne Inn. 4415 Pacific Way, Seaview; (360) 642-2442; www.theshelburneinn.com. Established in 1896, the Shelburne Inn has been spoiling its guests for over 100 years. Four-star dining, a stunning breakfast, and a pub serving fine wines and microbrews distinguish this world-renowned country inn retreat. $$.

appendix a: regional information

north

day trip 01

Vancouver USA Regional Tourism Office
101 East 8th St., Suite 240, Vancouver
(877) 600-0800
www.visitvancouverusa.com

day trip 02

South Columbia County Chamber
of Commerce
2194 Columbia Blvd., St. Helens
(503) 397-0685
www.sccchamber.org

northeast

day trip 01

Cowlitz County Tourism Bureau
105 Minor Rd., Kelso
(360) 577-3137
www.visitmtsthelens.com

east

day trip 01

Hood River Chamber of Commerce
720 E Port Marina Dr., Hood River
(541) 386-2000
www.hoodriver.org

Skamania County Chamber of Commerce
& Visitor Information Center
167 NW 2nd St., Stevenson
(800) 989-9178
www.skamania.org

day trip 02

Hood River Chamber of Commerce
720 E Port Marina Dr., Hood River
(541) 386-2000
www.hoodriver.org

day trip 03

The Dalles Area Chamber of Commerce
404 W 2nd St., The Dalles
(541) 296-2231, (800) 255-3385
www.thedalleschamber.com

southeast

day trip 01

Oregon's Mt. Hood Territory
Clackamas County Tourism
& Cultural Affairs
150 Beavercreek Rd., Suite 305,
Oregon City
(503) 742-5910
www.mthoodterritory.com

day trip 02

Maupin Area Chamber of Commerce
P.O. Box 220, US 197, Maupin
(541) 395-2599
www.maupinoregon.com

day trip 03

Confederated Tribes of Warm Springs
1233 Veterans St., Warm Springs
(541) 553-1161
www.warmsprings.com

Crooked River Ranch-Terrebonne Chamber
of Commerce
P.O. Box 1502, Crooked River Ranch
(541) 923-2679
www.crrchamber.com

Central Oregon Visitors Association
661 SW Powerhouse Dr., Suite 1301, Bend
(800) 800-8334
www.visitcentraloregon.com

day trip 04

Central Oregon Visitors Association
661 SW Powerhouse Dr., Suite 1301, Bend
(800) 800-8334
www.visitcentraloregon.com

south

day trip 01

Oregon's Mt. Hood Territory
Clackamas County Tourism
& Cultural Affairs
150 Beavercreek Rd., Suite 305,
Oregon City
(503) 742-5910
www.mthoodterritory.com

day trip 02

Travel Salem
181 High St. NE, Salem
(503) 581-4325, (800) 874-7012
www.travelsalem.com

day trip 03

Travel Salem
181 High St. NE, Salem
(503) 581-4325, (800) 874-7012
www.travelsalem.com

Silverton Chamber of Commerce
426 S Water St., Silverton
(503) 873-5615
www.silvertonchamber.org

day trip 04

Mill City Chamber of Commerce
North Santiam Chamber of Commerce/
Visitors Information Center
P.O. Box 222, Mill City
(503) 897-3183
www.nschamber.org

day trip 05

Travel Lane County
754 Olive St., Eugene
(541) 743-8760
www.travellanecounty.org

southwest

day trip 01

Travel Yamhill Valley
P.O. Box 774, McMinnville
(503) 883-7770
www.yamhillvalley.org

day trip 02

Travel Yamhill Valley
P.O. Box 774, McMinnville
(503) 883-7770
www.yamhillvalley.org

Travel Salem
181 High St. NE, Salem
(503) 581-4325, (800) 874-7012
www.travelsalem.com

McMinnville Area Chamber of Commerce
417 NW Adams St., McMinnville
(503) 472-6196
www.mcminnville.org

day trip 03

Corvallis Tourism
553 NW Harrison Blvd., Corvallis
(541) 757-1544
www.visitcorvallis.com

Corvallis Benton Chamber Coalition
420 Northwest 2nd St., Corvallis
(541) 757-1505
www.cbchambercoalition.com

day trip 04

Newport Chamber of Commerce
555 SW Coast Hwy., Newport
(541) 265-8801
www.newportchamber.org

west

day trip 01

Washington County Visitors Association
11000 SW Stratus St., Suite 170,
Beaverton
(503) 644-5555
www.visitwashingtoncountyoregon.com

day trip 02

Tillamook Area Chamber-Commerce
3705 US 101 N, Tillamook
(503) 842-7525
www.tillamookchamber.org

Nestucca Valley Chamber of Commerce
P.O. Box 75, Cloverdale
(503) 392-4340
www.pcnvchamber.org

day trip 03

Cannon Beach Chamber of Commerce
207 N Spruce St., Cannon Beach
(503) 436-2623
www.cannonbeach.org

northwest

day trip 01

Seaside Visitor's Bureau
Seaside Chamber of Commerce
7 North Roosevelt Dr., Seaside
(888) 306-2326
www.seasideor.com

day trip 02

Astoria Bicentennial 2011
No. 1 12th St., #5, Astoria
(503) 325-5889
www.astoria200.org

Astoria-Warrenton Area Chamber
of Commerce
111 West Marine Dr., Astoria
(503) 325-6311
www.oldoregon.com

day trip 03

Long Beach Peninsula Visitors Bureau
P.O. Box 562, Long Beach
(360) 642-2400, (800) 451-2542
www.funbeach.com

appendix b:
festivals & celebrations

The open road, no agenda, and free-form type exploration of a day trip can be fabulous, but sometimes it's just more fun to go somewhere you know there's going to be action. Festivals offer the opportunity to park the car in one spot and soak up music, food, and entertainment all at once. Luckily for you, the regions surrounding Portland love a good festival, and on just about any given weekend you can find a great party happening somewhere within a one- to three-hour drive of the city. These pages list festivals celebrating classic cars, seafood, wine, Leonardo Da Vinci, independent film, cranberries, kites, and more. No matter your interests, you're sure to find an appealing festival here. For more events, see www.traveloregon.com and www.oregonfestivals.org.

january

Oregon Truffle Festival. (503) 296-5929; www.oregontrufflefestival.com. Created to celebrate magnificent, world-famous Oregon truffle mushrooms as they reach the peak of ripeness, this is the first festival in North America dedicated to sharing the experience of chefs, foragers, and fans of Oregon's wild truffles. Three days of workshops indoors and outdoors, packages, and the Grand Truffle Dinner sell out quickly each year.

february

Newport Seafood and Wine Festival. (541) 265-8801; www.newportchamber.org. Held the last full weekend in February in Newport is this popular celebration of two of the things Oregonians love best—seafood and wine. Held outdoors south of town; tastings start at $1 each and free shuttle buses run from downtown.

march

Tulip Festival. (503) 634-2243; www.woodenshoe.com/tulip-fest. Held at the Wooden Shoe Tulip Farm outside of Woodburn, this festival lasts as long as the tulips are blooming—late March through May 1, typically. Enjoy more than 40 acres of tulips and daffodils on this farm, where you can also buy cut flowers, order bulbs for fall planting, and visit the children's acre and the gift shop.

The McMinnville Wine and Food Classic. (503) 472-4033; www.macwfc.org. Held in March at the Evergreen Aviation and Space Museum in the heart of Oregon Wine Country is this 3-day festival. This event showcases terrific food, beautiful arts and crafts, guest chef demonstrations, live musical entertainment, and wine tasting from some of the best wineries and vineyards in Oregon.

april

Astoria Warrenton Crab, Seafood and Wine Festival. (503) 325-6311; www.oldoregon .com. Enjoy a great spread of Northwest cuisine, arts and crafts, a selection of Oregon and Washington's finest wines, a beer garden, and more at this annual Astoria event. Try the traditional crab dinner all weekend long and hear live music.

Celilo Mid-Columbia River Pow Wow. www.powwowtime.com. A few times a year, Celilo Village throws a party and invites everyone in. Food, traditional Native American dance contests, and a royalty contest make these events lots of good fun. Located at the traditional Celilo Longhouse.

Columbia Gorge Fiddle Contest. www.columbiagorgefiddlecontest.com. Three days of music and fun in the Columbia River Gorge. Held at Hood River Middle School, this festival and contest consists of workshops, concerts, and jam sessions. There is a cafeteria on site with food, vendor booths, and more music. Camping available on site.

Hood River Valley Blossom Festival. (541) 386-2000; www.hoodriver.org. This festival has been going strong for more than 50 years, and celebrates the time each year when fruit trees bloom. Hood River Valley is the largest pear-growing region in Oregon, and is also home to an abundance of cherry and apple orchards. When they all bloom, it's a beautiful sight. Events typically include a Blossom Fest Craft Show, Blossom Fest Quilt Show, a farm "pansy party," a grange blossom dinner, and a fire department all-you-can-eat breakfast. Visitors can also get a real "taste" of the gorge at several wine and beer-tasting events.

Northwest Cherry Festival. (541) 296-2231; www.thedalleschamber.org. Held the fourth week in April in The Dalles, this whopper of a festival includes a lip sync contest, bicycle ride, parade, open air market, entertainment, car show, and coronation—all in celebration of the most famous local fruit.

may

Gorge Artists Open Studio Tour. (541) 478-0171; www.gorgeartists.org. Artists of the Columbia Gorge open their studios to the public annually at this event, held the first weekend in May. Participating artists will invite the public into their work spaces to view how and where they work, and to ask the artist questions. Tourists enhance their knowledge of art and culture in the Columbia Gorge, and view and purchase artwork not available in galleries.

McMinnville UFO Fest. (503) 472-8427; www.ufofest.com. For two days in May, it's all about aliens in McMinnville. McMenamins Hotel Oregon hosts this event, begun as a way to honor the famous 1950 Trent sighting in which two local citizens witnessed and photographed a UFO. With activities ranging from the serious (UFO experts speak) to the silly (costume contest), this event has become the second largest of its kind in the US.

Mother's Day Wildflower and Birding Weekend. (503) 873-8681; www.oregonstate parks.org. Flowers, birds, plant walks, and photography are celebrated at Silver Falls State Park during Mother's Day weekend each year. Join other families at the park's South Lodge all day both weekend days to enjoy nature with mom.

Wine Walk. (503) 717-1914; www.seasidedowntown.com. In Seaside in May, local wineries are invited into local shops to pour samples of their best wines. Each Wine Walk brings hundreds of people to the downtown area for an afternoon and evening of great wines, great food, and of course, great fun! Buy a commemorative wine glass and join in the fun. There's a second wine walk in November.

june

The Bach Festival. (541) 346-5667; www.oregonbachfestival.com. Headquartered in Eugene, this festival has grown to include Ashland, Bend, and Portland, and to encompass 11 days in June and July. Masterworks, guest stars, and up-and-coming musical artists are the heart of the Oregon Bach Festival, which pays homage to the music of the great Johann Sebastian Bach.

Balloons Over Bend. (541) 323-0964; www.balloonsoverbend.com. Hot air balloons fly over Bend for 3 days in June, launched from a park on the Deschutes River in the Old Mill District. Tether rides, balloon launches, breakfasts, and a night glow round out this celebration of color and beauty. There is also a marketplace with face painting, live music, and more.

Muscle N Chrome. (503) 717-1914; www.seasidedowntown.org. Those who love cars come together in Seaside each year to celebrate all things automobile. A poker run, beach party, and vendor area are part of this 2-day festival of the collector vehicle.

Northwest Garlic Festival. (360) 665-4448; www.opwa.com. Ocean Park on the Long Beach Peninsula knows there's a lot to love about garlic. Celebrate the passion for this exalted bulb with the faithful throngs who make their annual pilgrimage to the Northwest Garlic Festival, which is held each June in the seaside community of Ocean Park. Garlic games, garlic crafts, and—naturally—garlic food and condiments are on hand at this 2-day event, as well as live music. Festival motto: It's chic to reek.

july

Carlton's Walk in the Park. (503) 852-6572; www.carltonswalkinthepark.com. This 2-day event combines a fabulous selection of artists, musicians, and the region's top restaurants and wineries in an outdoor event in Carlton's Wennerberg Park. The North Yamhill River is a beautiful spot to taste great wine, beer, and food, as well as see great entertainment. Profits benefit local charities.

Columbia Gorge Bluegrass Festival. (509) 427-3980; www.columbiagorgebluegrass .net. Held on the fourth weekend of July, this festival attracts outstanding national talent as well as premier regional bands. Held on the picturesque Skamania County Fairgrounds, the festival offers 4 days of fun, music, dances, workshops, and jammin'.

Da Vinci Days Festival. (541) 757-6363; www.davincidays.org. This cerebral festival is held in Corvallis on the Oregon State University campus geographically; metaphorically it's located at the crossroads of art, science, and technology. There's music, entertainment, creative contests, exhibits, races of all kinds, a parade, food and beverages, and hands-on activities for kids and adults. Here's where you can geocache, stargaze, and computer program to your heart's content.

Dory Days Festival. (971) 998-6385; www.pacificcity.org. There's no other marine fishery exactly like the one at Pacific City anywhere in the world. The modern dory fleet of today has evolved from the boats that went to sea from Cape Kiwanda more than 100 years ago. This 3-day event celebrates that rich history with a parade, marine fair, and fish fry at Cape Kiwanda, and an artisan fair in the downtown area.

Fort Dalles Days Pro Rodeo. (541) 296-2231; www.thefortdallesrodeo.com. A parade, pageant, and a banquet are part of this 3-day event in The Dalles, as is a full-blown rodeo, of course. Come out and see real bullfighting and a royal rodeo court at this old-fashioned event. There is live music nightly, too.

The International Pinot Noir Celebration. (800) 775-4762; www.ipnc.org. For 3 lovely days in McMinnville, the pinot noir grape is exalted. For nearly 25 years, the IPNC has been uniting international pinot noir producers, journalists, pinot noir devotees, Northwest chefs, and foodies for a weekend of tasting, dining, learning, and celebrating together on the Linfield College Campus. Participants may also take a tour of Oregon wine country.

Jefferson Mint Festival and Frog Jump. (541) 981-8885; www.mintfestival.com. Jefferson calls itself the mint capital of the world, and celebrates that distinction each year with a frog jump and festival. There is even a royal mint festival court and parade at this 2-day event.

The Oregon Country Fair. Information: (541) 343-4298; www.oregoncountryfair.org. This 3-day event of nonstop costumed revelry has been an Oregon tradition for more than 40 years. Held each year in Veneta, west of Eugene, the Oregon Country Fair showcases world-class entertainment, handmade crafts, delectable foods, educational displays, and magical surprises at every turn of the path. The fair is an unforgettable adventure.

Red White and Blue Riverfront Festival. (541) 754-6624; www.visitcorvallis.com. This Corvallis event takes place over 2 days around July 4 and features lots of musical entertainment to get you up and dancing. A fireworks show is also included in the celebration, which is held on the riverfront.

Sisters Quilt Show. (541) 549-0989; www.sistersoutdoorquiltshow.org. Held the second Saturday in July in Sisters, this quilt show has become a must-see destination for thousands of visitors who descend on this small town this one day each year. Over 1,300 quilts from around the world cover this old-fashioned Western town in rich texture and color. Special exhibits and contests make the day even more fun.

St. Paul Rodeo. (800) 237-5920; www.stpaulrodeo.com. Held over the Fourth of July weekend in St. Paul, this rodeo has been going for more than 75 years and is ranked as one of the top in the nation with prize monies approaching $500,000 and nearly 1,000 competitors. This celebration underscores the grit and fortitude of those folks we know as cowboys and cowgirls.

august

Astoria Regatta Festival. (800) 875-6807; www.astoriaregatta.org. Five days of fun all about the greatest river in the west, the mighty Columbia. Sailboat races on the Columbia, live music and nightly concerts, a children's parade, fireworks over the Columbia, a salmon barbecue, a car show, and a grand parade bring out the folks in celebration.

Aurora Colony Days Old-Fashioned Family Day. (503) 939-0312; www.auroracolony .com. Downtown Aurora hosts this annual event, which includes a parade, kiddie carnival, local flavors market, art show and sale, live music, and historic tours. As does the city, the whole event has a deep flavor for the past.

Bend Brew Fest. (541) 322-9383; www.bendbrewfest.com. Bend knows beer, and would like you to know beer, too. This festival celebrates all things microbrewed. Held over 2 days at the Les Schwab Amphitheater, the Bend Brew Fest features more than 50 distinct craft beers for public tasting. There's great live music, as well as views of the mountains and the river.

Bridge of the Gods Kiteboarding Festival. (800) 989-9178; www.botgkitefest.com. Kiteboarders from across the nation converge on the Columbia River Gorge near Stevenson to compete in the nation's longest running amateur kiteboarding contest. The steep riverbanks make the Port of Skamania's East Point Kite Beach a natural grandstand for viewing the event.

Dufur Threshing Bee. (541) 467-2205; www.dufurthreshingbee.org. This old-time festival allows public enjoyment of wheat harvesting using old-time machinery and draft horses in the high desert community of Dufur. There is a parade, tractor pull, steak feed, grange breakfast, and classic car show to enjoy here, too.

Eugene Celebration. (541) 681-4108; www.eugenecelebration.com. This big fat celebration held in late summer each year has grown to include a car show, road race, sustainability village, health and wellness area, kid zone, 2 parades, and film festival, just for starters. In addition, there are all the things a good festival needs to please—food, beverages, entertainment, and shopping.

Huckleberry Festival. www.cgs-mthood.tripod.com/huck_festival. This annual festival on the slopes of Mt. Hood between Sandy and Zigzag celebrates tourism on the mountain and the local berry. Come and enjoy huckleberry pies and tarts, a Native American salmon bake, Native American storytelling, and live music.

Northwest Art and Air Festival. (800) 526-2256; www.airartnw.com. This celebration of art, flight, and entertainment happens the weekend before Labor Day each year in Albany. Hot air balloons kick off each festival morning, and art booths, demonstrations, a kid's village and live entertainment keep things going all day. At night, enjoy the night glow.

Vancouver Wine and Jazz Festival. (360) 906-0441; www.vancouverwinejazz.com. This 3-day festival is the largest of its kind in the Pacific Northwest. Internationally acclaimed jazz and blues musicians gather to entertain crowds of thousands, who also enjoy more than 200 wines, fine arts and crafts, and local cuisine.

Washington State International Kite Festival. (360) 642-4020; www.kitefestival.com. Voted Best Kite Festival in the World by Kite Trade Association, this weeklong festival on the Long Beach Peninsula includes competitions by professional and amateur kite flyers, choreographed kite flies, mass ascensions, fireworks, lighted night kite flies, vendors, and more. You can be sure the skies are full of color this week.

september

The Festival of the Forest. www.mthood.info/forestfest. A weekend-long celebration of Mt. Hood's culture, arts, and forest. Forest activities, nature crafts, food, beer and wine booths, and art booths all come together at the Wildwood Recreation area on US 26 E on the way to Mt. Hood.

Newport Jazz Festival. (541) 265-2787; www.jazzatnewport.org. Jazz and jazz lovers come together in Newport on the beautiful Oregon Coast each fall. Workshops and education accompany lots and lots of great jazz at this 3-day event.

River Fest. (541) 395-2222; www.maupinriverfest.com. Visit Maupin on the Lower Deschutes River for a day of terrific live music, great food, fun, and family-friendly activities. This festival celebrating the river has a 5k/10k walk/run, popular regional bands, a variety of food and beverage vendors, and the artwork of art vendors. Take a mini raft trip on the Deschutes, and cast some fly rods at a casting pond.

Shrewsbury Renaissance Faire. (541) 929-4897; www.shrewfaire.com. Come be thee blythe and merry at the Renaissance Faire! Just 15 miles and 500 years away from downtown Corvallis, enchantment awaits young and old alike as jousting knights and noble steeds clash on the tourney while minstrels, troubadours, jongleurs, dancers, and bards fill the lanes with delight. More than 125 artisan stalls and 1,000 costumed players entertain visitors as they browse the village for unique handmade goods and one-of-a-kind treasures.

Sisters Folk Festival. (541) 549-4979; www.sistersfolkfestival.org. The Sisters Folk Festival is a 3-day celebration of American roots music, from blues to bluegrass, held every year the weekend after Labor Day in beautiful Sisters. This little fest has a big reputation and attracts truly great performers each year.

The Vancouver Sausage Fest. (360) 696-2586; www.stjoevanschool.org. Hosted by St. Joseph Catholic School, this event offers food booths, a carnival, vendors, exhibits, and a beer and wine garden, accompanying lots and lots of sausages and happy people. Held every year the weekend after Labor Day, this Vancouver event draws attendance upwards of 100,000 over 3 days.

october

Bend Film Fest. (866) 261-7096; www.bendfilm.org. This 4-day celebration of independent film showcases more than 80 films from across the country and brings filmmakers, fans, and experts together in Bend for conversation, lectures, and a whole lot of film watching. It's a life-enriching experience that educates and entertains.

Cranberrian Fair. (360) 642-3446; www.columbiapacificheritagemuseum.org. This annual fall celebration of local harvest including all things cranberry takes place on the Long Beach Peninsula. During the local cranberry harvest, visitors enjoy vendors, live music, cranberry foods and traditions, and craft demonstrations, and ride the Cranberry Trolley to bog tours.

Hood River Harvest Fest. (541) 386-2000; www.hoodriver.org. Harvest Fest is held annually on the Hood River waterfront overlooking the Columbia River. Visitors shop for arts and crafts, including glass, wood sculpture, ceramics, photography, and fiber art; listen to music all day and find more entertainment in the evening; visit the kids' zone with a bounce house, face painters, bands, and balloon twisters; and partake of the food court with lots of local and traditional favorites.

Mt. Angel Oktoberfest. (503) 845-9440; www.oktoberfest.org. This American version of the "Old World" Oktoberfest takes place in Mount Angel, Oregon's answer to a Bavarian paradise. Oregon's largest folk festival lasts 4 days; has 50 alpine food chalets and a traditional biergarten, weingarten and alpinegarten; hosts more than 30 musical groups; and opens the streets for street dancing on Friday and Saturday nights.

Wild Seafood Weekend. (541) 574-5555; www.newportfishermenswives.com. The historic fishing town of Newport celebrates seafood at this massive celebration, which features a fish market, a cook-off, a harbor cruise, and a brunch made from seafood straight off of the boat. The festivities occur on the historic Newport Bayfront, where there's always something happening.

november

Oregon Bounty. (800) 547-7842; http://food.traveloregon.com. This statewide event celebrates all delicious things local. Coinciding with the August through November harvest season, Oregon Bounty features events and activities at craft breweries, wineries, artisan distillers, restaurants, and lodging properties in all seven regions of the state. Visitors have the opportunity to meet a variety of artisan producers including winemakers, brewers, distillers, and farmers who create Oregon's culinary wonders.

Stormy Weather Arts Festival. (503) 436-2623; www.cannonbeach.org. This Cannon Beach tradition offers a deluge of artistic and musical talent. Live music plays in shops, galleries, and restaurants all over town. There is an auction and demonstrations by local artists, too, during this 3-day festival.

Wine Country Thanksgiving. (503) 646-2985; www.willamettewines.com. More than 150 wineries from Portland to Eugene open their doors to visitors at this classic event. Barrel taste, sample new releases and older vintages, buy gift packages, enjoy music, and taste specialty foods. Request a list of activities and touring map at the website.

december

Christmas Along the Barlow Trail. (503) 622-4798; www.cgsmthood.com. The holiday season arrives at the village Rhododendron along the Oregon Trail with pioneer music, Native American flute music, storytelling featuring Christmas Tales From Old Oregon, Santa Claus, and much more. Come up to the slopes of Mt. Hood for this annual celebration.

Christmas Ships Parade. www.christmasships.org. A family tradition, this event presents a lighted holiday parade on the rivers around Portland. The Christmas Ships pageant includes two fleets that travel around, landing at many destinations including St. Helens, Milwaukie, Scappoose, Lake Oswego, and Hayden Island.

Oregon Coast Aquarium's Sea of Lights. (541) 867-FISH; www.aquarium.org. This holiday season tradition draws guests to the aquarium to see it adorned with holiday decorations, a large Christmas tree, and thousands of colorful lights. Enjoy face painting, holiday music, and a visit with Santa. Visitors come from all over the region to spend time together at the beach and enjoy the magic of the season.

Seaside Parade of Lights. (503) 738-6391; www.seasidechamber.com. This parade comes complete with Santa and takes place in downtown Seaside. Come and see the tree lighting, sing some carols afterwards, and partake in some cookies and a gift fair at the Convention Center.

index

INSIDERS' GUIDE ®

The acclaimed travel series that has sold more than 2 million copies!

Discover: Your Travel Destination.
Your Home. Your Home-to-Be.

Albuquerque

Anchorage &
  Southcentral
  Alaska

Atlanta

Austin

Baltimore

Baton Rouge

Boulder & Rocky Mountain
  National Park

Branson & the Ozark
  Mountains

California's Wine Country

Cape Cod & the Islands

Charleston

Charlotte

Chicago

Cincinnati

Civil War Sites in
  the Eastern Theater

Civil War Sites in the South

Colorado's Mountains

Dallas & Fort Worth

Denver

El Paso

Florida Keys & Key West

Gettysburg

Glacier National Park

Great Smoky Mountains

Greater Fort Lauderdale

Greater Tampa Bay Area

Hampton Roads

Houston

Hudson River Valley

Indianapolis

Jacksonville

Kansas City

Long Island

Louisville

Madison

Maine Coast

Memphis

Myrtle Beach &
  the Grand Strand

Nashville

New Orleans

New York City

North Carolina's
  Mountains

North Carolina's
  Outer Banks

North Carolina's
  Piedmont Triad

Oklahoma City

Orange County, CA

Oregon Coast

Palm Beach County

Palm Springs

Philadelphia &
  Pennsylvania Dutch
  Country

Phoenix

Portland, Maine

Portland, Oregon

Raleigh, Durham &
  Chapel Hill

Richmond, VA

Reno and Lake Tahoe

St. Louis

San Antonio

Santa Fe

Savannah & Hilton Head

Seattle

Shreveport

South Dakota's
  Black Hills Badlands

Southwest Florida

Tucson

Tulsa

Twin Cities

Washington, D.C.

Williamsburg & Virginia's
  Historic Triangle

Yellowstone
  & Grand Teton

Yosemite

**To order call 800-243-0495
or visit www.Insiders.com**

Getaway ideas for the local traveler

Need a day away to relax, refresh, renew?
Just get in your car and go!